THE RISE AND FALL
OF DÉTENTE

Issues in the History of American Foreign Relations

Series Editor: Robert J. McMahon, Ohio State University

Previously published titles in this series:

Amid a Warring World: American Foreign Relations, 1775–1815 (2012)
Robert W. Smith, Worcester State University

How the Cold War Ended: Debating and Doing History (2011)
John Prados, National Security Archive

John F. Kennedy: World Leader (2010)
Stephen G. Rabe, University of Texas at Dallas

The Triumph of Internationalism:
Franklin D. Roosevelt and a World in Crisis, 1933–1941 (2007)
David Schmitz, Whitman College

Intimate Ties, Bitter Struggles:
The United States and Latin America since 1945 (2006)
Alan McPherson, Howard University

The Color of Empire: Race and American Foreign Relations (2006)
Michael L. Krenn, Appalachian State University

Crisis and Crossfire: The United States and the Middle East Since 1945 (2005)
Peter L. Hahn, Ohio State University

THE RISE AND FALL OF DÉTENTE

American Foreign Policy and the Transformation of the Cold War

Jussi M. Hanhimäki

Potomac Books
Washington, D.C.

Library of Congress Cataloging-in-Publication Data
Hanhimäki, Jussi M., 1965–
    The rise and fall of détente : American foreign policy and the transformation of the Cold War / Jussi M. Hanhimäki. — 1st ed.
        p. cm. — (Issues in the history of American foreign relations)
    Includes bibliographical references and index.
    ISBN 978-1-59797-075-4 (hardcover : alk. paper)
    ISBN 978-1-59797-076-1 (pbk. : alk. paper)
    ISBN 978-1-61234-586-4 (electronic)
    1. United States—Foreign relations—1945–1989. 2. Detente. 3. Cold War. 4. International relations. I. Title.
    E840.H364 2013
    973.9—dc23

                                                                    2012031572

Potomac Books
22841 Quicksilver Drive
Dulles, Virginia 20166

First Edition

10 9 8 7 6 5 4 3 2 1

CONTENTS

Series Editor's Note   ix

Acknowledgments   xi

Introduction   xiii

CHAPTER 1.   Roots of Détente: Crises, Challenges,
              and the Quest for Stability   1

CHAPTER 2.   1968: Revolution, War, and the Birth of Détente   25

CHAPTER 3.   "Three for Three": Triangulation   43

CHAPTER 4.   Nixon, Kissinger, and Détente in Europe   61

CHAPTER 5.   Détente Halted: Domestic Critics and Regional Crises   77

CHAPTER 6.   Reason or Morality: Carter, Human Rights,
              and Nuclear Peace   101

CHAPTER 7.   Crisis and Collapse: Iran, Afghanistan,
              and the Carter Doctrine   125

CHAPTER 8.   Cold War Transformed: The Paradox of Détente   143

APPENDIX OF DOCUMENTS   155

  1. Khrushchev on the Need for Relaxation of Tensions,
      October 30, 1962   155

2. President John F. Kennedy's Commencement Address
   at American University, June 10, 1963 157

3. Memorandum of Understanding between the United States
   of America and the Union of Soviet Socialist Republics
   Regarding the Establishment of a Direct Communications
   Link, June 20, 1963 161

4. Test Ban Treaty between the United States, Great Britain,
   and the Soviet Union, August 5, 1963 164

5. Debriefing by the President on His Talks with Chairman
   Kosygin, June 23, 1967 165

6. Nixon's Address at the Bohemian Club in San Francisco,
   July 29, 1967 168

7. NATO Council on Future Relations with the Warsaw
   Pact Members (the Harmel Report), December 13–14, 1967 173

8. Nixon's Inaugural Address, January 20, 1969 176

9. Willy Brandt and Henry Kissinger on West German
   Ostpolitik, 1969–70 178

10. White House Background Press Briefing by the President's
    Assistant for National Security Affairs (Kissinger),
    February 16, 1970 181

11. Telegram from Ambassador Dobrynin to the Soviet Foreign
    Ministry, July 17, 1971 184

12. Basic Principles: The United States and the Soviet Union
    Agree on the "Rules" of Détente, May 1972 187

13. Jackson-Vanik Amendment to the 1974 Trade Law,
    January 3, 1975 188

14. Memorandum from the President's Assistant for National
    Security Affairs (Kissinger) to President Ford, July 1975
    (undated) 191

15. Cabinet Meeting, Memorandum of Conversation,
    August 8, 1975 195

16. Soviet Suppression of Dissidents, 1976   197

17. "To Restore America," Ronald Reagan's Campaign
    Address, March 31, 1976   198

18. Carter-Ford Debate about Détente, October 6, 1976   201

19. Jimmy Carter's Letter to Leonid Brezhnev, February 15, 1977   206

20. Jimmy Carter's Commencement Address at Notre Dame
    University, May 22, 1977   208

21. National Security Council Meeting on the Horn of Africa,
    March 2, 1978   212

22. Brezhnev's Speech to the Politburo on the International
    Situation, June 8, 1978   215

23. Ambassador Dobrynin on U.S.-Soviet Relations,
    July 11, 1978   218

24. NATO's Double-Track Decision, December 1979   221

25. Reasons to Invade Afghanistan, December 27, 1979   223

26. Jimmy Carter, Address to the Nation on the Soviet
    Invasion of Afghanistan, January 4, 1980   225

27. Soviet Analysis of the Impact of the Soviet Intervention
    in Afghanistan, January 20, 1980   229

28. Reagan's Televised Address, "A Strategy for Peace in the '80s,"
    October 19, 1980   231

29. Ayatollah Khomeini's Message, 1980   233

Notes   237
Selected Bibliography   253
Index   261
About the Author   275

Series Editor's Note

From the birth of the American Republic in the late eighteenth century to the emergence of the United States as a fledgling world power at the end of the nineteenth century, the place of the United States within the broader international system of nation-states posed fundamental challenges to American and foreign statesmen alike. What role would—and could—a non-European power play in a Eurocentric world order? The combination of America's stunning economic transformation and two devastating world wars helped shatter the old European order, catapulting the United States into a position of global preeminence by the middle decades of the twentieth century. Since the mid-1940s, it has become common to refer to the United States as a superpower. Since the collapse of the Soviet Union, America's only serious rival, and the concomitant end of the Cold War, it has become common to label the United States as the world's lone superpower, or "hyperpower," as a French diplomat labeled it in the late-1990s.

By any standard of measurement, the United States has long been, as it remains today, the dominant force in world affairs—economically, politically, militarily, and culturally.

The United States has placed, and continues to place, its own indelible stamp on the international system while shaping the aspirations, mores, tastes, living standards, and sometimes resentments and hatreds of hundreds of millions of ordinary people across the globe. Few subjects, consequently, loom larger in the history of the modern world than the often uneasy encounter between the United States and the nations and peoples beyond its shores.

This series, Issues in the History of American Foreign Relations, aims to provide students and general readers alike with a wide range of books, written by some of the outstanding scholarly experts of this generation, that elucidate key issues, themes, topics, and individuals in the nearly 250-year history of U.S. foreign relations. The series covers an array of diverse subjects spanning from the era of the founding fathers to the present. Each book offers a concise, accessible narrative, based upon the latest scholarship, followed by a careful selection of relevant primary documents. Primary sources enable readers to immerse themselves in the raw material of history, thereby facilitating the formation of informed, independent judgments about the subject at hand. To capitalize upon the unprecedented amount of non-American archival sources and materials currently available, most books feature foreign as well as American material in the documentary section. A broad, international perspective on the external behavior of the United States, one of the major trends of recent scholarship, is a prominent feature of the books in this series.

It is my fondest hope that this series will contribute to a greater engagement with and understanding of the complexities of this fascinating—and critical—subject.

ROBERT J. MCMAHON
OHIO STATE UNIVERSITY

ACKNOWLEDGMENTS

MANY PEOPLE CONTRIBUTED to the conception, research, and writing of this book. I would particularly like to acknowledge Robert McMahon, who implanted the idea in my head during a conference outside Washington, D.C., in the summer of 2007 and contributed to its gradual (and delayed) completion with his insightful comments. I am glad that my work is part of the series of investigations into the history of American foreign policy that Bob is overseeing for Potomac Books. I would further like to thank Jeremi Suri, who took time from his busy schedule to provide detailed comments about an early version of the manuscript. Others who offered commentary and criticism about the various portions of this book include Anne Deighton, John Gaddis, Geir Lundestad, Melvyn Leffler, Piers Ludlow, Voitech Mastny, Olav Njolstad, Thomas Schwartz, and Odd Arne Westad.

At Potomac Books I would like to thank Hilary Claggett and Kathryn Owens for their attention to my manuscript, and Julie Kimmel for an expert job at copyediting (and for saving me from a number of embarrassments).

Most of all I would like to thank those closest to me, including Barbara for her critical support and love, despite the many complications, professional and personal, that occurred throughout the years that it took to complete this book. Without her I would not have bothered. Meanwhile, my son Jari provided much-needed perspective by repeatedly asking that all-important and basic question: do you really need to spend all that time on another book? I thought yes. We disagreed. For now.

INTRODUCTION

JANUARY 20, 1973, WAS A COOL AND CLOUDY DAY in Washington, D.C. But that did not disturb the buoyant mood of Richard Milhous Nixon, at the peak of a turbulent career. As the thirty-seventh president mounted the podium to deliver his second inaugural address, there was much to be celebrated, particularly in the area of foreign policy. And Nixon was not one to be tempted by false modesty:

> As we meet here today, we stand on the threshold of a new era of peace in the world. . . . This past year saw far-reaching results from our new policies for peace. By continuing to revitalize our traditional friendships, and by our missions to Peking and to Moscow, we were able to establish the base for a new and more durable pattern of relationships among the nations of the world. Because of America's bold initiatives, 1972 will be long remembered as the year of the greatest progress since the end of World War II toward a lasting peace in the world. . . . Let us continue to bring down the walls of hostility which have divided the world for too long, and to build in their place bridges of understanding—so that despite profound differences between systems of government, the people of the world can be friends. Let us build a structure of peace in the world.[1]

Nixon's larger-than-life rhetoric was not without foundation. The early 1970s had been characterized by high-level negotiations, arms control agreements, and superpower summitry. Such events as the Strategic Arms Limitation Talks

(SALT) I Agreement of 1972 and the Nixon-Brezhnev summits of 1972–74 high-lighted the way in which Soviet-American relations, while not amicable, had at least moved toward a new level of civility. As the United States simultaneously moved to break away from its earlier nonrecognition policy vis-à-vis the People's Republic of China (PRC), the view of the Cold War as a bipolar confrontation had, it seemed, become a thing of the past. In Paris, only days after Nixon's second inaugural, Henry Kissinger initialled the agreements that ended the United States' direct involvement in the Vietnam War (the upholding of such agreements is another matter). In Europe, the German problem moved toward normalization with the advent of inter-German relations, a four-power agreement on the status of Berlin, and a series of bilateral treaties between the Federal Republic of Germany (FRG), on the one hand, and the Union of Soviet Socialist Republics (USSR), Poland, and other Soviet bloc countries, on the other. In the early 1970s, moreover, the talks that eventually led to the Conference on Security and Cooperation in Europe (CSCE)—and the signing of the Helsinki Final Act in 1975—finally got under way. A new era in East-West relations appeared to be emerging, not least because of changes in the American approach to the Soviet Union. Some even talked about the Cold War as history.

By the late 1970s, however, Soviet-American détente was all but dead. In the mid-1970s the policy of reducing military tension through negotiations and agreements with countries based on dramatically different ideological foundations came under increasing criticism. The 1980 election of Ronald Reagan, who openly called for a more belligerent American foreign policy vis-à-vis the Soviet Union, signaled the end of the era of negotiations that Nixon had announced a decade earlier. In short, within a few years the optimistic climate of the early part of the decade had been replaced with what some scholars see as the Second Cold War in the early 1980s.

While focusing on the evolution of American foreign policy, this book will survey the reasons for the rise of détente, explore the highlights of this era of reduced East-West tensions, and explain the causes for its demise. It will address such questions as, What were the long- and short-term causes of détente? Was it a policy "invented" in the United States or adopted because of pressures from abroad? Did it represent a radical break with the past (a move, perhaps, from idealism to realism), or was it simply an attempt to prolong the Cold War bipolarity within the international system? Was détente a policy that grew from weakness and doubt (caused particularly by the Vietnam War)? What were its main achievements and shortcomings? What caused its demise? Did détente ultimately make a difference?

In exploring these questions, this book will make three interconnected arguments. First, détente was, essentially, a conservative policy, aimed at stabilizing a situation that was (particularly because of the Vietnam War, the escalation of the nuclear arms race, and the breakdown of the domestic consensus over U.S. foreign policy) threatening the proper functioning of American foreign policy. Second, détente's immediate results were at times spectacular (opening to China, SALT agreements with the Soviets), but the policy itself lacked domestic support and international respect (even relevance). As a result, it did not provide the lasting "structure of peace" that Nixon had called for. Third, while détente as conceived in the early 1970s did not last, it did introduce certain elements (such as the idea of human security) that ultimately—at times unintentionally—worked to undermine the validity of the Cold War itself. That is, détente ultimately—ironically—discredited the international system it was meant to stabilize.

The system in question was, simply, the Cold War international system. It had grown from the ashes of World War II. It defined and was responsible for the role of the United States as the world's leading power in the second half of the twentieth century. This was not by accident. After 1945 the United States was the world's greatest economic power; the nation was responsible for roughly half of the world's industrial production and in subsequent years helped others (for example, Western Europe via the Marshall Plan) to recover from the devastation of the war. After 1945 the United States was also the world's greatest military power—the sole nation on earth to possess not only atomic weapons but also troops stationed in the heart of Europe (Berlin) and Asia (U.S. troops occupied Japan). Moreover, American ideas and culture—as well as Americans in general—were popular around the world. World War II had been the transformative conflict that made it possible for America to take its place as the leading nation in the world.

In the first decade and a half of the postwar era, the dominant American position became a central feature of the international system. The United States forged alliances across the globe (the North Atlantic Treaty Organization [NATO] for Europe, Rio Treaty for Latin America, Southeast Asia Treaty Organization

[SEATO] for Southeast Asia, and Australia–New Zealand–United States Treaty [ANZUS] for Oceania) and concluded bilateral alliances with such key countries as Japan and South Korea. American military bases were omnipresent from the Western Hemisphere to the Far East. The United States remained economically dominant; neither Western European recovery and integration nor the Japanese economic miracle could shake America's role as the leading industrial democracy in the first two decades after World War II. And while American ideas and culture were occasionally resisted and even rejected, the 1950s were nothing if not the peak of what *Time* publisher Henry Luce had in 1941 called "the American Century." Measured by virtually any indicator, the United States entered the 1960s as the world's great superpower, the uncontested leader of the so-called free world.

But, of course, there was the Soviet Union. Without the USSR and the challenge of socialism, the Cold War international system could not have emerged. Without the Soviet presence in Eastern Europe after World War II, it is doubtful that the United States would have launched the Marshall Plan for Western Europe in 1947 or become the key member of NATO, founded in 1949. Although the Soviet role in subsequent events—the establishment of the PRC in 1949 and the Korean War of 1950–53—remained indirect, the Cold War system soon covered most of the earth as the United States countered what most American policy-makers perceived as a global communist threat emanating from the Kremlin. Indeed, from the late 1940s onward, American policy vis-à-vis the Soviet Union was dominated by the notion summed up best by George F. Kennan in his famous "Mr. X" article published in *Foreign Affairs* in July 1947: "The main element of any United States policy toward the Soviet Union must be a long-term, patient but firm and vigilant containment of Russian expansive tendencies." Kennan added, "Soviet pressure against the free institutions of the Western world is something that can be contained by the adroit and vigilant application of counterforce at a series of constantly shifting geographical and political points, corresponding to the shifts and maneuvers of Soviet policy, but which cannot be charmed or talked out of existence."[2]

But even a formidable superpower like the United States could overreach. By the late 1950s the "vigilant application of counterforce" was proving to be increasingly costly and potentially dangerous (if not even self-defeating). For example, slightly under forty thousand American soldiers had died in what had turned out to be an unpopular war in Korea in the early 1950s. After 1949, when the Soviet Union tested the first atomic bomb, the U.S. government expended billions upon billions to develop and build nuclear weapons to stay ahead—both in numbers and quality—of the USSR. But the nuclear arms race continued to spiral and cause repeated scares in the collective American psyche. Indeed, one of the Cold War's most unfortunate by-products in the United States was the ways in which the national security state limited—not always within reason—domestic individual freedoms. Anticommunism, when taken to its extremes, produced the series of political witch hunts known collectively as McCarthyism. Even Nixon, the peacemaker of the 1970s, started his political career as an unabashed "red baiter."

The emergence of détente was in part a reaction to the excesses of early Cold War containment and anticommunism. In the 1960s the need for more destructive nuclear weapons was beginning to be questioned as the idea of actually using such weapons became progressively more preposterous. Sending American troops to Vietnam to support an anticommunist regime became a hotly contested policy that called into question both the morality and wisdom of the very idea of containment. While most Americans continued to believe in the need for their country to lead the free world and stand up for such broad principles as democracy and economic liberalism, they were less enthusiastic about the methods by which containment was being applied. This was particularly the case as no one in the 1960s could see, or offer, a road map to victory. As it matured, the Cold War appeared increasingly "normal." And if it were here to stay, then it was high time to reduce the dangers the Cold War had produced by taking steps toward a more predictable world order in which the possibility of a thermonuclear war could also be contained. The only realistic way to do so was by direct negotiations with—to use Nixon's terminology—"subject A: the Soviet Union."[3]

As the first two chapters of this book make clear, Nixon was not the first American president to push for negotiations with the Soviet Union. Indeed, throughout the 1960s, the Kennedy and Johnson administrations engaged in a series of initiatives that lay the groundwork for the emergence of détente. These initiatives fell short of delivering the kind of breakthroughs that Nixon and his major adviser, Henry Kissinger, were able to achieve in large part because of America's growing engagement in Vietnam. But not even the Warsaw Pact's invasion of Czechoslovakia in 1968 could ultimately prevent the momentum—both

American and Soviet—toward negotiation. Chapters 3 and 4 provide an account of the diplomatic maneuvering of the high tide of détente in the early 1970s. By the time Nixon left office as a result of the Watergate crisis, his administration had indeed compiled a significant foreign policy record.

Watergate was not directly linked to foreign policy, but by discrediting Nixon, it did play a part in the demise of détente. Chapters 5, 6, and 7 explore this process. While acknowledging the role of domestic factors—such as the criticism that détente was either morally repugnant or an expression of an acceptance of weakness—I also emphasize the continued Soviet-American competition in the context of various regional conflicts. Indeed, one of the shortcomings of the Soviet-American détente process was the superpowers' inability to come to any significant agreement on how to limit their involvement (let alone cooperate) in the many crises that in the 1970s rocked the so-called third world. In Africa, the Middle East, and Central Asia, the United States and the Soviet Union competed over influence, donated aid to allies, and supported various proxies. Meanwhile, public rhetoric—which had become less confrontational and apocalyptic in the early 1970s—saw a revival of the antagonistic excesses of the early Cold War.

In the concluding chapter of this book, I will attempt to place détente in its broader historical context by specifically addressing the question of the impact of the 1970s on the overall development of the Cold War.

It is important to note that "détente"—much like the "Cold War"—is a term that defies easy definition or periodization. There was no official declaration of détente, no official starting point, no clear-cut end. I have chosen, perhaps rather conventionally, the early 1960s—the twin crises over Berlin and Cuba in 1961–62 and the subsequent calls for negotiations—as the time when the Soviet-American relationship began its gradual evolution toward the "golden era" of the early 1970s. Equally conventionally, I end the narrative in 1979–80 with the Soviet invasion of Afghanistan and the election of Ronald Reagan, both of which highlighted the increased tensions of what has been called the "Second" or "New" Cold War.

I am fully cognizant, moreover, of the elasticity of any concept, particularly in the hands of policymakers. Détente is no exception. Indeed, one of the key difficulties of détente was that it meant different things to different people in different places. The Soviets, for example, rarely used the term "détente," preferring "peaceful coexistence" instead. In American rhetoric, "détente" became almost a dirty word by 1976, and Gerald Ford banned its use in his presidential campaign ("peace through strength" became the favored, if less than meaningful, phrase à la mode). When the West German chancellor, Willy Brandt, spoke of détente, he meant something other than what his East German counterpart, Walter Ulbricht, meant. The very fact that the term's origin was French did not mean that Charles de Gaulle could claim special ownership of its content.

Thus, I have chosen to employ the term "détente" somewhat loosely. In this book "détente" refers to an era when subsequent American administrations attempted to redefine their relationship with the Soviet Union in order to increase predictability and reduce the potential of direct military confrontation. This did not mean that American policymakers suddenly began ignoring the differences in the two nations' social and economic systems or accepted some form of convergence between capitalism and socialism. While there may have been broad agreement on negotiations, for example, the substance of any negotiation was always contested. While some thought of détente as a broad set of rules of international behavior, others chose to limit it to the direct bilateral relationship.

Ultimately, détente can be understood as both an era and a strategy. As an era, it stretches from the early 1960s to the late 1970s and incorporates a transformation in the interstate relationship between the two superpowers, the end to the PRC's virtual isolation from international affairs, and the transformation of East-West relations in Europe. All this, however, took place against the backdrop of violent conflicts in the third world that gave zest to the ongoing confrontation between the United States and the Soviet Union, between East and West, between capitalism and socialism. As an American strategy, détente was a constantly evolving approach to foreign policy that represented an adjustment to the means and methods by which the Cold War was waged. In the end, despite Nixon's soaring rhetoric in January 1973, détente was never a policy aimed at ending the Cold War. While its consequences—like those of many other foreign policy strategies— were unpredictable, détente represented a distinct phase in the context of that long twilight struggle.

CHAPTER 1

ROOTS OF DÉTENTE: CRISES, CHALLENGES, AND THE QUEST FOR STABILITY

"ICH BIN EIN BERLINER," JOHN F. KENNEDY MEMORABLY ANNOUNCED in his speech in the German capital on June 26, 1963. It was a superb performance from that most gifted of American orators of the Cold War era. Today, a visitor to Rathaus Schöneberg, the city hall of Berlin's Tempelhof district, can find a plaque erected to commemorate the event and the spot where Kennedy aroused the adulation of thousands of West Berliners less than a year after the building of the Berlin Wall commenced. Kennedy, by identifying Berlin as the frontier of the free world and standing shoulder to shoulder with West Berlin's mayor and future chancellor of the Federal Republic of Germany, Willy Brandt, thus seemed to issue an open challenge to the Soviet and East German regimes. His national security adviser, McGeorge Bundy, even thought that Kennedy had gone "too far" with the speech's challenging tone.[1]

In retrospect, though, one can see a different symbolism at work. Kennedy, undoubtedly, meant to identify himself with the cause of the free world. For him, the statement "Ich bin ein Berliner" (not a jelly donut, but a citizen of the venerable city) was aimed at expressing American support for those left staring at a wall that divided the city into East and West. It was a shot in the propaganda war of the Cold War. But it was also a hint that Kennedy, like everyone else, was a prisoner of the Cold War. He acknowledged that the division that the wall symbolized was something beyond his capacity to change. And since he could not change it, Kennedy was clearly tilting away from antagonism and toward a modus vivendi with the USSR.

Kennedy's successors faced an even more disturbing phenomenon that impressed to them the necessity of a new type of relationship with the Soviet

1

Union: as the 1960s wore on, America appeared to be growing weaker. Lyndon Johnson thought he could offer both guns and butter by fighting a war in Vietnam and combating poverty through generous welfare programs at home. He was wrong. Although reelected in 1964 by a virtual landslide, the years that followed saw Lyndon Johnson beleaguered at home and abroad. He could triumph in neither a hot (Vietnam) nor a cold war and found his treasured domestic agenda—the dream of building the Great Society—attacked by critics on the left and right. He was being challenged not only by adversaries abroad and critics at home, but also by allies as French president Charles de Gaulle distanced his country from America's leadership. The stability of the Cold War international system could not be taken for granted.

All these pressures pointed to a growing need to find new approaches to American foreign policy. The Cold War was not about to end. Few questioned its basic rationale: that the Soviet Union and communism represented a threat to both U.S. national interests and the "American way of life." But the methods used to fight the Cold War—the means of containing communism and the Soviet Union—needed to be redefined if America's damaged prestige and diminished power were to be rescued from a seemingly inevitable decline. The 1960s began with a confident note. But it proved to be a troubling decade for the United States at home and abroad.

Berlin

The wall that was built to separate the eastern and western halves of Berlin was the result of a prolonged crisis. After a brief thaw in the mid-1950s, symbolized by the so-called Spirit of Geneva, the Soviet-American relationship had soured. In Europe, the focus of the confrontation became Berlin, where American, British, and French forces retained their postwar control over the western part of the city. In November 1958 Nikita Khrushchev suddenly demanded the evacuation of the Western allies' military installations from Berlin by the following summer; otherwise, the USSR would sign a separate peace treaty with the German Democratic Republic (GDR). Such unilateral action, in turn, would mean that the Western powers would either have to recognize the GDR and negotiate an access agreement with it or accept the absorption of Berlin into East Germany. Neither alternative was appealing: the former would have created a crisis between the United States and the FRG. The latter would have meant a damaging blow to America's prestige.[2]

Khrushchev's ultimatum had several objectives. First, it was a response to growing GDR demands to cut the brain drain of talented young East Germans via the open access route from East to West Berlin. In the 1950s thousands of young East Germans were taking advantage of the one remaining hole in the Iron Curtain; between 1949 and 1961, 2.6 million East Germans moved via West Berlin to the FRG (this represented roughly 15 percent of the total East German population after World War II). Not even a decision in December 1957 to punish anyone leaving East Germany without permission with up to three years of prison could stem the flow.[3]

For the East Germans and Soviets, the exodus was an economic and political disaster. Indeed, not only was the GDR deprived of many of its most promising and best-educated citizens, but the constant movement from East to West also provided a welcome propaganda asset to Konrad Adenauer's West German government and its American supporters. Accordingly, the secondary aim of the Berlin ultimatum was to cause some rifts in the close (from the Soviet perspective, disturbingly so) American–West German relationship. Finally, the Soviets hoped to create doubts within NATO at a time when the alliance was considering whether to deploy medium-range missiles in Western Europe. Confident that the increasing Soviet nuclear capability would raise questions about the reliability of an American deterrent, Khrushchev thus seized the opportunity both to solve an embarrassing local problem and to alter the delicate balance in Europe in the Soviet Union's favor.

The problem for Khrushchev was that the United States and the West European powers simply rejected Khrushchev's 1958 ultimatum. Moreover, he could not make any progress on the issue when he met with President Dwight Eisenhower at Camp David in September 1959. The first Soviet leader to visit the United States, Khrushchev seemed to abandon the controversial issue for the duration of his trip in favor of friendly banter. The following year, however, Khrushchev's tone changed again. In May 1960 he stormed out of the Four Power Paris summit meeting that had been convened to deal with such unresolved issues as the Berlin question. The Soviet leader cited as his reason a series of American U-2 spy flights, one of which had been shot down (and the pilot, Francis Gary Powers, captured and tried) shortly prior to the summit. In his opening remarks at Paris, Khrushchev demanded that Eisenhower publicly apologize for such violations of Soviet airspace. The American president, who had probably expected to end his presidency on a hopeful note, refused to oblige. Charles de Gaulle, host of the shortest high-level summit of the Cold War, saw no alternative to ending the summit. "I'm just fed up!" Eisenhower yelled as he arrived at the U.S. ambassador's residence later on.[4]

In 1961, the first year of the Kennedy presidency, the Berlin crisis headed for a dramatic climax. With more than a hundred thousand East Germans fleeing via Berlin in the first half of 1961, East German complaints increased. Concerned over his credibility, Khrushchev clearly felt that the issue had to be settled. But the Soviet-American summit in Vienna in June 1961 accomplished little, and the war of words intensified. Khrushchev set the end of 1961 as the deadline for a solution, while Kennedy shot back by reaffirming America's commitment to West Berlin and asking the U.S. Congress to increase defense expenditures. As tensions mounted, the Soviets and East Germans resorted to the only solution that was unlikely to provoke an open military confrontation: on August 13, 1961, East German police forces started to construct a barbed-wire fence that separated East and West Berlin. They followed this up by erecting a concrete wall. Access between East and West Berlin was soon restricted to a number of tightly controlled checkpoints.[5]

The building of the Berlin Wall had mixed effects. In the short term, it diffused the crisis by removing its source, for East Germans now found it virtually impossible to move to the West via Berlin (in 1962–89 a mere five thousand were able to do so). The Western powers, especially the United States, protested loudly. But Kennedy did not attempt to remove the wall; he realized that this would risk war. As a result, the Berlin question, while by no means solved, soon occupied a far less central position as a source of Cold War tension. In a sense, the Berlin Wall thus symbolized the acceptance of the status quo in Europe by both sides. To the West, Berlin was clearly not an adequate cause for going to war. To the Soviets, West Berlin's existence was acceptable as long as it no longer drained the best and the brightest from the GDR. However, Khrushchev's decision to build the wall was also indicative of the tightrope act that the Soviet premier was performing. On the one hand, he had been pressed by his East German allies to take action, but on the other hand, he was no more eager than Kennedy was to risk a nuclear exchange. In Berlin, at least, a calm of sorts—however bizarre a concrete wall dividing the former capital of the Third Reich was in the nuclear age—had set in. For all its grotesque nature, the wall actually served a stabilizing function.

In the long run, the wall's more significant symbolic value was not the stability it seemed to provide, but the way in which it clarified the differences between the two political systems it separated for all to see. As Cold War propaganda wars continued, the West never stopped using to its advantage the fact that the East had had to build a wall to keep its people in. Over subsequent decades, the Berlin Wall became *the* symbol of the Cold War's endurance, and the ultimate unanswerable indictment of communism.[6]

From Cuba to MAD

Just over a year following the erection of the Berlin Wall, the world's attention was transfixed on an island not far from the Florida peninsula. This time a crisis prompted by Soviet action truly had the potential for transforming the Cold War into a hot one. In the end, though, its resolution—the upholding of the status quo—was such that future historians may well be excused for not treating the Cuban missile crisis as the moment when the future of all mankind was hanging in the balance.

Before the late 1950s Cuba was an unlikely setting for a major superpower confrontation. Ever since the Spanish-American War of the late nineteenth century, this small island had effectively been a *protectorate* of the United States. The repeated interventions of U.S. marines (1898–1902, 1906–9, 1912, 1917–22) and the domination of American business and trade interests (in the 1920s American companies owned 60 percent of Cuban sugar plantations and imported 95 percent of Cuban sugar) over the island's economy had ensured this stranglehold for decades. But they had also added to the extreme economic and social divisions within Cuba and prompted widespread anti-Americanism. To many Cubans, the U.S.-supported dictatorship of Fulgencio Batista, in power since the early 1930s, symbolized foreign domination and inequality. Finally, after years of guerrilla warfare, the revolutionary forces (the *Fidelistas*) headed by a young lawyer, Fidel Castro, entered Havana in January 1959. However, Castro knew that his success depended in large part on the willingness of the United States to tolerate his new regime. This, as well as memories of the American role in the 1954 overthrow of a leftist government in Guatemala, made the leader of the new Cuba extremely anxious about a prospective military intervention from the United States. By 1960 these concerns made Castro turn increasingly toward the USSR for support. The new Kennedy administration responded by approving the ill-fated *Bay of Pigs* invasion of April 1961.[7]

Although the Fidelistas successfully defeated the invasion force, the Bay of Pigs experience and growing concerns about continuing American attempts to remove Castro from power made the Cuban leader receptive to further offers of Soviet military support. The result was one of the most dangerous crises of the Cold War era, when, a year after the Bay of Pigs, Khrushchev offered to deploy Soviet nuclear missiles in Cuba. Castro accepted, and by the summer of 1962 Soviet ships started delivering the necessary materials, including missiles, to their new ally. Hoping that a future public announcement about the presence of Soviet missiles stationed a mere hundred miles from the American heartland would amount to a substantial propaganda coup, Castro ordered that the installation of these weapons be undertaken in secrecy.[8]

What prompted the Soviets to make this offer has been a subject of much debate. Yet, two essential reasons can be detected. On the one hand, the Soviets undoubtedly saw the survival of the Cuban revolution—the creation of a socialist state in close proximity to the United States—as a significant development in the context of the Cold War. At the minimum, the Fidelistas represented a thorn in the flesh for the Americans; at the most, Castro's Cuba was a harbinger of a series of "liberations" that could align the third world decisively on the Soviet side. On the other hand, having Soviet missiles in close proximity to the United States was bound to upset what remained, from the Soviet perspective, an unfavorable nuclear arms imbalance.

Indeed, despite the launch of Sputnik in 1957 and Khrushchev's bombastic rhetoric about Soviet nuclear prowess, the USSR remained far behind the United States in nuclear arms development. American superiority in terms of the two countries' respective nuclear stockpiles remained massive and proportionately unchanged on the eve of the Cuban missile crisis. According to the best estimates, in 1956 the American lead in nuclear warheads had been 3,620 to roughly 400; by 1961 the difference was 23,200 to 2,450 in the United States' favor. The Soviets' ability to develop a functional intercontinental ballistic missile (ICBM) capability was particularly lagging: according to William Burr and David Rosenberg, Moscow had only four ICBMs that could reach the United States. This and the Americans' decisive edge in the field of long-range strategic bombers, nuclear warheads in NATO countries (for example, in Turkey), and plan to deploy hundreds of Minutemen ICBMs in the 1960s meant that the Soviets were strategically vulnerable. In simple terms, in 1962 the Americans could "hit" the Soviets more easily than the other way around. The Soviets had, though, hundreds of medium-range ballistic missiles that, if stationed close enough to the U.S. mainland, could reach various American cities with relatively accuracy.[9]

The crisis erupted after American U-2 spy planes flying over Cuba spotted the ballistic missile sites under construction in mid-October 1962. Kennedy formed a special inner cabinet of advisers, the Executive Committee of the National Security Council (ExCom), to discuss the situation. They initially considered several options, including a possible military invasion of Cuba and aerial attacks against the missile bases. In the end, though, the Kennedy administration chose to "quarantine" Cuba by erecting a naval blockade to stop any further Soviet shipments from reaching their destination. On October 22 Kennedy went public in a televised address, disclosing the discovery of Soviet missiles in Cuba and announcing that a blockade was in force against all ships bound there. He also demanded the removal of the missiles from Cuba.

For the next few days, the United States and the Soviet Union appeared to be moving toward a nuclear war. The Kennedy administration took its case to the UN and prepared for air strikes and a massive invasion of Cuba. The Castro government called up more than a quarter million Cubans to repel an American invasion, and the Soviet forces on the island, with their nuclear-tipped tactical missiles, were placed on full alert. In the United States, a wave of panic buying swept across the country as people tried to prepare for a possible nuclear holocaust. In the Soviet Union, some news about the crisis reached the public, causing a more limited panic. In Western Europe, America's NATO allies prepared for the implications of a potential nuclear war that might easily spread to Berlin and elsewhere.

After some bargaining, under increasingly tense conditions, the crisis was finally resolved. On October 26 Khrushchev offered to withdraw his missiles from Cuba in return for an American pledge not to invade the island. While Kennedy was considering this compromise, the Soviet leader suddenly made another demand: that the Americans also remove their missiles from Turkey. Meanwhile, the situation was made more ominous when an American U-2 was shot down over Cuba on October 27. On the same day, however, Robert Kennedy, the attorney general and the president's brother, struck a deal with Soviet ambassador Anatoly Dobrynin, whereby Soviet missiles would be removed from Cuba in return for a subsequent, unpublicized removal of missiles from Turkey. On Sunday, October 28, Khrushchev announced the withdrawal of the Soviet missiles from Cuba. Under close American surveillance, Soviet ships took the missiles back home.

Although the Soviets had achieved two important goals—the U.S. pledge not to invade Cuba and the removal of American missiles from Turkey—Kennedy was proclaimed the hands-down "winner" of the crisis. Khrushchev's decision to trust the secret American pledge to remove their missiles from Turkey in part caused the general impression that it was the Soviets that had "blinked." However, as Dobrynin would later put it in his memoir, "The terms of the final settlement were neither a great defeat nor a great victory for Kennedy or Khrushchev."[10]

If anything, the outcome of the Cuban missile crisis confirmed that, as a result of the development of nuclear weapons, the two superpowers had come to a turning point in their bilateral relationship. War against each other was simply not an option; avoiding situations that might provoke a war with catastrophic consequences—nuclear annihilation—was a necessity. While many world leaders called for détente, no one did so more famously than Kennedy in his commencement address at American University in June 1963. Five months prior to his assassination, the president was admonishing the United States and the Soviet Union for being "caught up in a vicious and dangerous cycle, with suspicion on one side breeding suspicion on the other, and new weapons begetting counter-weapons." He offered the following conclusions and recommendations:

> Both the United States and its allies, and the Soviet Union and its allies, have a mutually deep interest in a just and genuine peace and in halting the arms race. Agreements to this end are in the interests of the Soviet Union as well as ours. . . . So let us not be blind to our differences, but let us also direct attention to our common interests and the means by which those differences can be resolved. And if we cannot end now our differences, at least we can help make the world safe for diversity. For in the final analysis, our most basic common link is that we all inhabit this small planet. We all breathe the same air. We all cherish our children's futures. And we are all mortal.[11]

By the time of his assassination, many historians have contended, Kennedy was ready to move toward détente. Indeed, the Kennedy administration took the first steps toward improved crisis prevention and nuclear arms control. The first concrete expressions of this newfound cautiousness were the 1963 Test Ban Treaty and the establishment of a direct telephone link between the White House and the Kremlin.

Whether Kennedy really wished to end the Cold War is impossible to prove. On the Soviet side, however, it seems clear that the impression that Khrushchev had "lost" the Cuban crisis played an important role in his ouster in 1964. Yet, even before Khrushchev was sent to early retirement, the Soviets had made a key strategic decision: to catch the American lead in nuclear weapons. They moved fast. By 1966–67 the Soviets had caught up to the United States in the number of ICBM launchers. Although the Americans still held a number of qualitative and quantitative leads—an edge in the development of multiple warhead technology and more strategic bombers, for example—the reality was very different from that of the pre–Cuban missile crisis years. As the USSR reached virtual parity with the United States in nuclear weapons, however, Kennedy's call for halting the arms race became ever more pertinent.

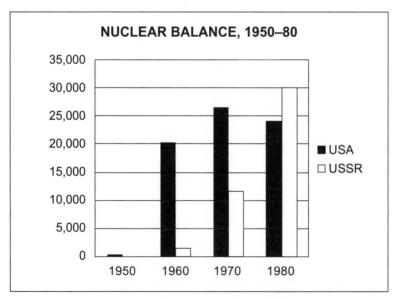

Number of nuclear warheads in American and Soviet stockpiles. Data source: "Global Nuclear Stockpiles," *Bulletin of the Atomic Scientists* 62, no. 4 (July–August 2006): 66.

Given the hostility that had produced the arms race in the first place, however, the road to genuine negotiations about nuclear arms stockpiles was far from easy. To be sure, the Johnson administration tried to pursue better relations with the Soviet Union. In June 1967 Soviet prime minister Alexei Kosygin and Johnson even met in Glassboro, New Jersey, to discuss ways of taming the ongoing arms race between the superpowers. But this potentially important step toward launching détente was overshadowed by the Six-Day War in the Middle East, in which the American-backed Israelis soundly defeated the Soviet-supported Arab states. Johnson's prospective follow-up visit to the Soviet Union in 1968 never took place. While the recognition of the futility of developing ever-growing arsenals of nuclear weapons was sinking in, the stage was simply not yet set for serious Soviet-American negotiations.

Like the Berlin crisis a year earlier, the 1962 Cuban missile crisis had a mixed impact on American foreign policy. Ultimately, however, its resolution was proof that no matter how severe tensions between Washington and Moscow were, neither side wished to risk Armageddon in the form of a nuclear war. In essence, the leaders of the two superpowers had come to realize that the world of mutually assured destruction (MAD) had arrived, and while brinkmanship was ripe, neither, fortunately, was willing to take the ultimate risk.

Transatlantic Dilemmas

The crises over Berlin and Cuba were not merely bilateral Soviet-American skirmishes. Already in the early 1960s, but increasingly as the decade matured, the United States found itself in a difficult position vis-à-vis its NATO allies.

Within NATO, Charles de Gaulle caused severe headaches to both the Kennedy and Johnson administrations. The French president advocated a more independent European policy (led by France) and eventually withdrew France from the alliance's integrated military structure in 1966. Having been in power since 1958, de Gaulle wished to raise France into a new position of prominence in Europe. The flip side of this was, of course, that he wished to limit the American and (if less obviously so) Soviet roles on the Continent. In addition to severing his ties with NATO, de Gaulle pursued the development of an independent French nuclear capability, strengthened the Franco-German special relationship (e.g., the 1963 Franco-German Treaty), and embarked on independent initiatives vis-à-vis

Eastern Europe (Romania in particular) and the Soviet Union.[12] De Gaulle even stirred up trouble in America's backyard: while visiting the city of Montreal in 1967, he declared that the Francophone province of Quebec should move toward independence from Canada. There were many other tense moments over Vietnam, over foreign investment, and over de Gaulle's decision to recognize the PRC without consulting the United States.[13]

De Gaulle was not alone. In the years following the Berlin crisis, West German policymakers expressed increased skepticism about American leadership. The first steps toward Ostpolitik, the policy of movement—the search for improved relations with Eastern European countries and the Soviet Union—was in large part a reaction to the wall and the apparent lack of Western commitment to German unification. There was, moreover, a strong sense in West Germany that the foreign policy of the postwar chancellor, Konrad Adenauer, had only served to strengthen the division of the country. In simple terms, the Hallstein Doctrine of not dealing with countries that recognized the GDR had strengthened, not undermined, the East German state. To Chancellors Ludwig Erhardt (1963–66), Kurt Kiesinger (1966–69), and most obviously, Willy Brandt (1969–74), unification could only be brought about by closer contacts with the Soviet bloc, which would, in turn, reduce the security concerns of many of Germany's eastern neighbors and, in particular, the Soviet Union. Some observers even predicted in the aftermath of the Franco-German friendship treaty of January 1963 that a strengthening of the Bonn-Paris axis might result in the rupture of NATO and the unification-neutralization of Germany.[14]

Such an axis never emerged. In fact, it was clear that neither the Germans nor other Western Europeans were taken by de Gaulle's anti-American sentiments. Nevertheless, by the mid-1960s the Western European interest in détente was clearly growing. In February 1966, for example, British prime minister Harold Wilson visited the Soviet capital to develop trade and technological exchanges (and to discuss possible ways of ending the Vietnam War). De Gaulle visited Moscow in June 1966. The Italians, in turn, invited Soviet president Nikolai Podgorny to Rome in early 1967. Among the large European countries, Germany—whose position was the most delicate—was the odd man out. The Germans' rampant activism would have to wait until the election of Willy Brandt to the chancellorship in the fall of 1969.

European East-West détente therefore did not break out in the 1960s. However, de Gaulle's challenge and the general Western European interest in improving East-West relations forced the Johnson administration to adapt its policies and resulted in a significant shift in NATO's strategy. In part as a response to de Gaulle's independent initiatives toward the Soviet Union and his concept of a "Europe from the Atlantic to the Urals," the alliance adopted in late 1967 the Harmel Report, a policy document that emphasized the need to search for a détente with the Warsaw Pact. While arguing that the alliance members should continue military preparedness, the Harmel Report also stressed that negotiations with the Warsaw Pact could enhance European security. This codification of a loosely coordinated dual-track policy—maintaining military strength and pursuing détente—can be seen as a road map to a different kind of East-West relationship in Europe. But, for the Americans, it was also a way of meeting the challenges posed to NATO's unity in the 1960s. In a sense, the Harmel Report was a reflection of the flexible nature of NATO and America's leadership role in it, as well as a method of linking French and West German initiatives toward the East by forging a unified, but modified, NATO policy. Or, as Andreas Wenger puts it, the Harmel exercise represented, quite simply, the "multilateralization of détente." In June 1968, at a NATO foreign ministers meeting in Reykjavik, the alliance's détente goal was further affirmed with a declaration in favor of mutual force reduction talks with the Warsaw Pact.[15]

The major point in all this was that the United States—in part willingly, in part by necessity—gradually aligned its policies with those of the more détente-minded Western Europeans. In the context of de Gaulle's challenge, this realignment was the best way of ensuring that the damage done to America's leadership role in the Western alliance would remain limited.

Unity and Division in the East

To a lesser degree than in Western Europe, the Soviet bloc experienced its own centrifugal tendencies in the 1960s. This was the case even though contemplating an exit from the Soviet-led military alliance could have bloody consequences; the Hungarians had experienced this in 1956. But the repression ultimately underlined the fragility of the alliance or, as one historian puts it, showed that the American "empire" in Western Europe was built upon a multilateral invitation by the founding members of NATO; the Soviet empire, in contrast, was based upon a unilateral imposition of Moscow's hegemony.[16]

The 1960s saw, though, an effort on the part of Eastern European leaders to find room for independence. As early as 1960, Enver Hoxha, the Stalinist dictator of Albania, openly criticized the USSR. As a result, his country was subjected to Soviet economic pressure but turned to China for economic aid instead. Although Albania remained nominally a member of the Warsaw Pact until 1968, its "defection" was symbolic of the—admittedly minor—cracks in the Soviet hold on Eastern Europe. Leaving the Warsaw Pact did average Albanians little good. Chinese aid was limited, and Hoxha used the increased isolation of his country to strengthen his personal hold on power. In 1966 the Albanian dictator even launched his own cultural revolution, thus emulating Mao Tse-tung's model. Hoxha's policies, however, only confirmed Albania's status as Europe's poorest country and hardly troubled the Soviets.[17]

Potentially more disconcerting than Albania's defection to the Chinese camp was Romania's independent course. Romanian leaders Gheorghe Gheorghieu-Dej and, after 1965, Nicolae Ceauşescu were ruthless authoritarians who combined repression at home with an independent foreign policy. The latter, at least partly geared toward increasing their domestic popularity, resulted in Romania's consistent resistance to any kind of economic integration in the Soviet bloc. In 1967 Ceauşescu ventured toward risky territory by recognizing the FRG and thus breaking Soviet bloc unity on this issue (the USSR had, though, recognized the FRG earlier). Yet, while refusing to participate in the 1968 Warsaw Pact invasion of Czechoslovakia and inviting President Richard Nixon for a state visit the following year, Romania remained a member of the alliance. It was no wonder that Ceauşescu was often described as the eastern version of de Gaulle, someone willing to issue a challenge to the dominant superpower in the name of national pride but unwilling to risk a complete breakdown in relations.[18]

The apparent loosening of Soviet bloc unity did not go unnoticed in Washington. Already in the first half of the 1960s, many in the United States and Western Europe thought that the time had arrived for a policy of bridge building based on the assumption that by gradually increasing economic, cultural, and human contacts with Eastern Europe and the Soviet Union, the West could undermine the Communist parties' hold on power. In 1961 Zbigniew Brzezinski and

William Griffith called for a policy of "peaceful engagement" vis-à-vis Eastern Europe that would result "in the creation of a neutral belt of states" in East-Central Europe. In his famous June 1963 speech at American University, Kennedy called on Americans to "reexamine our own attitude toward the possibilities of peace, toward the Soviet Union, toward the course of the cold war."[19]

The Johnson administration developed these ideas further. On February 25, 1964, Secretary of State Dean Rusk pointed out that "the Communist world is no longer a single flock of sheep following blindly one leader" and that, in particular, "the smaller countries of Eastern Europe have increasingly asserted their own policies." A few months later, Lyndon Johnson called for extending bridges of "trade, travel and humanitarian assistance" to Eastern Europe. In 1965 the so-called Miller Committee (the Special Committee on U.S. Trade Relations with Eastern Europe and the Soviet Union, headed by J. Irwin Miller, chairman of the Cummins Engine Company) reported to Johnson that expanded trade with the Soviet bloc would give the United States great political leverage and called for a relaxation of the export licenses imposed on the Soviet bloc.[20]

At about the same time, the State Department's Policy Planning Staff concluded that loosening restrictions on East-West trade would yield political advantages to the United States. The basic assumption behind the recommendation was simple: American trade restrictions had forced Eastern Europeans to become more economically and politically dependent on the Soviet Union. Therefore, a relaxation of such sanctions would "prove a significant factor in preserving the national identity of the satellite countries and the Western orientation of the satellite peoples."[21]

By 1966, however, the momentum toward peaceful engagement and bridge building collapsed in the United States. The Johnson administration's most ambitious item on this agenda was the East-West trade bill, submitted to Congress in May 1966. American involvement in Vietnam had deepened significantly that year, and it was difficult to argue that while fighting communism in Asia required the sacrifice of American lives, the United States should simultaneously trade more with Soviet bloc countries in Europe. The idea of increased trade with Communist countries even prompted grassroots protests and boycotts of various Eastern European goods. One and a half million Americans signed the John Birch Society's petition opposing increased trade with Communist countries. The East-West trade bill never made it.[22]

The Johnson administration did not, however, abandon the quest for building bridges to Eastern Europe. To be sure, the collapse of the East-West trade bill severely limited the growth of American–Eastern European trade in the 1960s.[23] Unable to use American trading power as a tool for building bridges, however, the Johnson administration shifted to a more multilateral approach to its overall policy toward Europe. An early expression of this came in July 1966, when the Johnson administration issued National Security Action Memorandum 352, which called, "in consultation with our allies," for the United States to "develop areas of peaceful cooperation with Eastern Europe and the Soviet Union."[24]

Significantly, it appeared that the other side was readying itself for détente as well. In addition to the unilateral Soviet contacts with a number of Western European countries, there had, in fact, been movement toward pursuing détente with the West. In the summer of 1966 the Warsaw Pact issued the Bucharest Declaration, which reaffirmed its interest in an all-European security conference, an idea that had first been pushed in 1954. The following year—a month after Romania's recognition of the FRG—another Warsaw Pact foreign ministers meeting repeated this call. Although the Warsaw Pact declarations undoubtedly encouraged NATO to move toward the adoption of the Harmel Report, the fact that the member states continued to exclude the United States (and Canada) from pan-European security talks discouraged the West. But such sticking points appeared minor when compared with the tensions of the early 1960s. The Iron Curtain stood firm, yet minor cracks were already appearing as renegade leaders—from de Gaulle to Ceauşescu—made forays across the East-West divide. Although such centrifugal tendencies resulted in growing pressure toward détente in Europe, however, American foreign policy was being forged in the shadow of war.

Vietnam, a War without End

It is difficult to overestimate the dramatic impact that America's experience in Vietnam had on the overriding confidence that had been so evident in John F. Kennedy's inaugural address in 1961. The young president had called his countrymen to "bear any burden" in what he described as the "hour of maximum danger" in the struggle against totalitarian communism. In subsequent years Southeast Asia became the setting where that struggle was supposedly fought, as the United States pulled out virtually all the stops to try and secure the survival of South

Vietnam as a noncommunist state. By 1968 it had become clear, however, that the awesome military might of the United States was incapable of defeating a materially far inferior force. American hubris—or what Senator J. William Fulbright (D-AR) called the arrogance of power—produced a quagmire that threatened to destroy the very fabric of American society and foreign policy alike.[25]

Although most of the blame for Washington's overcommitment to South Vietnam is usually placed on Kennedy's successor, there was actually a great deal of continuity in U.S. policy from the Eisenhower administration to the Johnson administration. Already in the 1950s the Eisenhower administration had committed American power and prestige to the survival of the Republic of Vietnam (RVN), which had been created in the aftermath of the 1954 Geneva Conference. The United States had refused to endorse the July 1954 Geneva Accords (which called for a nationwide referendum in 1956) and started supporting the construction of an independent noncommunist regime in South Vietnam under Ngo Dinh Diem. In 1955 Diem won an astonishing—and clearly fraudulent—98.2 percent of the vote (including 600,000 votes from the Saigon electoral district, which had only 450,000 eligible voters) in a referendum calling for South Vietnam's independence. The Eisenhower administration not only supported Diem with financial aid and a growing cohort of military advisers but also established SEATO in September 1954. The major purpose of SEATO—whose membership included the United States, France, Britain, Australia, New Zealand, Thailand, Pakistan, and the Philippines—was to "contain" the PRC and its efforts to support communist revolutionaries in Indochina. In short, by the mid-1950s the United States had extended the containment doctrine to Southeast Asia. The inevitable result was that in subsequent years the division of Vietnam—as well as the future of Laos and Cambodia—became the linchpin of the increasingly globalized Cold War.

Within a few years everything started to go wrong. Diem's regime received generous American aid but failed to initiate significant political and economic reforms. Instead, the government repressed any form of dissent and, by doing so, played into the hands of its opponents, both in the South and the North. In 1959 the northerners, having managed to solidify their own internal situation, began sending aid to southern rebels. In December 1960 a number of anti-Diem organizations joined forces to form the National Liberation Front (NLF), a

Communist-dominated political group that became the major southern force fighting against the Saigon regime and for the unification of Vietnam. Using guerrilla tactics and taking advantage of growing rural discontent, the NLF quickly grew into a major force throughout South Vietnam. By the early 1960s the Diem regime in South Vietnam was losing its ability to control the country.

Initially the Eisenhower and Kennedy administrations tried to control the situation by increasing aid packages and sending more military advisers, including special forces trained in guerrilla warfare and counterinsurgency methods, to help the South Vietnamese army (the Army of the Republic of Vietnam, ARVN). However, the record was far from encouraging: in October 1961 the American military estimated that the Diem government had lost its ability to control 80 to 90 percent of South Vietnam's rural areas. To stop further deterioration of the situation, the Kennedy administration ultimately raised the number of American "advisers" in Vietnam from 900 in 1961 to 16,700 in the fall of 1963. By then, though, civil unrest had spread into the major cities, where students and Buddhists launched protests throughout 1963 (the most famous of which was the self-immolation of a Buddhist monk, Thich Quang-Duc, in Saigon in June 1963).

The Kennedy administration's response to the deteriorating situation in South Vietnam was to support, or at least not discourage, a military coup against Diem and his entrenched family oligarchy. On November 1, 1963, Diem and his brother, Nhu, were arrested and killed. This dramatic move did not do anything to stem the hemorrhaging of power from the RVN regime. The problem was that no effective replacement could be found for Diem; instead he was succeeded by what amounted to a series of military juntas that lacked both political legitimacy and administrative competence. Moreover, recognizing the RVN's weakness, now that Diem had been removed, Hanoi decided to increase its support for the NLF in December 1963. This in turn allowed the latter to begin to engage in larger unit actions against the ARVN, and as a result, the situation on the ground grew steadily worse for the Saigon regime.

A more confident leader might have considered finding a negotiated solution to avoid further U.S. commitment in Vietnam. Lyndon Johnson was not that leader. Although he initially postponed any major decisions regarding withdrawal or escalation, the passing of the August 1964 Gulf of Tonkin Resolution—following highly contested reports of North Vietnamese patrol boats' unprovoked attacks against two

American destroyers—gave him the legislative license to use all necessary measures to counter and prevent any further such military attacks. In part because of the U.S. presidential election a few months later, Johnson authorized only a short, sharp attack on North Vietnam's naval facilities. However, after his reelection to office, and with both the military and political situation in South Vietnam deteriorating rapidly, he used his new powers in February 1965 to order the beginning of a limited bombing campaign against the Democratic Republic of Vietnam (DRV) and the dispatch of American marines to defend the air base at Da Nang in South Vietnam. Even this escalation, however, was not enough to stem the communist flood. By the late spring both the NLF and, for the first time, regular army units from the DRV escalated the ground war in the South, believing that Saigon's collapse might be imminent. Faced with the urgent need to stabilize the situation in the South, Johnson was therefore forced to raise the level of American troops quickly and markedly, and in July 1965 he agreed to a deployment of 200,000 men.

Three years later the war was still on. Johnson had committed more than 500,000 American troops to the war in South Vietnam and engaged in a massive bombing campaign against targets throughout Vietnam, as well as neighboring Laos and Cambodia. The United States also tried to bolster South Vietnam through further injections of economic aid. Overall, while not expanding the ground war to North Vietnam because of concerns that the Chinese might enter the war and create a situation similar to that of the Korean War, the United States pursued the conflict with few limitations after 1965. By 1968 the war had become a focal point of not only international criticism but also growing domestic discontent, which marked the 1960s as perhaps the most significant decade of reform in the post–World War II era.

Race, Poverty, and American Foreign Policy

Even before the February 1968 Tet offensive, American domestic opinion had become deeply divided over Vietnam. Public protests, for example, grew gradually in size: whereas in 1964 approximately 25,000 people protested the war in Washington, D.C., two years later the number of participants had increased to several hundred thousand. In 1967 a group of internationally well-known academics, headed by the English philosopher Bertrand Russell, set up the International War Crimes Tribunal, which criticized the American conduct in the war. A few

American pacifists followed the example of the Buddhist monks in Saigon and immolated themselves in protest of the war; thousands of other young men risked jail sentences by burning their draft cards in open defiance of government policy. In 1967 disillusioned soldiers founded a group called the Vietnam Veterans Against the War that would later count among its members such distinguished politicians as the Massachusetts senator and 2004 Democratic presidential candidate John F. Kerry. At college campuses so-called teach-ins proliferated, and antiwar activists clashed repeatedly with the supporters of the government's policies. Although most protesting throughout the 1960s was nonviolent, the war was clearly dividing American society in the second half of that decade, with the supporters of the war slightly outnumbering opponents at the end of Lyndon Johnson's presidency.[26]

The antiwar movement did not, however, represent a truly revolutionary challenge to the social order that the Democratic administrations had inherited from their predecessors. Burning of draft cards may have seemed like a radical form of civil disobedience to those who had grown up in relatively well-to-do white suburban America. But the true challenge was presented by questions of race. For despite some early efforts to end racial segregation in the 1950s, America entered the 1960s as a fundamentally segregated society. In the South, African Americans were habitually denied the right to vote by a system of discrimination that resembled apartheid in South Africa. Throughout the rest of the country, racial discrimination may not have had the same legalized basis as it had in the old Confederate states, but economically and socially there were clearly two Americas in the 1960s. Racism and poverty were twin evils that mobilized various political movements and propelled the careers of a number of activists in the 1960s. The connection between race relations in the United States and the image of itself that the country portrayed abroad during the Cold War has been a particularly active field of research since the 1990s.[27]

The basic question that haunted many U.S. policymakers was simple enough: How does one reconcile the glaring contradiction between the idea of America as a model of democracy and the reality of America as a segregated, racist society? As the Cold War became increasingly globalized in the 1950s and 1960s, as the United States engaged itself in a battle over the hearts and minds of non-Europeans emerging from colonialism, the question became increasingly central to those policymakers trying to ensure that the collapse of European empires did not result in the rise of an anti-American, socialist third world. In a nutshell, the problem was that, viewed from abroad, the United States simply did not practice what it preached.

In her book *Cold War Civil Rights*, the historian Mary Dudziak illustrates the problem effectively. In 1958 an African-American man, Jimmy Wilson, was sentenced to death in Alabama. Wilson had stolen two dollars. The state's governor, James E. Folsom, quickly found himself inundated by mail from around the world. Naturally, he was under fire from such U.S. organizations as the Congress on Racial Equality (CORE) and the National Association for the Advancement of Colored People (NAACP). But among the thousand pieces of mail the governor received each day were letters from Europe, Canada, and Africa. In a press conference, Folsom complained of being "snowed under with mail from Toronto demanding clemency" for Wilson. The internationalization of the protest became clearer when the Trades Unions Congress of Ghana urged that the conviction be overturned "to save the United States of America from ridicule and contempt." U.S. racial segregation was compared with the lack of political and civil rights in Communist countries. And yet, the Alabama Supreme Court upheld Wilson's conviction. In the end, it took an intervention from Secretary of State John Foster Dulles for Folsom to decide to grant Wilson clemency.[28]

The Wilson case was symptomatic of the way in which U.S. foreign policy and civil rights activism interacted. Until the 1950s and 1960s, there had been limited change in the Jim Crow system of the South; domestic "normalcy"—read "legalized racial discrimination"—had been favored in the aftermath of both world wars. At the onset of the Cold War, many civil rights groups, in fact, found themselves under attack from those segregationists who were willing to discredit civil rights activism as a communist-inspired menace to traditional values. Eager to minimize any attacks on the nature of American society that might be harmful to the image of America abroad, the U.S. State Department curtailed the international travel of such open critics as Paul Robeson and W. E. B. DuBois, and instead encouraged international speaking tours by such liberal anticommunists as NAACP leader Walter White (himself only partially of African ancestry) and Edith Sampson, the first African-American U.S. delegate to the United Nations (UN). In short, the U.S. government did its best to present a rosier-than-real picture of American race relations.[29]

Nevertheless, the reality filtered through. The reason why Soviet accusations of American racism—much like American criticism of the lack of democracy in the Soviet bloc—reached wide audiences was simple: they were based in fact. Even as foreign observers hailed the advances in civil rights legislation—such as the *Brown v. Board of Education* decision of 1954 and the Civil Rights Acts of 1964 and 1965—they were outraged by news of the violence that accompanied many acts of protest, whether in Little Rock or Birmingham. Similarly, the racial violence and riots of the late 1960s—as well as the assassination of the most potent icon of desegregation, Martin Luther King Jr., in 1968—confirmed to the outside world that America remained a racially divided nation.

The external image of the United States was particularly influenced by events in the 1960s. In the first half of the decade, the civil rights movement was characterized by nonviolent protests, aimed at ending all forms of legalized discrimination. Under the charismatic leadership of Martin Luther King Jr., who received the 1964 Nobel Peace Prize for his efforts, the civil rights movement scored its biggest successes. In August 1963 an estimated 200,000 to 300,000 people participated in the March on Washington during which King gave his famous "I Have a Dream" speech while standing in front of the Lincoln Memorial. In 1964 President Johnson signed into law the Civil Rights Act, which outlawed segregation in schools, public places, and employment. The following year Congress passed and Johnson approved the Voting Rights Act, which outlawed discriminatory voting practices that had disenfranchised much of the African-American population in the South. A hundred years after the end of the American Civil War, discrimination based on race had finally been outlawed in the United States.

Civil rights activists now turned their attention to other issues, including widespread poverty and the Vietnam War. King, for example, became a strong critic of the war. In a speech called "Beyond Vietnam," delivered in April 1967, he even maintained that the United States was occupying South Vietnam as a colony and that the American government was "the greatest purveyor of violence in the world today." Significantly, he also linked the massive spending on the war with what many considered the inadequate funds allocated to fighting poverty at home. As King put it, "A nation that continues year after year to spend more money on military defense than on programs of social uplift is approaching spiritual death."[30]

The exact impact of the civil rights movement or other social movements on U.S. foreign policy is difficult to measure. It seems clear, though, that the links were more than purely implicit. That African decolonization coincided with the mass popularity of the civil rights movement was hardly coincidental. Within the context of the Cold War, the allegiance of the newly independent nations was viewed as an important asset; the denial of such allegiances to the USSR was considered equally necessary. But domestic racism did not endear Americans to African leaders; propagating the American way of life to audiences whose recent historical experience was one of domination by white European imperialists was difficult. Without taking anything away from the decisive role of civil rights activists in the United States, it seems that both the Kennedy and Johnson administrations were more positively disposed toward promoting racial equality at home because they recognized the need to clean up America's external image as a racially divided society.[31]

In the end, the 1960s were indeed a crucial decade in the United States. The civil rights movement and the movement against the war in Vietnam were two mass challenges to the status quo that had seemingly characterized Cold War America in the 1950s. Although the targets of the two movements were different, both spoke of widespread discontent, particularly among the postwar generation. Both had an impact. Changes in domestic policies—certainly in terms of getting rid of legalized forms of racial discrimination—began to unfold as early as in the first half of the 1960s. The changes in foreign policy took a bit longer.

End of Moral Certainty in Foreign Policy

"When we were kids the United States was the wealthiest and strongest country in the world; the only one with the atom bomb, the least scarred by modern war, an initiator of the United Nations that we thought would distribute Western influence throughout the world. Freedom and equality for each individual, government of, by, and for the people—these American values we found good, principles by which we could live as men. Many of us began maturing in complacency." This quotation from the 1962 Port Huron Statement—the founding document of Students for Democratic Society (SDS)—sums up a certain longing for an era that, in the minds of many members of the baby boom generation, had disappeared by the time they entered university during the Kennedy and Johnson administrations. The students who founded SDS identified themselves as "people of this generation, bred in at least modest comfort, housed now in universities, looking uncomfortably to the world we inherit." America had, SDS cofounder Tom Hayden and his colleagues maintained, lost its claim to being the idealistic beacon of the modern world. As the statement put it, "To be idealistic is to be considered apocalyptic, deluded. To have no serious aspirations, on the contrary, is to be 'tough-minded.'"[32]

At first glance, the Port Huron Statement's message appears somewhat out of place. It was issued, after all, at a time when John F. Kennedy's larger-than-life rhetoric was filling many American hearts with pride in their country, and the civil rights movement was at the height of its "heroic era" of sit-ins, freedom rides, and other forms of nonviolent resistance. The Vietnam War had yet to become headline news; self-immolations were still to come.

The SDS's message can be read, however, as a portent of a widespread feeling of disillusionment—not only in the United States but throughout much of the West—regarding the moral certainties that had helped America cement its unchallenged leadership role in the Cold War world. Such sentiments were naturally strongest among young activists who were searching for a cause that would provide radical and positive change at home or abroad. The ideology of the Cold War was clearly losing its "radical" nature by the early 1960s; the building of the Berlin Wall and the standoff over Cuba offered little but confirmation that the lines that had been drawn in the postwar era were to remain as they were. In subsequent years, the Vietnam War helped to destroy much of the remaining appeal of the ideological underpinnings of American Cold War policy. The baby boomers were simply not convinced by the need to "bear *any* burden."

In fact, they were hardly alone. There were also plenty of those—shortly to be dubbed the "silent majority"—who yearned for the stability and predictability that had characterized the postwar era. But even they appreciated the fact that in the world of the 1960s certain things were not worth the ultimate prize. What the more conservative sectors of American society yearned for was not radical change in American goals but more measured means in their promotion. In this sense, most Americans increasingly agreed on one thing: the war in Vietnam needed to end. The differences—and they were manifest—were over how this was to come about.

In 1968—a presidential election year in the United States—a series of profound challenges to the existing moral certitudes that lay behind American foreign policy became evident. Ironically, they also ushered in an administration that was far from sympathetic to the architects of the Port Huron Statement or the need that the 1960s generation felt for a new type of idealism. Instead, the leadership that would take over in early 1969 searched for a way to build a new domestic consensus by modifying the means, if not the ultimate goals, of American foreign policy.

CHAPTER 2

1968: REVOLUTION, WAR, AND THE BIRTH OF DÉTENTE

"WORLD BIDS ADIEU TO A VIOLENT YEAR," the *New York Times'* headline read on January 1, 1968. The article expressed hopes that the year just beginning would bring about, among other changes, a resolution to America's war in Vietnam.[1] Such high expectations were soon shattered, and 1968 turned into a truly memorable year. It was a year of tragedy, turning points, youthful revolt, military suppression, and hairsplitting political drama.

Foremost among the tragedies were the assassinations of two charismatic political leaders in the United States. Martin Luther King Jr. and Senator Robert F. Kennedy (D-NY)—the most important leader of the civil rights movement and the most popular political figure of the Democratic Party—were gunned down within a few months of each other. Their deaths produced domestic upheaval and widespread disillusionment in a country that was already deeply divided across racial lines and over a war that many believed was the outgrowth of a misconceived foreign policy.

In reality, the Vietnam War had seen its most important turning point several months before the King assassination in early April. The late January Tet offensive, launched by the South Vietnamese NLF with the support of their North Vietnamese allies, did not end the war, but it marked the beginning of an end to America's gradual extrication from Southeast Asia. It also marked the end of the Johnson presidency, as the Texan announced—two months after the offensive had begun—that he would not seek another term as president.

While U.S. forces fought back the Tet offensive and Americans were shocked by the political upheavals in their country, the Prague Spring was in full bloom.

25

Under the leadership of Alexander Dubček, the Czechoslovakian government aimed to reinvent socialism by giving it a "human face." The movement met its much predicted fate when Czechoslovakia's Warsaw Pact allies, headed by the USSR, invaded the country in August 1968. The Johnson government responded meekly: after mild protest, it resumed its efforts to stage a major Soviet-American summit before the American presidential election in November. Military intervention could not kill the Johnson administration's hopes for détente. Only politics could do that. But only briefly.

Indeed, Richard Nixon and Hubert Humphrey were much closer in their foreign policy ideas than either would ever have admitted. Both recognized that the Vietnam War had to be brought to an end; neither gave a clear indication of how that end was likely to come about (Humphrey was advocating a negotiated solution; Nixon supposedly had a secret plan). Both thought that the NATO alliance was a key ingredient of American foreign policy and required some reform; neither could give a clear road map to show how this would be done. Both hinted that America's policy of nonrecognition of the PRC would have to end; neither indicated when. Most importantly, both were bound to pursue a foreign policy course that would require some form of negotiations and agreements with America's foremost nemesis. Although both clearly played politics with foreign policy during the election, both Nixon and Humphrey were likely to pursue détente and an end to the Vietnam War after the election.

The crises of 1968 robbed Lyndon Johnson of the opportunity to forge ahead with his plans for an East-West rapprochement. After the extremely close election in November, it became Richard Nixon's historic task to assemble the team and define the specific program that brought about détente.

Tet

For Lyndon Johnson, 1968 got off to a very bad start. On January 30, the NLF initiated a series of attacks throughout South Vietnam. Within days, thirty-six out of forty-four provincial capitals and five of the six major cities were under fire. Most spectacularly, the NLF attacked the American embassy in Saigon and briefly occupied parts of this symbol of U.S. presence in Vietnam. In Hue, the old imperial capital of Vietnam located just south of the 17th parallel, the NLF, supported by large numbers of North Vietnamese troops, was even more successful. After capturing the city on January 31, it held back an American–South Vietnamese counteroffensive for three weeks.[2]

The NLF had launched the Tet offensive with two political aims in mind. Its primary goal was to cause the complete collapse of the Saigon regime. Given the presence of a half million American troops who supported the South Vietnamese government, such a result would have been virtually impossible. In a sense, the NLF's attack turned into a suicidal act: its casualties were extremely heavy (approximately forty thousand Vietcong guerrillas were killed in the fighting) compared with the number of American and ARVN regular army troop casualties (totaling approximately eleven hundred). The NLF's organization in large parts of South Vietnam was virtually destroyed, making those who survived increasingly dependent on their northern allies.[3]

However, such setbacks were balanced by the successful achievement of the offensive's secondary aim: the U.S. government and general population could only conclude that the war was far from over. By 1967, with close to thirty thousand Americans dead, the antiwar movement had gathered strength and fielded high-level spokespeople, including Senator Eugene McCarthy (D-MN), Robert Kennedy, and Martin Luther King Jr. In November 1967 Robert McNamara, the secretary of defense, had resigned owing largely to his disenchantment with the Vietnam policies that he had personally overseen. Still, at the end of 1967, as internal and external pressure was mounting for an American withdrawal, the Johnson administration claimed that "victory" in Vietnam was just around the corner. The Tet offensive dramatized what was already called the "credibility gap," the wide chasm between what the government was saying about the war and the reality on the ground. Thus, while the NLF might have lost militarily, the Tet offensive illustrated to critical politicians and most of the general public in the United States exactly what the front wanted it to: the hollow nature of the Johnson administration's policy. Johnson's claims that the situation was under control were refuted; instead Tet suggested that further bloodletting would be necessary. When news leaked to the press that Gen. William Westmoreland, the American commander in Vietnam, had requested more troops—a remarkable 200,000 of them—the Johnson administration lost even more of its fragile credibility.[4]

The biggest casualty of the Tet offensive was the president himself. By late March President Johnson became convinced that further escalation could not be sanctioned. In a dramatic television appearance on March 31, he declined to seek reelection, announced a bombing halt, and underlined his intention to seek a peaceful resolution of the war. The beleaguered Johnson solemnly explained,

> With American sons in the fields far away, with America's future under challenge right here at home, with our hopes and the world's hopes for peace in the balance every day, I do not believe that I should devote an hour or a day of my time to any personal partisan causes or to any duties other than the awesome duties of this office, the presidency of your country. Accordingly, I shall not seek and I will not accept the nomination of my party for another term as your president.[5]

Ultimately, the main beneficiary of Johnson's decision was Richard Nixon, the former vice president who narrowly defeated the sitting vice president, Hubert Humphrey, in November 1968. Before that, though, dramatic events in Europe preempted Johnson's early efforts to launch détente.

Prague

Centrifugal tendencies within the Soviet bloc had become increasingly evident during the 1960s. The adoption of more independent policies by some Eastern European countries (such as Romania) hardly meant the erosion of Soviet hegemony in the region. Developments in Czechoslovakia, however, ultimately resulted in a violent crackdown that was reminiscent of previous Soviet military interventions in 1953 (East Germany) and 1956 (Hungary). The August 1968 crackdown also presented a test case for the United States on how to respond to an internal Soviet bloc development. Hopes for détente and questions about the stability of the East-West division were at stake when Johnson considered the proper response to the events in East-Central Europe.

The Czech reform movement did not spring up from nowhere. Throughout the 1960s discontent had been building up in the Czechoslovakian Communist Party (Komunistická Strana Československa, KSČ). The reformers scored an important victory in January 1968 when Alexander Dubçek was chosen as the first secretary of the KSČ. In subsequent months, Dubçek led efforts to give his country "socialism with a human face," through a gradual process of economic decentralization and democratization. His reforms were by no means meant to end the power of the local communist party or to wrest Czechoslovakia from the USSR and Warsaw Pact's embrace (as had been the case with the Hungarian revolution of 1956). Rather, the so-called Prague Spring resembled the reforms initiated by Mikhail Gorbachev in the Soviet Union almost two decades later. Among the freedoms granted were a loosening of restrictions on the freedom of speech. Dubçek, himself a Slovak, also federalized the country into two separate republics and thus lay down the basis for the 1990s division of Czechoslovakia into two independent countries (the Czech and Slovak Republics).[6]

The Soviet Union and other Warsaw Pact nations grew gradually more concerned about the popular cause that Dubçek pioneered. Already in March the Warsaw Five (Bulgaria, East Germany, Hungary, Poland, and the USSR) expressed doubts about the loosening of media controls in Czechoslovakia. In July the Soviet Union and Czechoslovakia began bilateral discussions during which Dubçek defended his reforms but vouched that the Czechs would remain loyal members of the Warsaw Pact and would not permit the legalization of new political parties. On August 3 these agreements were seemingly reenforced by the Bratislava Declaration of the Warsaw Pact members (save Romania), which emphasized the continuation of the struggle of proletarian internationalism against "bourgeois" ideology. The Soviet Union did, however, express its determination to intervene in the affairs of a socialist country if it were threatened by the sinister forces of capitalism. Given that Soviet troops were at the time stationed close to the eastern borders of Czechoslovakia, many interpreted the Soviet stand as a last warning to the Czech reformers.[7]

A few weeks later, Operation Danube unfolded. On the night of August 20–21, 1968, roughly 200,000 troops of the Warsaw Five invaded and occupied Czechoslovakia. Dubçek and his closest aides were arrested, although Dubçek, who was taken to Moscow for "negotiations," was allowed to remain in office after signing the Moscow Protocols. Reforms were gradually cancelled, and Dubçek was eventually forced to resign in April 1969, when a new government headed by Gustav Husak took over. Although "normalcy" returned, Czechoslovakia witnessed large-scale emigration in the aftermath of the Warsaw Pact invasion. There were numerous, mostly peaceful, anti-Soviet demonstrations, including large-scale riots throughout Czechoslovakia in March 1969, after the Czech ice hockey team beat the Soviet team in the world ice hockey championships. The most dramatic form of resistance, though, took place in January 1969. In a scene eerily reminiscent of Saigon in 1963 or the United States some years earlier, a Czech student, Jan Palach, immolated himself in protest.[8]

The Prague Spring, Warsaw Pact crackdown, and subsequent long-term Soviet occupation of Czechoslovakia (the last troops were not withdrawn until 1990) were evidence of the limited legitimacy that local communist parties could muster in Eastern Europe as well as the perceived need for the Soviet leadership to crack down on political movements that had a potentially erosive impact on its control of the region. In a speech to the Polish United Workers' Party on November 13, 1968, Soviet leader Leonid Brezhnev summed up the argument in favor of intervention as follows: "When forces that are hostile to socialism try to turn the development of some socialist country toward capitalism, it becomes not only a problem of the country concerned, but a common problem and concern of all socialist countries."[9] This so-called Brezhnev Doctrine—a term invented in the West—was later called the Soviet version of the Monroe Doctrine. As the Americans had assumed a right to intervene in the internal affairs of Latin American countries to prevent an excess of "foreign" influences, so did the Soviet Union have a right to intervene in Eastern Europe if socialism was under threat. Moreover, if you removed the ideological principles from these statements, the Brezhnev Doctrine—much like the Monroe Doctrine—could easily be seen as a realpolitik statement, aimed at justifying one country's—in this case the USSR's—sphere of influence.[10]

The timing of the Warsaw Pact intervention and the Brezhnev Doctrine was unfortunate for the Johnson administration's desire for détente. One of the immediate results of the Warsaw Pact intervention was that the planning for a Soviet-American summit had to be aborted at short notice. On August 19, only a day before the intervention began, Soviet ambassador Dobrynin approached Secretary of State Dean Rusk with a note suggesting that Johnson could visit the Soviet Union in the beginning of October 1968 for discussions on various issues. Talks about the details of a potential nuclear arms limitation and agreement were also scheduled to begin in late September in Geneva. The White House had even prepared a press release to announce these moves, including the summit, on August 21. When Dobrynin informed Johnson of the invasion of Czechoslovakia on the evening of the twentieth, however, the potentially embarrassing announcement was rapidly cancelled.[11]

In the next few days, U.S. foreign policy makers immersed themselves in trying to understand the motivations behind the Soviet move. There was concern that the Warsaw Pact intervention would not be limited to Czechoslovakia but extended to other "renegade" countries. Romania and Yugoslavia in particular were anticipated to be on the hit list. As these fears dissipated, Johnson and Rusk continued to wonder whether the intervention in Czechoslovakia meant a definite shift in Soviet policy that would not allow the pursuit of détente. The Americans protested the intervention before the UN Security Council and limited any contact with Soviet diplomats, but overt American military intervention was never seriously considered. President Johnson's comments at a Nation Security Council meeting on August 22 sum up the confusion—but also the caution—that characterized the administration's response:

We have no commitment to intervene militarily.
- It would not be in Czech interests or ours.
- The "Cold War" is not over.
- Our relations with Soviets are in transition.
- We would go anywhere at anytime to further interests of peace.
- We have thought at times we have made progress.
- We have the NPT [Non-Proliferation Treaty], Outer Space agreement and the Consular Treaty.
- Soviets thought a pause would enable them to do something in Vietnam. We tried a 37-day pause in the bombing.
- There are some plusses and some minuses.
- We have been disillusioned if not deceived.[12]

Disillusionment did not last long. In September Johnson resumed contacts with Ambassador Dobrynin. The Soviet leadership could hardly have missed the administration's eagerness for détente and responded positively to the idea of a superpower summit. The potential agenda, reflecting preinvasion exchanges, were to consist of a wide variety of issues from the Middle East and Vietnam to nuclear weapons. The Soviets refused, however, to set a firm date for the withdrawal of their troops from Czechoslovakia. In the end, a summit would have to wait. The Warsaw Pact invasion did halt the development of Soviet-American détente.

To argue that the stalling of détente was a result of moral considerations would, however, be faulty. Of course, it would not look good if Johnson shook hands with Soviet leaders immediately after they had ordered a bloody invasion. It would clearly imply that as far as the United States was concerned, Czechoslovakia did not matter. But in addition to bad publicity and moral dilemmas, the Czech invasion actually opened an opportunity for the Johnson administration to address the ruptured unity of NATO. Most significantly, the crushing of the Prague Spring reminded Western Europeans of their vulnerability in light of the Warsaw Pact's conventional military superiority and their dependency on American military support. Within the United States, the Warsaw Pact intervention also served to undercut demands for reducing U.S. troop levels in Europe.

In simple terms, by intervening to crush the Czech reform movement, the USSR and its allies had reminded the West why NATO existed in the first place. In this sense, August 1968 resembled October 1956, when the Spirit of Geneva had evaporated as Soviet tanks rolled into Hungary to crush an earlier reform movement. Again, a military intervention reversed the course exactly at the moment when it appeared that a serious East-West breakthrough was in the offing. Unlike in 1956, however, the crushing of the Prague Spring did not produce anything other than a reassessment of strategy. It caused a delay in the implementation rather than an abandonment of détente.

1968 Elections

Foreign policy was an important part of the 1968 presidential election. Or, more accurately, Vietnam was a significant foreign policy issue that made a crucial impact on the outcome of the election. Other external issues hardly appeared in the campaign slogans of the major candidates of either party. Détente was never mentioned; the Prague Spring and its suppression received almost formalistic condemnation from all candidates, Democratic and Republican, in the field. And yet, the implication was that foreign policy was about to change no matter who occupied the White House in 1969. Serious questions were raised regarding basic assumptions of the U.S. containment policy by cohorts of young people demonstrating against the war. To an extent, the Democratic Party's presidential hopes were dashed by its standard-bearer's association with the specific policies that had, for the first time since World War II, raised serious questions about the validity behind the principles of America's Cold War grand strategy.

On the Democratic side, the race for the nomination was filled with high drama. At the beginning of the electoral season, the general assumption was that the race was to be but a coronation for the candidacy of the incumbent president. In the New Hampshire primary on March 12, however, Eugene McCarthy, an openly antiwar senator from Minnesota, gave Johnson a severe warning by claiming 42 percent of the vote. Although the president received 49 percent, the result probably prompted New York senator Robert F. Kennedy to enter the race four days later. When Lyndon Johnson withdrew from the campaign on March 31, Vice President Hubert Humphrey joined the campaign as a "replacement incumbent." Unlike McCarthy and Kennedy, Humphrey did not contest the primaries (only thirteen were held in 1968) but relied upon the support of the party machines to carry him into the candidacy.

Over the next few months, the United States experienced some of the worst urban violence in its history. The immediate cause for the race riots that erupted in April and May in sixty cities across the country was the assassination of Martin Luther King Jr. On April 4 King was gunned down in Memphis. The news was received with shock and anger across the nation, and the National Guard was called on to restore order in many of the most-affected urban centers, such as Washington, D.C., and Baltimore. Upon learning of King's assassination, Robert Kennedy, traveling in Indianapolis, made a moving impromptu speech in which he, in keeping with a major campaign theme, called for racial reconciliation. His words did little to quell the violence throughout the country, but they may have kept an incipient riot from erupting in the Indiana capital. Two months later Kennedy, after narrowly defeating McCarthy in the California primary, gave his last speech. As he prepared to leave a Los Angeles hotel in the early morning hours of June 5, he was shot in full view of television cameras.[13]

The Kennedy assassination pushed the already divided Democratic Party into complete disarray. Humphrey's lackluster campaign was given an indirect boost by the entry of Senator George McGovern (D-SD), a Kennedy supporter in the early primaries, into the race. Perhaps most importantly, McGovern's challenge created the context in which the August 1968 Chicago Democratic Convention—which opened on August 22, the day following the Warsaw Pact intervention in Czechoslovakia—descended into an open battle between the supporters of McCarthy and those of Humphrey. Although the vice president eventually clinched the nomination with a comfortable majority of delegates, the most memorable images—and ones that dominated media coverage—were the violent clashes between the Chicago police and antiwar demonstrators that took place on the city's streets and outside the convention hall throughout the week. Numerous arrests were made. Some of the more prominent leaders of the protests, the so-called Chicago Seven, were charged with conspiracy (they would be tried but acquitted in 1970). To make matters worse, another former Kennedy supporter, Senator Abraham Ribicoff (D-CT), made a much quoted comment in his speech nominating McGovern. "If George McGovern were president," Ribicoff said, "we wouldn't have these Gestapo tactics in the streets of Chicago." Hubert Humphrey did not appreciate the implication.[14]

Ultimately, the major beneficiary of the Democrats' "civil war" in 1968 was Richard Nixon. The Republican would later be remembered for his foreign policy feats, but in 1968 he did not campaign for détente. He did promise an end to the Vietnam War but refused to yield details of his secret plan. Nixon's ultimate triumph was not, in short, the result of any promise that he would reinvent the wheel when it came down to managing U.S. foreign affairs. Rather, he benefited from a significant amount of name recognition and a consistent message of restoring order. Also, because he was selected at an orderly Republican convention in early August, Nixon's campaign had a significant edge over Humphrey's when it came to attracting voters longing for an end to domestic turbulence.

Nixon was the best known of the Republican candidates, but he did not run unopposed. The two most important challenges came from California governor Ronald Reagan and New York governor Nelson Rockefeller. Positioning himself in the middle between a right-wing conservative (Reagan) and a left-wing moderate (Rockefeller), Nixon was able to attract enough delegates from both camps to clinch the nomination of his party in the first ballot. He then surprised most observers by choosing, as a way of assuring conservative voters, Maryland governor Spiro T. Agnew as his running mate.[15]

It was Nixon's message of "law and order" that secured him the presidency. Throughout the Republican primaries, in the aftermath of the Democrats' convention, and all the way up to the November election, Nixon took advantage of the mounting tide of civil disobedience. In the end he won by a relatively narrow margin—43.4 percent over 42.7 percent—over Humphrey. The rest of the votes, including majorities in five southern states, went to the third-party candidate, Alabama governor George Wallace. The candidates spent a noticeably limited amount of time discussing foreign policy on the campaign trail, however. Nor did Humphrey and Nixon—in the manner of most later presidential races—debate each other in public. Yet, as became clear in the months after Nixon's triumph, he was ultimately interested more in making his mark as foreign policy president than anything else. By year's end Nixon had assembled a team headed by Harvard professor Henry Kissinger.

Nixon, Kissinger, and New Diplomacy

The two men who dominated U.S. foreign relations after the debacles of 1968 came from dramatically different backgrounds. Richard Nixon was the consummate American politician, a man who for most of his adult life had focussed on achieving the position he finally assumed in January 1969. Born in 1913 in California, he had been trained as a lawyer, served in the Navy during World War II, and was elected to the House of Representatives in 1946. For the next fourteen years, his political career had been meteoric: elected senator in 1950, vice president in 1952 and 1956, and selected as the Republican Party's presidential candidate in 1960. After two demoralizing defeats—to Kennedy in 1960 and to Pat Brown for the governorship of California in 1962—Nixon spent a few years in a political wilderness. He had sat out the 1964 election, when Barry Goldwater was crushed by Lyndon Johnson. The triumphant return in 1968 could not have been more satisfying for the fifty-five-year-old Nixon.[16]

Henry Kissinger was never a politician. Born in 1923, he was a Jewish refugee from Germany who had built a remarkable career as an academic and foreign policy consultant. In 1968 Kissinger was a professor of international relations at Harvard University with numerous books, including the bestselling *Nuclear Weapons and Foreign Policy* (1957), to his name. He had worked briefly for the Eisenhower, Kennedy, and Johnson administrations and was also a longtime associate and chief foreign policy adviser to Nixon's chief nemesis in the Republican Party, Nelson Rockefeller. When he was asked to take charge of Nixon's National Security Council staff, though, Kissinger was unburdened by any potential mixed loyalties. While winning the presidency was the ultimate prize for Nixon, playing a crucial role on world stage as an architect of U.S. foreign policy was clearly a dream come true for Kissinger, who had, during the Republican convention, called Nixon's selection a "disaster" for the party and, potentially, for the country.[17]

They may have been an odd couple on the surface, but a deeper look reveals a number of important—personal and substantial—symmetries between Nixon and Kissinger. Both were outsiders, or considered themselves as such. Both were driven by a deep sense of insecurity that did, however, manifest itself in different ways. Nixon, although he had made a career on populist anticommunism, was neither a gifted speaker nor comfortable among people. He loved politics, no question about that. But he was not a charismatic personality, like John F. Kennedy, Ronald Reagan, Bill Clinton, or Barack Obama. Nor was Nixon particularly comfortable or successful in backroom political haggling; he was no Lyndon Johnson. Nixon loved politics because it was the only vehicle he could use to gain distinction. But, throughout his remarkable career, Nixon was, it seems, constantly on the brink of some catastrophe or another: from accusations that he had taken bribes in the early 1950s to the ultimate disaster, the Watergate scandal, in the 1970s. The former he countered effectively on national television with the so-called Checkers speech. The latter drove him out of office for good, in part because he was caught lying so repeatedly on national television.[18]

In contrast, Kissinger had made his career in academia at a time when Jewish intellectuals were just starting to break into the Ivy League establishment. If Nixon turned his "outsider" status into a political asset of sorts, Kissinger undoubtedly benefited from the fact that he was of European origin at a time when the postwar transatlantic bond was being cemented. His Jewishness, however, always meant that, as Jeremi Suri puts it, Kissinger was part of the establishment but never a true member thereof. In fact, even as a high-ranking member of the Nixon White House, Kissinger had to repeatedly swallow the bitter pill of anti-Semitism. Like Nixon, he was subjected to numerous accusations of wrongdoing and immoral acts as a policymaker. In contrast to Nixon, however, Kissinger was one of the main beneficiaries of the Watergate scandal, which essentially made him the prime foreign policy maker in 1973–75. The recipient of the 1973 Nobel Peace Prize and a worldwide celebrity for the remainder of his life, Kissinger's career—

notwithstanding various efforts to paint him as a war criminal—had a far happier trajectory than Nixon's.[19]

The bond between these two men of very different backgrounds is the stuff of endless speculation and volumes of articles and books. Suffice it to say here that aside from any psychological explanations (that both men repeatedly refuted), there were two substantial reasons why the two men established such a close—if not always happy—relationship. First, Nixon wanted to be a great foreign policy president. But his experience from years in the Eisenhower administration had taught him that large bureaucracies, such as the State Department, could not be trusted to carry out an effective foreign policy. There was simply too much inertia, too many vested interests, too much red tape, and in particular, too many difficult diplomats with careers on the line to allow a president hoping to be his own secretary of state to control. Thus, Nixon built his own foreign policy operation. After appointing Kissinger as his national security adviser, Nixon charged him with implementing a coup d'état of sorts. With Kissinger at its helm, the National Security Council started operating a series of back channels to key countries (such as the Soviet Union, China, West Germany, and Israel). With his close physical proximity to Nixon, chairmanship of a number of key interdepartmental committees, and a small tight-lipped staff, Kissinger gradually established himself as the foreign policy czar of the Nixon administration, thus outflanking the secretary of state, William P. Rogers.[20]

The second substantial factor that helped forge the bond between Nixon and Kissinger was their essential agreement on where U.S. foreign policy should be heading. In general, both believed that American foreign policy was in trouble and could best be rescued by a policy that was less ideologically driven than in previous years. While concerned over the loss of that much-overvalued commodity known as "prestige" should America appear to be defeated, both Kissinger and Nixon recognized the need to find some way out of the Vietnam War. In fact, Kissinger had acted as an emissary for the Johnson administration in a 1967 secret but ultimately unsuccessful negotiation effort code-named Pennsylvania. At the end of 1968 the Nixon-Kissinger team faced the unattractive task of somehow extricating more than a half million American troops from Vietnam without admitting the obvious: that the United States had lost a war. The often tragic details of ending America's longest war became a major part of the foreign policy of the Nixon administration. However, Vietnam seemingly also taught Nixon and Kissinger an important lesson about the limits of military power. In a speech in May 1968 Nixon claimed, "It is time to develop a new diplomacy for the United States, a diplomacy to deal with future aggression—so that when the freedom of friendly nations is threatened by aggression, we help them with our money and help them with our arms; but we let them fight the war and don't fight the war for them. This should be the goal of a new diplomacy for America."[21] The germ of a key part of what would later be known as the Nixon Doctrine was here: the United States would support allies through material aid but not—as in Vietnam—by putting U.S. troops in harm's way. Kissinger— although he would have some tactical problems with such logical outcomes of the Nixon Doctrine, such as Vietnamization (see chapter 3)—clearly agreed on the necessity to emphasize diplomacy over power.

Another key issue on which Kissinger and Nixon were in agreement was the opening to China. While he talked little in public about this possibility, Nixon had made some hints to this effect, most famously in an article published in *Foreign Affairs* in 1967 where he wrote, "We simply cannot afford to leave China forever outside the family of nations, there to nurture its fantasies, cherish its hates and threaten its neighbors." In a speech to the Bohemian Club that same year, Nixon had also hinted at the possibility that the United States might take advantage of the Sino-Soviet split. For his part, Kissinger had toyed with similar ideas when drafting Nelson Rockefeller's foreign policy platform during the New York governor's failed 1968 presidential campaign. In 1968 neither of them had a clear idea how the opening could come about or whether it was even possible to achieve it during the Nixon presidency. Neither knew much about China. But it is equally clear that the possibility of an opening became a virtual obsession for both men after they entered office.[22]

The central issue, though, was neither Vietnam nor China. Both were ultimately subservient to what Nixon, in his Bohemian speech, called "subject A, the Soviet Union."[23] Even Kissinger, while making noises about a politically multipolar world, was essentially convinced that the continued military bipolarity— whether measured in forms of alliance leadership or nuclear parity—made the United States and the Soviet Union the true leading powers. Although he wrote in 1968 that "for the first time, foreign policy has become global," Kissinger clearly emphasized that on that global scene the USSR was the only serious rival facing the United States.[24] While in office, Kissinger's diplomacy in regional crises—from Vietnam and the Middle East to Southern Africa and Europe—was constantly driven by concerns about Soviet intentions. The idea of "triangulation"—of using the "China card" as a diplomatic tool to influence Soviet behavior—would send him on the historic secret trip to Beijing in the summer of 1971. The Soviet Union would indeed remain subject A, a threat to be contained. In this fundamental way, the primary goals of American foreign policy would not change dramatically with the ascendancy of Richard Nixon and Henry Kissinger. Containment remained the key. The methods, however, would change. To a large extent, détente would be the major tool of managing America's global rivalry with the Soviet Union.

"New Approaches to Friend and Foe"

In February 1969 Henry Kissinger's face appeared on *Time* magazine's cover for the first time. "Bonn, London, and Paris may disagree on a score of issues, but they are in happy unanimity in their respect for him; even Moscow is not displeased," the article commented. It went on to describe how Kissinger "knows more foreign leaders than many State Department careerists." With Kissinger at the helm, there would be "new approaches to friend and foe," *Time* announced.[25] Some of his critics have since hinted that Kissinger's memoirs are best read as novels rather than as true historical accounts. Within a month of Nixon's inauguration, the media had clearly figured out who would make the decisions about foreign policy in years to come.

In subsequent months and years there were, indeed, numerous new policies toward the Soviet Union, the Vietnam War, the PRC, and Western Europe. The realpolitik approach advocated by Richard Nixon and his chief foreign policy adviser seemed to offer a more viable (and less costly) alternative for safeguarding American interests. At its basis lay the notion that America's international adversaries, most specifically the Soviet Union and China, acted more out of national interest than ideological convictions. Given the military clashes between the two Communist powers, which climaxed in a severe border conflict in March 1969, the United States had a particularly tempting opportunity to play the Chinese and Soviets off each other through a careful application of rewards and pressures. Among other things, the Nixon administration hoped to use the USSR and the PRC to help bring about an "acceptable" end to the Vietnam War. By the end of Nixon's first term, Kissinger had orchestrated the seemingly impossible breakthroughs with China, the Soviet Union, and Vietnam. By 1972 the edifice of the "structure of peace" that Nixon had promised in his inaugural address was erected.

Before entering into a detailed discussion of the various aspects of the Nixon-Kissinger grand design, it is worth raising two questions. First, were these policies truly new? Were Nixon and Kissinger simply continuing policies already pursued by their predecessors and demanded by their domestic audience? Second, how important was the role of American policymakers in the unfolding of détente? If America had indeed lost much of its prestige and some of its power in the 1960s, if the world had become global and multipolar, had Washington's ability to dictate the course of events also been dramatically cut down?

The answer to the first question seems relatively straightforward. There was little new in the pursuit of détente. The Nixon administration essentially picked up where the Johnson administration had left off on the first tentative nuclear arms negotiations and the planning of a superpower summit. In fact, Johnson had come tantalizingly close to making a visit to the USSR in his last year as president. Granted, the Nixon administration spent far more time preparing the substance of the summit that ultimately took place in May 1972. But the Nixon administration's foreign policy was actually much more conservative in its overall goals than the shapers of that policy would later admit. Most significantly, the Cold War mind-set—present in American foreign policy since the 1940s—remained relatively unchanged. That the Soviet Union was, as Nixon put it, "subject A" was incontestable and drove the president, his national security adviser, and others to pursue détente as a new way of containing the Soviet Union. In fact, as John Gaddis puts it, "There were striking similarities in the approaches to containment advocated by George Kennan in the 1940s and by Henry Kissinger in the early 1970s. . . . On the underlying assumptions that informed the American approach to the world, the congruence in viewpoint was impressive."[26] In short, the continuity in American foreign policy reached farther back in history than Nixon and Kissinger's immediate predecessors.

The second question is more difficult. Yet, as will become obvious on the pages that follow, numerous other players had an equally, if not more, significant influence on the subsequent course of events. Without the policies pursued by such Soviet leaders as Leonid Brezhnev, for example, détente had no chance of being erected. Without such initiatives as West German Ostpolitik, pursued relentlessly by Chancellor Willy Brandt, European détente would hardly have taken the shape it did. And to make but an obvious and closely related point: without Mao's consent, there would not have been an opening to China.

With Nixon's inauguration in January 1969, American foreign policy indeed changed. But the era of negotiation that followed was neither a dramatic and unprecedented break from the past nor a course entirely reliant on those charged for its conduct.

CHAPTER 3

"Three for Three": Triangulation

Richard Nixon rarely inspired audiences with his oratorical gifts. But on January 20, 1969, he came close. On that cold Monday afternoon, the new president lay down, in larger-than-life rhetoric, his vision of American foreign policy. "Let us take as our goal: where peace is unknown, make it welcome; where peace is fragile, make it strong; where peace is temporary, make it permanent," he proclaimed. He then added the best-remembered phrase of his first inaugural address by announcing, "After a period of confrontation, we are entering an era of negotiation." And he did not stop there. "Let all nations know that during this administration our lines of communication will be open," Nixon offered. He promised that all countries could join the United States in a joint effort "to reduce the burden of arms, to strengthen the structure of peace, to lift up the poor and the hungry." In his effort to outperform his former nemesis, John F. Kennedy, Nixon truly sounded like the prince of peace, a worthy successor of his hero, Woodrow Wilson.[1] But, there was a catch: "All those who would be tempted by weakness, let us leave no doubt that we will be as strong as we need to be for as long as we need to be."[2] In short, we are ready to talk but do not try to push us around.

Nixon had essentially summarized the two basic principles driving his foreign policy. He was, first of all, keen to negotiate and reach agreements with America's Cold War adversaries. His comment about reducing "the burden of arms" could easily be read as an invitation for the USSR to engage in serious negotiations over limiting the size of the two countries' nuclear arsenals. He also made a less-than-muted reference to his interest in developing the U.S. relationship with China by asserting that the United States was promoting the creation of "a world in which no people, great or small, will live in angry isolation."³ He was probably not thinking mainly about the North Koreans or the Albanians.

From the American perspective, the new approach succeeded in the early 1970s. The United States—after more than two decades—finally opened a relationship with the PRC in 1971–72. At the same time, the Soviets, apparently concerned over the new Sino-American relationship, agreed to a Nixon-Brezhnev summit in May 1972, which led to the signing of the SALT I Agreement. Although it did not bring an end to the nuclear arms race, SALT I symbolized the long road that the United States and the Soviet Union had traveled during the decade following the Cuban missile crisis of 1962.

One should not, of course, read too much into Nixon's inaugural address when exploring the successes his administration enjoyed vis-à-vis the USSR and the PRC. In fact, if it had not been for the undeclared war between the Soviet Union and the PRC, two months' after Nixon took office, the famed opening to China might never have taken place and the PRC's "angry isolation" could have continued for some time into the future. More importantly, the successes with China and the Soviet Union—as well as Nixon's political fortunes at home—were connected to what was the most acute issue that the new administration had to address: the Vietnam War.

Vietnam: The Symptom

The Soviet Union may have been "subject A," but the overriding immediate problem of American foreign policy in early 1969 was Vietnam. Nixon had no miracle solution. Like his predecessors, he held onto the idea of a "peace with honor" as the only acceptable solution to the war he had inherited. Kissinger shared this idea as he prepared to take office as the national security adviser. He did not see Vietnam as crucial in its own right. To Kissinger, Vietnam was a complication, a nuisance, a possible obstacle to bigger achievements. Thus, like most everyone else, he was convinced that the war had to be ended. But the caveat was crucial: if the endgame was not handled properly, Vietnam could undermine American credibility in its dealings with foe and friend alike. The war's importance did not lie, Kissinger thought, in anything concrete and certainly not in Vietnam's geostrategic significance in the nuclear age. "Vietnam was not a cause of our difficulties but a symptom," Kissinger wrote in his memoir. The central problem—and the reason why an exit from Vietnam was necessary—was that "the war had stimulated an attack on our entire postwar foreign policy."[4] To accept defeat would thus imply that U.S. foreign policy since 1945 had in fact been based on false assumptions. To avoid this interpretation, Americans needed, in effect, a peace that would leave no doubt that the United States had achieved its main objective of sustaining an independent state south of the 17th parallel. Defeat was not an option.

There was another basic continuity from the Johnson years: Kissinger and Nixon believed for quite some time that North Vietnam could be pressed into making an acceptable peace agreement by the use of superior American military force. In the early days of the administration, Kissinger relentlessly pressured Nixon to approve a secret bombing campaign against Vietcong facilities in Cambodia. As would be the case many times in the future, Kissinger's ability to take advantage of Nixon's own inclinations and perceived need to appear tough won the day over the State Department's objections. The result was the Operation Menu bombing campaign that commenced on March 17, 1969. The following day Kissinger was, according to Nixon's chief of staff Bob Haldeman, "beaming" as early reports showed that the campaign was a success. Such delight on Kissinger's part later turned to frustration as the bombing campaigns ultimately had seemingly little impact on Hanoi's position, a fact Kissinger discovered in his first secret meetings with North Vietnamese negotiators Le Duc Tho and Xuan Thuy in August 1969 and February–April 1970.[5]

To break this deadlock, the Nixon administration chose further escalation. In late April 1970, after a coup d'état that removed the neutralist Prince Norodom Sihanouk from power, American and South Vietnamese troops poured into Cambodia to obstruct the Ho Chi Minh Trail and destroy the elusive Communist headquarters, the Central Office for South Vietnam (COSVN).[6] For a couple of months, the ARVN and U.S. forces, numbering eighty thousand at their peak, trekked throughout eastern Cambodia, wreaking havoc on the countryside as they captured enemy supplies. But they rarely made contact with the enemy and merely managed to drive the Communists farther west. As a consequence, the operation created a large flood of refugees, most of them searching for sanctuary in Phnom Penh. Internal political, social, and economic instability became endemic in Cambodia and opened an opportunity for the Khmer Rouge—now allied with the deposed Prince Sihanouk—to increase its influence in the beleaguered country.

As Cambodia sank into further chaos, Kissinger's peace talks in Paris did not progress. In another series of negotiations that began in September 1970, Kissinger made little progress with the North Vietnamese. Exasperated and under pressure at home, Nixon called for a standstill cease-fire and an American bombing halt throughout Indochina in a televised speech on October 7, 1970. He then proposed a comprehensive peace conference to end the fighting throughout the region and offered to negotiate a complete U.S. withdrawal from Indochina. It was, in Kissinger's view, "a comprehensive program that could well have served as a basis for negotiation except with an opponent bent on total victory." His point has some merit: amid applause in the United States for what many considered a generous offer, the North Vietnamese refused the latest Nixon proposal on October 10. They demanded a political solution that would begin with an American-initiated removal of the key figures in the Saigon administration.[7]

The explanation for Hanoi's resistance lay in the Nixon administration's own policies. Vietnamization, the gradual withdrawal of U.S. troops coupled with enhanced U.S. aid to and training of the ARVN, had commenced in 1969. Nixon had approved the policy in principle at about the same time he approved the secret bombing of Cambodia.[8] The policy was aimed at silencing domestic critics on the left and the right. Although the antiwar critics could not charge that Nixon was simply continuing the war effort as before, because the withdrawals were coupled with increased U.S. aid, the hawks would find it difficult to accuse Nixon of abandoning an ally. After all, was it not logical to let the Vietnamese themselves fight their own war? In other words, while fewer body bags were likely to mean fewer antiwar demonstrations, more material aid should have satisfied the concerns of those who could not stomach the reality that the United States was being gradually smoked out of Vietnam. That Nixon was not completely behind Vietnamization, however, was evident in the delay before the plan became operational. The American president's first public announcement of troop withdrawals was made after his first meeting with South Vietnam's President Nguyen Van Thieu on Midway Island in June. The actual policy was announced on the island of Guam at the start of Nixon's around-the-world trip in July.[9]

Although it applied, in the first instance, to Vietnam, the Nixon (or Guam) Doctrine quickly acquired broader meaning. Nixon was essentially saying that American troops would no longer be sent in large numbers to take part in regional conflicts. The president made three basic points in his speech:

First, the United States will keep all of its treaty commitments.
Second, we shall provide a shield if a nuclear power threatens the freedom of a nation allied with us or of a nation whose survival we consider vital to our security. Third, in cases involving other types of
aggression, we shall furnish military and economic assistance when
requested in accordance with our treaty commitments. But we shall
look to the nation directly threatened to assume the primary responsibility of providing the manpower for its defense.[10]

In other words, the United States would help allies and other friendly
nations that were in trouble with every means possible other than committing
large numbers of American troops. In years to come, these principles would be
applied elsewhere, perhaps most significantly in the Middle East. They were meant
to counter what many had considered an overextension of direct American commitments. But the Nixon Doctrine by no means signaled a sudden retreat of the
United States from the global arena; it merely redefined the means by which
American power was to be exercised.

One of the realities of the practical application of the Nixon Doctrine was
that it removed Hanoi's incentive to accept a negotiated settlement. As American
troops declined from a high of 540,000 in early 1969 to just more than half of
that by the end of 1970 (280,000), to 140,000 in late 1971, and to a mere
24,000 by the end of 1972, Kissinger's effort to pressure his interlocutors in Paris
was not backed up by any meaningful threat. No matter what carrots he offered,
he had very few sticks to wield.[11] As Kissinger put it in his memoir, he had "great
hope for negotiations," but with Vietnamization, U.S. policy "ran the risk of
falling between two stools. With Hanoi we risked throwing away our position in
a series of unreciprocated concessions. At home, the more we sought to placate
the critics, the more we discouraged those who were willing to support a strategy for victory."[12]

In fact, the emphasis of Nixon and Kissinger's diplomacy had already gravitated toward the "great game," the emerging triangular relationship between United
States, the Soviet Union, and China. But Vietnam remained intricately tied to the
broader goals of the first Nixon administration. In fact, a large part of the attrac-
tion of triangular diplomacy was that it provided the means for achieving a decent

interval with minimum of loss to American prestige. By 1971–72 the Nixon administration had not only reduced Vietnam's importance in U.S. domestic politics by a steady withdrawal of American troops. The simultaneous breakthroughs in relations with the Soviets and the Chinese also dramatically showed the benefits of diplomacy and negotiations in the conduct of U.S. policy toward its major adversaries.

Dealing with "Subject A"

The Soviet Union had been on top of the new administration's agenda from the very beginning. Indeed, while Nixon made public offers of negotiation, Kissinger thought that the moment was ripe to engage the USSR. The goal of such engagement, though, was peculiar: Kissinger insisted that the new administration could use diplomacy to manage Soviet behavior, to channel it into certain directions by using a policy of linkage. As he wrote to Nixon early on in the presidency, "Moscow wants to engage us. . . . We should seek to utilize this Soviet interest . . . to induce them to come to grips with the real sources of tension, notably in the Middle East, but also in Vietnam."[13] In subsequent months and years, Kissinger and Nixon aimed at building a structure of relations in which the Soviets, should they cooperate in defusing a number of regional crises, would be offered economic and other rewards.

In developing détente, the Nixon administration had to contend with U.S. public opinion accustomed to viewing the USSR as a permanent menace. To be sure, Nixon's rhetoric did cause a gradual shift in attitudes. According to a Harris poll, in late 1968 only 34 percent of voters—and many of those presumably had voted for the Democrats—thought that agreements and cooperation between the United States and the Soviet Union was possible. In the summer of 1971 this figure had gone up to 52 percent. Still, almost half of Americans remained skeptical and would not be swayed without concrete evidence of Soviet-American cooperation.[14] As the start of the 1972 presidential campaign loomed and the situation in Vietnam remained gloomy, Nixon was under considerable pressure to deliver something that would prove that his high-flying rhetoric about a structure of peace was not a mere pipe dream.

The actual practice of détente and linkage with the USSR became a matter of a highly centralized machine centered around the president and his national security adviser. To pursue linkage and détente, Kissinger and Nixon established the back channel to the Kremlin via Ambassador Anatoly Dobrynin. Although much has been made about the foot-dragging on both sides, the real problem at the beginning was not the general principle of linkage. Rather, the Soviet ambassador objected to the type of linkage that Kissinger and Nixon aimed to pursue. During the meeting in the White House on February 17, 1969, that effectively established the back channel (attended by Kissinger and Malcolm Toon of the State Department in addition to Dobrynin and Nixon), the Soviet ambassador called for serious negotiations "on various subjects and at various levels." When prodded by Nixon, Dobrynin mentioned SALT and the Middle East as the key issues. Nixon responded by stressing that one should separate SALT from "the settlement of larger political issues" but did not foreclose the possibility of holding "parallel" talks. Dobrynin was curious and pressed for clarification on "the linkage between arms talks and negotiations on political issues," and Nixon asserted that "progress in one area is bound to have an influence on progress in all other areas." Further clarifying his central point, Nixon explained that it was his hope that the Soviets would "do what they can to get the Paris talks [on Vietnam] off dead-center." Dobrynin was evasive and maintained that if a true era of negotiation were to be launched, "it would be wise not to begin with the most difficult issues."[15]

Aside from establishing the Kissinger-Dobrynin back channel, the meeting set the tone for Soviet-American negotiations for the next few years. Linkage was real. The bilateral relationship was to be pursued over a number of issues ranging from SALT to Vietnam. And yet, as they sparred over Berlin, the Middle East, Vietnam, and many other issues, Kissinger and Dobrynin reached no agreements. The same was true of the more "formal" Soviet-American negotiations that began in the fall of 1969 over nuclear weapons (that is, SALT). Not until May 1971, when Kissinger announced the conceptual breakthrough in the SALT process—the decoupling of discussions about offensive and defensive nuclear arms—was any major step toward the eventual SALT agreements taken. And even then, two and a half years into the Nixon administration, it was difficult to argue that the much-vaunted structure of peace was irrevocably in the making.

In fact, linkage was largely to blame for the slow progress of détente in 1969–71. The Soviet reluctance—and inability—to pressure the North Vietnamese to be more forthcoming in the Paris peace talks made the Nixon administration less willing to accommodate Soviet interests in the Middle East (and press the Israelis to accommodate Egyptian interests). In the fall of 1970 concerns that the Soviets were in the process of building a submarine base in Cuba produced a minicrisis that revealed an atmosphere of mutually assured suspicion. In discussions over formalizing the status of and access rights to Berlin, neither wished to give in, and it was the West Germans who—under the leadership of Willy Brandt—pushed the process ahead. In a similar vein, although the Soviets accepted American participation in the discussions leading to the CSCE in 1969, the Nixon administration—suspicious of the Soviet initiative—linked U.S. commitment to progress in other areas, most notably discussions on mutually balanced forced reductions (MBFR). As a result, the initial multilateral preparatory talks of the CSCE did not commence before November 1972 (discussed in chapter 4).

All told, progress was slow and, for the most part, hidden from the public view. In fact, the May 1971 announcement of the conceptual breakthrough was followed by further stalling as the Soviets were unwilling to be pinned down to a date for a Soviet-American summit during which the nuclear arms agreements would be signed. To be sure, the outline of the Berlin agreements was ready by early June 1971. But Kissinger decided to hold back; only in August 1971 would the Soviets suddenly yield on both of these fronts. In intervening months, the focus was on something more dramatic.

Triangulation

Despite the apparent success of the Warsaw Pact invasion of Czechoslovakia, the USSR was not the unchallenged leader of the socialist bloc when the Nixon administration entered office. The Communist monolith that American policymakers had fretted about since the late 1940s had been permanently split by the increasingly independent course of the PRC. Since Joseph Stalin's death in 1953, the Sino-Soviet relationship had soured. For the Soviet leadership, Mao's China represented the clear and present danger of the late 1960s. Ideological differences—based largely on different socioeconomic setups in the USSR and China—spelled a very different view of the road to a socialist society. In the 1960s the Chinese developed a nuclear capability and then embraced the Cultural Revolution, which—on top of the catastrophic Great Leap Forward of the 1950s—confirmed to the technocrats of the Brezhnev generation that their former allies had, in essence, gone mad. Or, as Odd Arne Westad puts it, "Believing themselves to be rational policymakers and the Chinese to be heavily ideological and under the spell of Mao's apocalyptic visions, the Kremlin had to fight the remaining part of the Cold War always looking over its shoulder."[16]

But if the Soviet leaders feared a "yellow horde" in the late 1960s and began to amass large numbers of troops on the Sino-Soviet border, the Chinese held a similar threat perception of the Soviet Union. To them, the Brezhnev Doctrine and the Prague invasion were clear examples of Soviet "socio-imperialism." But even before 1968 China's hostility toward the USSR had been evident. Indeed, the split had become public in 1960 at a Romanian Communist Party Congress in Bucharest. In 1964, following Khrushchev's fall, Mao asserted that there had been a counterrevolution in the USSR. In 1967 the Red Guards seized the Soviet embassy in Beijing.

Finally, in March 1969—only two months after the inauguration of Richard Nixon—Soviet and Chinese troops clashed along the Ussuri River. Further clashes in August and rumors that the Soviets were contemplating a nuclear strike against China confirmed the seriousness of the split. In the end, Alexei Kosygin visited Beijing secretly to meet with Chinese premier Zhou En-lai. Discussions of the border conflict commenced the following month. While they would remain inconclusive, the two sides had drawn back from the brink of war.[17]

Increased tension in Sino-Soviet relations did not go unnoticed in Washington. In the months that followed the Ussuri clashes, Nixon and Kissinger discussed the implications and possibilities that the open rift between Beijing and Moscow offered. In fact, it would have been difficult to feel otherwise: on March 10, 1969, Ambassador Dobrynin asked Kissinger whether the Americans were "going to take advantage of the Soviet Union's difficulties" with the PRC. After relaying this information to the president, Nixon mused how "sometimes events that we could not have foreseen may have some helpful effect" on the contours of American foreign policy.[18] As the tension between the Soviets and Chinese continued to simmer and encouraging reports about China's potential interest in an opening to the United States began to filter to Washington, the administration began a series of exploratory moves toward Beijing.

The actual progress toward the famed opening to China was, though, rather slow. The first secret messages sent via Pakistan in the late summer of 1969 were accorded no immediate response. Then, in December 1969, contacts between the new administration and China recommenced in Warsaw, one of the few cities where both the United States and the PRC had diplomatic representatives. But these were soon broken off as the White House—Kissinger and Nixon—took over the handling of the China initiative. Efforts to forge a link yielded no fruit until early 1971. Undoubtedly, the Chinese were reluctant because of the Nixon administration's aggressive tactics in Vietnam; the 1970 Cambodian invasion resulted in particularly harsh rhetoric from Beijing. But there were also unmistakable signs, such as the opening of Canadian-Chinese relations in October 1970, of the PRC's desire to break away from its diplomatic isolation. In late 1970 and early 1971 a series of secret messages—received via Pakistan and Romania—arrived in Washington indicating China's willingness to receive an envoy from the United States.

These exchanges ultimately culminated in Kissinger's secret trip to China on July 9–11, 1971. Accompanied by a small group of advisers, the national security adviser landed in Pakistan and then secretly boarded a plane to Beijing. After two days of detailed discussions with Chinese premier Zhou En-lai, Kissinger and his entourage returned to Islamabad and continued on to Paris and, ultimately, to Nixon's San Clemente residence in California. On July 15, from NBC studios in Burbank, Nixon delivered what amounted to one of the most shocking announcements of his presidency. He told a national audience about Kissinger's trip and explained that the PRC had extended, and Nixon had accepted, an invitation to visit Beijing the following spring.

When Air Force One eventually landed in Beijing on February 21, 1972, however, the world was transfixed. Nixon called this trip "the week that changed the world," and he was not far off the mark. To be sure, the major significance of the trip was symbolic. There were few concrete details and agreements: the Shanghai communiqué, which the leaders of the two countries endorsed at the end of the trip, was a set of broad principles, not a treaty. It acknowledged the disagreements between the two countries—particularly over Vietnam and Taiwan—and announced that the countries considered the expansion of trade and other exchanges desirable. The communiqué was, in fact, an accurate reflection of the Nixon visit and of the immediate future of Sino-American relations. The Chinese, without saying so publicly, indicated that reuniting Taiwan with the mainland (a centerpiece of the PRC's foreign policy since 1949) was not a question of crucial

urgency. Nixon and Zhou agreed that the Soviet Union was a menace to bo[ ]
United States and the PRC. Ultimately, the visit established that neither Chin[ ]
the United States was, in 1972, interested in the relationship for its own sake; it
was a strategic tool to be used in dealing with the Soviet Union, the reluctant
third party in triangular diplomacy. In bilateral terms, however, there were no
major concessions on either side. The main outcome of Nixon's "journey of peace"
was to establish the necessary basis for a future relationship.

The opening to China and Nixon's trip had meaning, of course, beyond the
establishment of a bilateral Sino-American relationship. Although Nixon and
Kissinger insisted that the trip was not "directed against any other nation," the
Soviets were clearly implicated. In a phone call to Ambassador Dobrynin a few
hours before the official announcement of his secret trip, Kissinger had made this
clear. The Soviets had a choice, the NSC adviser indicated: to "advance quickly"
in the stalled negotiations over the Berlin agreement and settle the timing of a
Soviet-American summit or "retreat to a painful reassessment of our relations."[19]
Soon after this conversation, the Soviets responded in much the way Kissinger
and Nixon had hoped. The final details of the Four Power Agreement on Berlin
were ironed out, and the pact was signed on September 3, 1971. Negotiations on
nuclear arms moved toward a conclusion. And Moscow issued a formal invitation for Nixon to visit the Soviet Union.

Moscow, 1972: "An Extraordinary Opportunity"

In clear contrast to the content-poor but symbolically rich trip to China in
February 1972, the Soviet-American summit three months later was overloaded
with concrete agreements. Most importantly, the SALT I Agreement and the Anti-
Ballistic Missile (ABM) Treaty set a standard for the regulation of the nuclear arms
race. SALT I was an interim five-year agreement on offensive missiles (ICBMs
and submarine-launched ballistic missiles [SLBMs]), while the ABM Treaty reg-
ulated defensive systems. (Concluded without an expiration date, the ABM Treaty
would remain in force for thirty years.) The result of years of haggling—some of
it at the summit itself—these were landmark treaties. Yet, they produced plenty
of criticism that would undermine the chances for concluding future agreements.

To be sure, the ABM Treaty of May 1972, which limited the number of
ABM sites each side could have to two (one around the capital, the other around

a missile site), was generally considered a positive achievement. It certainly allowed each side to cut down spending on an expensive and unproven program. Indeed, as long as the ABM Treaty remained in force—until 2002—the United States and the Soviet Union were committed to not developing a national missile defense system.

But the five-year interim agreement on offensive weapons was something else. The final terms of the agreement allowed the Soviets higher ceilings on ICBMs (1,618 to 1,054) and was apparently asymmetric in another way: while the number of U.S. SLBMs was frozen at 656 (on 44 submarines), the Soviets were allowed to build up to 740 (on 62). To many critics in the United States, it was thus easy to charge that Nixon and Kissinger had, in effect, given up U.S. missile superiority. Already on May 24, for example, John M. Ashbrook, a conservative Republican member of the House of Representatives from Ohio, had denounced the agreement as one that would "lock the Soviet Union into unchallengeable superiority, and plunge the United States and its allies into a decade of danger."[20] The most outspoken critic, however, was Senator Henry "Scoop" Jackson (D-WA). The SALT I Agreement was "a bad one," the senator charged. Realizing that he would not be able to gather enough votes to defeat the ratification of the treaty, however, Jackson opted for a different course. In mid-August 1972 he introduced the Jackson Amendment to the SALT I Agreement which stated that in negotiating the next nuclear arms agreement, the president must make sure that the United States would not commit itself "to levels of intercontinental strategic forces inferior to the limits provided for the Soviet Union." It was a brilliantly worded amendment: could any responsible official or U.S. senator commit to negotiating something that would make the United States "inferior"? The amendment was adopted by the Senate on September 14, 1972, by a sizable majority (56–35). But the demand that the United States would either have to have equal (or superior) "levels of intercontinental strategic forces" was also the opening shot in the domestic criticism that overshadowed the next round of SALT negotiations.

The reality was more complex than such critics as Jackson publicly argued. The interim agreement did not cover a number of issues, which, in effect, guaranteed the United States an advantage for years to come. For example, the exclusion of multiple independently targetable reentry vehicles (MIRVs) from the agreement meant that the United States could go ahead with "qualitative" improvements and use its technological advantage to arm missile launchers with multiple warheads. As a result, over the next five years, the United States continued to hold a significant advantage in the overall number of nuclear warheads. (In late 1972 the United States had 4,146 warheads whereas the USSR had only 1,971.) In addition, the Soviets did not insist on counting either long-range bombers equipped with nuclear weapons (in which Washington had a 450 to 155 advantage) or U.S. forward base systems (that is, medium-range missile launchers based in Europe) as part of the overall American offensive capability. While pointing out that the continued U.S. superiority overall may have satisfied some hawkish critics at home, however, it also raised a different type of criticism: The SALT I Agreement had done little to curb the arms race. It had merely shifted it to other types of weapons. As one of Kissinger's own advisers, William Hyland, later pointed out, the SALT I Agreement "actually produced a sizeable buildup in strategic weaponry."[21]

The critics were on the mark: the Moscow summit produced an imperfect nuclear arms control agreement. But this criticism also misses a major point: to Nixon and Kissinger, the SALT agreements were not about numbers of missiles or about stopping the nuclear arms race dead in its tracks. SALT and the summit produced a politically significant deal, which set Nixon apart as the president who had concluded the first such agreement, while ensuring Kissinger's position as— at least in the public perception—the premier diplomat of his era. And while they were less spectacular in their public relations value than the Shanghai communiqué, the SALT agreements—both the ABM Treaty and the five-year interim agreement on offensive missiles—were at the same time more concrete than anything Nixon and Kissinger had brought home from China. When added to all the other bilateral agreements that were signed in Moscow in May 1972— on science and technology, medicine and public health, environmental protection, space exploration—and the creation of a joint economic commission, it was hard to escape the conclusion that the Moscow summit was another "journey for peace." Indeed, it seemed most appropriate that on the last day of the summit, May 29, the United States and the Soviet Union signed what Raymond Garthoff calls the "charter for détente."[22]

Officially called the "Basic Principles of Relations between the United States and the Union of Soviet Socialist Republics," the charter of détente was negotiated by Kissinger without the State Department's knowledge. It was a wide-ranging and, to many, alarming document. It referred to "peaceful co-existence"—a term usually employed by the Soviets, not the Americans—as the key principle of the bilateral relationship. The role of security interests was highlighted while ideological differences were downplayed. One of the basic principles was that the two countries would not seek "unilateral advantage" at the expense of the other country. This was no treaty. Rather, as Kissinger put it during a news conference on departing Moscow, "I think we are talking here about a general spirit which regulates the overall direction of the policy."[23]

That spirit, however, was notably absent in discussions about the ongoing conflicts in Vietnam and the Middle East. On the latter, the Soviets' call for a comprehensive approach by the two superpowers went entirely unheeded by Nixon and Kissinger. Instead, the Americans chose to play a waiting game; Nixon proposed that Kissinger and Dobrynin continue discussions on the back channel. By the morning of Monday, May 29, all Nixon would promise to Brezhnev was to "do my best to bring about a reasonable solution" to the ongoing Arab-Israeli crisis.[24]

On the topic of Vietnam, differences of policy were more acute. The North Vietnamese spring offensive—supported by Soviet arms shipments—launched in March 1972 had almost derailed the Moscow summit. In April and May the Nixon administration had responded with the heaviest bombing campaigns of the war so far (Linebacker I) and a blockade of the Haiphong Harbor, the main supply route used by Soviet ships. Kissinger's secret visit to Moscow in April had defused some of the tension, but it had not changed the simple fact that in Southeast Asia, the Soviets and Americans remained enemies, supporting proxies in a bitter struggle that—if linkage was real—had the potential of derailing the progress of détente.

In the end, the Vietnam War did not prevent the Soviet-American rapprochement. Even as Soviet arms were used to shoot at American targets and U.S. bombs sank Soviet ships, Nixon and Brezhnev were joking and drinking at the Soviet leader's dacha outside Moscow. Kissinger, in talks with Soviet foreign minister Andrei Gromyko, implored the Soviets to press the North Vietnamese to be reasonable in future negotiations and offered what would amount to the so-called decent interval between the eventual American exit and the final settlement of the inter-Vietnamese conflict. As he put it on May 27, "All we ask is *a degree of time so as to leave Vietnam for Americans in a better perspective*. . . . We are prepared to leave so that a communist victory is not excluded, though not guaranteed."[25] This "offer" summed up a fundamental lesson of the American approach to the 1972 summit and Soviet-American détente: improvements in superpower relations far outstripped the fate of a long-standing American ally, South Vietnam.

When Nixon and Kissinger left Moscow on Monday, May 29, they did not go straight to Washington. Instead, they flew to Kiev, stayed overnight, and continued on Air Force One to Tehran for another historic meeting, this one with the shah of Iran. On the afternoon of May 31, the presidential party arrived in Warsaw, where Nixon met with Prime Minister Eduard Gierek. On June 1, 1972, Nixon and Kissinger finally headed back to the United States. After arriving at Andrews Air Force Base on that Thursday evening, the president did not go directly to the White House but instead chose to dramatize the results of his whirlwind trip by taking a helicopter to Capitol Hill. At 9:40 p.m. he gave a televised speech in front of a joint session of Congress. "We have before us an extraordinary opportunity," Nixon proclaimed. He went on to catalogue the recent agreements with the Soviets and the significance of the opening to China, and added, "The summits of 1972 . . . are part of a great national journey for peace."[26]

Nixon did not mention that the 1972 presidential elections were only five months away or that the fighting in Vietnam continued.

"Three for Three"

"You've got three for three Mr. President," Kissinger told Nixon on the evening of October 12, 1972. Having just returned from Paris after the latest negotiation marathon with North Vietnamese diplomat Le Duc Tho, Kissinger was confident that he had secured a deal that would end the Vietnam War. Kissinger argued that the treaty was far better than anyone could have expected. It guaranteed a cease-fire in place by the end of October. This would be followed by the withdrawal of U.S. troops and the return of American prisoners of war (POWs) within sixty days. After Nixon's historic trip to China and the signing of the SALT agreements in Moscow, the end of America's longest war was to be the crowning achievement of the administration's foreign policy. With the presidential elections less than a month away, Nixon could only be elated that his foreign policy had been a great success.[27]

The October agreements fell apart. Only in January 1973—after a heavy bombing campaign (Linebacker II) that even exceeded the one in May 1972

(Linebacker I)—was the peace agreement initialed in Paris. Even then Vietnam would not see a day of peace, as the fighting continued all the way into late April 1975, when, finally, the country was unified after a successful North Vietnamese offensive against the South. By then Nixon was gone and Kissinger was blaming weak-kneed senators and members of Congress for failing to support their former allies in South Vietnam with adequate military support. The relationship between Vietnam and Watergate, South Vietnam's collapse and Nixon's fall, remains among the most hotly debated in the historiography of American foreign policy.

The fact of the matter, though, was that by the end of 1972 Nixon's call for a structure of peace had been successfully implemented. The war in Vietnam remained a controversial issue at home and abroad, but it had lost its centrality as an issue against which the administration's record was measured. Indeed, 1972 was a year of Richard Nixon's great triumphs. As he visited China and the Soviet Union, the president could easily claim that he had changed the course of history, that the structure of peace he had publicly clamored for was truly in the making. This was, surely, what most Americans thought as they reelected Richard Nixon over George McGovern by a wide margin—more than 60 percent of the popular vote, the fourth-largest margin in the history of U.S. presidential elections—on November 7.[28] And yet, problems remained. Despite hopes to the contrary, the Vietnam War remained unresolved on Election Day. A crisis in the Middle East that would eventually undermine détente was left brewing by an administration focused on other issues. Most fatefully, Nixon had approved the use of clandestine strategies in his 1972 reelection campaign; the scandal that would eventually prove to be his undoing began to unfold immediately after his second inauguration. Indeed, the seismic nature of Nixon's foreign policy triumphs would forever be overshadowed by the drama of Watergate, which would soon be the focus of most everyone's attention.

At the time of his second inauguration in January 1973, however, the tragedies were still to come. Instead, the thirty-seventh president could claim that he had restored perspective to American foreign policy in his four years in office. The prospects were great; the possibilities enormous. As Nixon put it, "The time has passed when America will make every other nation's conflict our own, or make every other nation's future our responsibility, or presume to tell the people of other nations how to manage their own affairs."[29] Détente and the opening to China had showed the way forward to an era of a "new and more durable pattern of relationships among the nations of the world," Nixon added. This trend toward a new "pattern of relationships" was most evident in the continent that Nixon failed to mention: Europe.

CHAPTER 4

NIXON, KISSINGER, AND DÉTENTE IN EUROPE

"EUROPE HAS VERY WEAK LEADERSHIP right now. . . . They don't unite and they don't take farsighted views. . . . In any case, what Europe thinks is basically irrelevant." With such customary bluntness, Henry Kissinger summed up his views of America's NATO allies' role in international relations in February 1973.[1] To be sure, he was talking to his Chinese counterparts and may have used such disparaging language mainly to highlight the unparalleled significance of America's—and Kissinger's own—role in determining the course of international affairs. Yet, his imperious attitude was not unique among American policymakers (or among the Soviet or Chinese ones).

At the time Kissinger made such comments, détente—the kind of détente that included the high-stakes game of triangular diplomacy and Soviet-American nuclear arms talks—appeared, indeed, to be ruling the day. Europe was a sideshow. If anything, détente—the apparent acceptance of the East-West division—appeared to make the old continent downright irrelevant. Of course, in 1989 the Cold War ended in Europe with a dramatic, if virtually bloodless, revolution, which swept away geriatric communist dictatorships and even reform-minded socialist leaders. By then, Europe's irrelevance was gone, and the continent was basking, however briefly, in the limelight. Indeed, Europe was never irrelevant to the contours of the Cold War.

At the time that the Nixon administration came to office, American policy toward Europe reflected two, often contradictory, goals. On the one hand, successive American administrations had encouraged European economic integration through such policies as the Marshall Plan and subsequent support to the

European Economic Community (EEC) and British membership in the community. On the other hand, Washington was concerned about the effects of European political integration and independent European policy initiatives that jeopardized—or had the potential of undermining—America's unquestioned leadership of the transatlantic alliance. As Henry Kissinger put it, Americans constantly asked themselves, "How much unity should we want? How much diversity can we stand?" From this premise, it followed that "adjusting the balance between integration and autonomy will be the key challenge [for American policy vis-à-vis Europe]."[2]

The challenge of finding the right balance between integration and autonomy was exacerbated in the 1960s and early 1970s within the context of an emerging East-West (Soviet-American) détente and the first enlargement of the EEC in 1973. While détente signaled the reduction of Cold War tensions, it also—at least in theory—meant that the Western Europeans' reliance on America's military power became less of a determining factor in the policy calculations of the leaders in Bonn, Paris, and elsewhere. Meanwhile, the 1973 introduction of Great Britain, Ireland, and Denmark to the EEC raised the specter of serious economic competition with potentially difficult political consequences. In Kissinger's terms, Western "unity" seemed vulnerable, as a decreasing threat from the East and the forward momentum of European integration translated to increased European "autonomy." The challenge to the Nixon administration was to try and adjust policies to the changing environment in a way that would prevent a fundamental challenge to Western unity. In the end, as Nixon told British prime minister Harold Wilson, NATO was a "blue chip investment" for U.S. foreign policy.[3]

From the commanding heights of Nixon's Oval Office or Kissinger's globe-trotting jet, Europe may not have been at the cutting edge of international relations in the early 1970s. Yet, a number of coinciding developments from détente to further European integration meant that U.S. policy toward Europe had to be continuously fine-tuned. While détente flourished, transatlantic relations often suffered.[4]

Nixon's Détente and Brandt's Ostpolitik

Although Western Europe was clearly not at the top of the Nixon administration's foreign policy agenda, the president and Kissinger did focus on certain aspects of

European policy. In particular, they worried about the possible proliferation of independent European initiatives toward détente. In this regard, France's Charles de Gaulle set an example through a series of diplomatic maneuvers vis-à-vis the East (*politique a l'est*). Already in 1964 de Gaulle recognized the PRC, thus openly breaking with U.S. policy. In 1964–65 de Gaulle started publicly arguing that overcoming the Cold War division was possible only by questioning the very logic behind the existence of the two blocs. His motto was catchy: "Détente, entente, and cooperation."[5]

For a few years de Gaulle pushed for his *politique a l'est* with some gusto. The peak year was undoubtedly 1966, when France withdrew from NATO's unified military command structure and de Gaulle embarked on a high-profile visit to Moscow. By 1968, however, de Gaulle found himself besieged and outmaneuvered. By approving the Harmel Report, which called for the pursuit of détente with the Warsaw Pact (see chapter 1), NATO effectively adopted (or co-opted) some of de Gaulle's *politique a l'est*. At home, the May 1968 student riots were the most serious symptom of a deep internal crisis. Although he was able to restore order in Paris rather quickly, de Gaulle resigned in April of the following year. By this time, however, the August 1968 Warsaw Pact invasion of Czechoslovakia had further undercut de Gaulle's foreign policy. His successor, Georges Pompidou, was unable to efficiently rekindle the initiatives toward détente set by de Gaulle.

In the late 1960s, however, Germany, not France, presented the most serious Western European challenge to American foreign policy. The major watershed in the FRG's official foreign policy came when Willy Brandt's Social Democratic Party (SDP) won the September 1969 elections to FRG's national parliament, the Bundestag. However, the ideas that lay behind Brandt's Ostpolitik (or Neue Ostpolitik, to distinguish it from the original 1920s version) were already well established. They bore many hallmarks of de Gaulle's politique a l'est and the Johnson administration's idea of bridge building. But Ostpolitik had a more specific ultimate aim: the unification of Germany.

Brandt and his closest foreign policy adviser, Egon Bahr, had been thinking about new ways to pursue unification at least since the building of the Berlin Wall in 1961. In 1963 Bahr coined the term "change through rapprochement" (*Wandel durch Annäherung*), which captured the central message of Ostpolitik. The basic notion was straightforward: a policy of engagement with the Warsaw Pact nations would bring about a gradual change in the East German regime, decrease the perception of a possible revival of the German threat that remained widespread in the Soviet bloc, and hence remove a major obstacle to unification. If combined with improving the stability of East-West relations in Europe, Brandt and Bahr argued, the dream of unification could be turned into a reality.

As the foreign minister of Kurt Kiesinger's Grand Coalition government in 1966–69, Brandt repeatedly discussed the need for changes in both NATO and the overall organization of European security. He was a supporter of NATO's 1967 Harmel Report and its call for a policy of détente. But he even went further, initiating, also in 1967, a Franco-German study group on "European security problems in the 1970s" and suggesting in a radio interview that "something new" in place of NATO and the Warsaw Pact would provide a better system of guaranteeing European security. Chancellor Kiesinger's opposition to any effort at undermining FRG's NATO pillar and the Warsaw Pact invasion of Czechoslovakia in 1968, however, kept Brandt's broader ambitions under check during his tenure as foreign minister.[6]

When Brandt was elected chancellor in September 1969, he and Bahr set out to practice Ostpolitik. Much Annäherung (rapprochement) followed. In the early 1970s a number of treaties were signed: the Non-Aggression Pact with the USSR in August 1970, the West German–Polish Treaty recognizing the Oder-Neisse line in December 1970, a Four Power agreement on the status of Berlin in 1971, and finally, the Basic Treaty between East and West Germany in 1972. In a span of a few years, the uncertainties about the postwar division of Germany were transformed, laying the basis for further East-West détente in Europe. In 1971 Brandt received the Nobel Peace Prize for his efforts.[7]

Kissinger and Nixon worried about Brandt's diplomacy. Although pursuing détente with the Soviet Union himself, Kissinger thought that Ostpolitik might, if it proved successful as an independent West German policy, become a new form of "Gaullism."[8] And he and Nixon faced the same problem the Johnson administration had faced vis-à-vis de Gaulle. The United States could not, without risking an adverse reaction from the FRG, move to block the progress of Ostpolitik. Moreover, if it had objected to the overwhelming desire for détente in Europe, the Nixon administration would have played into Soviet hands by promoting further disunity within NATO. As Kissinger put it in February 1970, [while] there is no necessary incompatibility between alliance and integration with the West on the one hand, and some degree of normalization with East, on the other . . . assuming Brandt achieves a degree of normalization, he or his successor may discover before long that the hoped-for benefits fail to develop. Instead of ameliorating the division of Germany, recognition of the GDR may boost its status and strengthen the Communist regime. . . . More fundamentally, the Soviets having achieved their first set of objectives may then confront the FRG with the proposition that a real and lasting improvement in the FRG's relations with the GDR and other Eastern countries can only be achieved if Bonn loosens its Western ties.[9]

In other words, Kissinger worried mainly about the leverage that Ostpolitik might give to the Soviet Union.

The answer was, as Kissinger wrote in his memoir, "to channel [West German foreign policy] in a constructive direction by working closely with Brandt and his colleagues." Indeed, Kissinger saw as his main task the need to coordinate the onset of U.S.-Soviet détente with the unfolding of Ostpolitik. In Kissinger's words, "If Ostpolitik were to succeed, it had to be related to other issues involving the Alliance as a whole; only in this manner would the Soviet Union have incentives for compromise."[10]

The way to get the West Germans on board was to point out the disastrous consequences to NATO and American presence in Europe should Ostpolitik be practiced too independently. Thus, during his February 1969 trip through Europe, Nixon warned then–Foreign Minister Brandt that the Soviets' interest in Ostpolitik was part of "a major Soviet objective to weaken the [NATO] alliance and especially the FRG."[11] Happily, Brandt had much the same concern. He had no intention of breaking away from NATO but wanted to find a way of aligning Ostpolitik with NATO policy, most specifically with the 1967 Harmel Report. Brandt was after a new kind of equilibrium between the East and West in Europe, an equilibrium in which the United States played a key role by maintaining its presence on the old continent.

Brandt also well understood the need to coordinate his policies with the United States. And he did not have any illusions as to who, aside from Nixon, was the prime foreign policy maker in Washington. In October 1969 Brandt sent Bahr to meet Kissinger, not Secretary of State William Rogers, thus creating another Kissinger back channel. In the October discussions, Bahr outlined to Kissinger his vision of Ostpolitik, detailing the planned West German overtures to the USSR, Poland, and East Germany. In his report to Nixon, Kissinger warned that the planned German initiatives "could become troublesome if they engender euphoria, affect Germany's contribution to NATO and give ammunition to our own détente-minded people here at home. The Germans may also become so engaged in their Eastern policy that their commitment to West European unity may decline. The Soviets, and with some apparent prodding by Moscow, [East German leader Walter] Ulbricht, seem willing enough to receive Bonn's overtures." Yet, Kissinger's talks with Bahr also implied that the United States held significant leverage that could be used to co-opt Ostpolitik. Bahr had expressed concern about unilateral U.S. troop cuts in Germany. Kissinger had promised that this would be done only after consultations, but that there were likely to be some cuts over the next two years. At the end of their meeting, Bahr had said that there was likely to be "less of a guilt complex in Bonn under Brandt and hence more self-reliant and not always compliant attitude toward us." Kissinger agreed and promised Bahr that the United States would "deal with Germany as a partner, not a client." According to Bahr, Kissinger added, "Your success will be ours."[12]

By the spring of 1970, however, it was clear that the Brandt-Bahr Ostpolitik had claimed the forerunner's role in East-West détente. Because Kissinger had been unable to make significant progress in his back channel negotiations with Soviet ambassador Anatoly Dobrynin, the NSC adviser became increasingly concerned that the Soviets were playing an intricate balancing act of selective détente: deliberately stalling in their talks with the Americans while moving ahead with the Germans. Thus, when Brandt visited the United States in April 1970 hoping to obtain the Nixon administration's formal endorsement of Ostpolitik, Kissinger was distinctly recalcitrant and counseled Nixon against endorsing any specific element of Ostpolitik in public.[13]

Nixon, while siding with his national security adviser, decided that confronting Brandt was ultimately futile and potentially counterproductive. During his meeting with the chancellor on April 11, Nixon simply warned that Ostpolitik might create some uncertainty in France and Britain, as well as among the old-style cold warriors in the United States. Still, Nixon told Brandt that "the main point was the understanding between us that we would keep in close touch over all East-West questions." According to Kissinger, Brandt was "greatly relieved" by American reassurances.[14]

The American insistence for coordination and unity became even clearer after the signing of the Non-Aggression Pact by the USSR and West Germany in Moscow on August 12, 1970. Walter Scheel, Brandt's foreign minister and the head of the Free Democrats, had negotiated some important caveats to this treaty in his July talks with Soviet foreign minister Andrei Gromyko. In particular, Gromyko agreed to an accompanying statement expressing support for German unification (through peaceful means). Moreover, the conclusion of a new agreement on Berlin—negotiated between the four occupying powers and the two Germanys—was understood to be a condition for the eventual FRG ratification of the treaty.[15]

The Berlin negotiations allowed Kissinger to become directly involved in the shaping of Ostpolitik via two sets of back channels that smoothed the way to the Four Power Agreement on Berlin of September 3, 1971. On the one hand, Kissinger negotiated throughout the spring of 1971 on a weekly basis, and without the knowledge of the State Department, with Soviet ambassador Anatoly Dobrynin. On the other hand, Kissinger engaged Kenneth Rush, the American ambassador to Bonn, as his special link to Egon Bahr. Rush, to Kissinger's great satisfaction, managed to keep the rest of the State Department uninformed. By early June an agreement was basically ready. But, in an ironic twist of fate, its finalization was postponed by two months until after Kissinger's secret foray to Beijing in July (creating the false impression that the opening to China resulted in Soviet accommodation on Berlin).[16]

Although Kissinger would later overemphasize his own role in the Berlin negotiations, they had accomplished one significant fact: the Americans and the West Germans cooperated closely throughout the negotiation process. As a result, by September 1971, the concerns of an independent German-Soviet détente that would undermine Western unity no longer colored American evaluations of the transatlantic relationship. The specter of West German "Gaullism" was all but gone. Indeed, in 1972 Kissinger and Nixon played scant attention to Europe, let alone Germany, focusing their energies on the historic summits in Moscow and

Beijing and the tortuous negotiations that ended U.S. troop involvement in the Vietnam War. After the commencement of Nixon's second term, however, Europe was back on the agenda.

Integration, Unity, and the "Year of Europe"

On October 27, 1970, the EEC published the Davignon Report. Named after Étienne Davignon, the Belgian diplomat who chaired the committee that drafted the document, the Davignon Report made a number of proposals regarding political cooperation among EEC countries. A key idea was to encourage the member states to speak with a single voice on international problems; this proposal was approved by all six member governments. "Europe must prepare itself to discharge the imperative world duties entailed by its greater cohesion and increasing role," the Davignon Report expansively stated. The report was linked to the prospects of EEC enlargement. Indeed, the charge given to the commission that drafted the report was defined in December 1969 as follows: "to study the best way of achieving progress in the matter of political unification, within the context of enlargement."[17] The spark was the successful accession negotiations between the EEC, Great Britain, Ireland, Denmark, and Norway, which resulted, in January 1973, in the first successful enlargement (all but Norway joined) of the EEC. Statistics were rewritten: the combined population of the community of nine member countries totaled 256 million compared with the 211 million of the United States.

Time magazine ran a cover story, titled "America's New Rival," that featured the nine flags of the member states. Exaggerated though such alarm was, from the American perspective the changes in Europe were potentially troubling. The much awaited widening of the EEC in particular raised the specter of competition at a time of economic downturn, one that would be further highlighted with the onset of the oil crisis in the fall of 1973. In Kissinger's view it was thus necessary to prevent a serious challenge to Western unity by strengthening Atlanticism.

The Nixon administration responded with the "Year of Europe"—an unfortunate title for a commendable initiative. There was no question in 1973 that the Atlantic relationship required a reassessment. The international situation had, after all, changed dramatically. In addition to Ostpolitik and changes in U.S. policy vis-à-vis the Soviet Union and China, the last American troops were withdrawing from Vietnam. The enlargement of the EEC and the launching of various initiatives of deepening political cooperation among member states raised the possibility of a united, more confident, and influential Europe on the world stage. In contrast, the May 1972 SALT I Agreement had raised European concerns about the bilateral nature of superpower détente (even a possible Soviet-American "condominium"); these would be further heightened in the summer of 1973 when the United States and the Soviet Union signed the Agreement on the Prevention of Nuclear War (PNW). Questions of autonomy and unity were thus firmly on the transatlantic agenda in 1973.

U.S. concerns over the Soviet Union influenced the Year of Europe initiative, as they had Kissinger's approach to Ostpolitik. While Europeans worried that the Americans would decrease their presence on the old continent, Americans remained doubtful about their NATO partners' commitment to the transatlantic alliance at a time of decreased East-West tensions. In October 1972 a national intelligence estimate had summed up the Nixon administration's concern as follows: "The Soviet leaders hope that while maintaining their position in the East they can wean West Europeans away from their close relations with the US . . . and ultimately clear the way for the USSR's emergence as the dominant power on the continent as a whole."[18] Viewed from this perspective, European autonomy remained a threat to transatlantic unity *and* to U.S. standing vis-à-vis the USSR.

In the spring of 1973 Kissinger set out to address this issue. He stressed to Nixon the need to open a substantive dialogue with European leaders. And, he argued, it was important that the Americans take the initiative because "we cannot expect the Europeans to enter this dialogue with much unity or clarity of purpose." Thus it was important to explain to European leaders "as precisely as possible what we expect of the Europeans and what we are willing to do in return." In other words, the United States was willing to work together with the Europeans on various East-West security issues and willing to keep its strong commitment to European defense, but only if "the Europeans are willing to make reasonable economic concessions and sacrifices."[19]

After months of consultation, Kissinger attempted to open this new dialogue with his Year of Europe speech. Delivered on April 23, 1973, in New York, the speech included little that was not known to any observer of transatlantic relations; Kissinger touched on the revival and economic unification of Western Europe, the approximate strategic parity between the United States and the Soviet

Union, and the onset of détente. He then stressed that "problems have arisen, unforeseen a generation ago, which require new types of cooperative action." Kissinger then called for the leaders of Europe to join the United States in setting down "the basis for a new era of creativity in the West [and in] reinvigorating shared ideals and common purpose with our friends."

Few would have objected to such a high-minded call, reminiscent of Kissinger's writings in the 1960s. But then Kissinger effectively asked for trouble by stressing, in an unnecessarily crude way, the difference between America's "wider international" responsibilities and the EEC's "regional personality." The ultimate, and oft-quoted, faux-pas, however, was the following: "The United States has global interests and responsibilities. Our European allies have regional interests." In other words, not only did the United States appear to have the monopoly on "responsibilities," it was the only country in the West with legitimate interests outside its own continent.[20]

The speech and the diplomacy surrounding it might have been meant as an opening of a new era in transatlantic relations. Kissinger might not have said anything that was not true: Europeans were hardly capable of playing a significant role outside of their own continent. There surely was a need to rethink common policies and find ways of keeping potential trade wars from erupting. But in the United States, where Watergate commanded headlines, the speech passed virtually unnoticed. Those Americans who did pay attention, moreover, tended to respond positively. In a fit of hyperbole, *New York Times* columnist James Reston even compared the Year of Europe speech to George C. Marshall's June 1947 commencement address at Harvard University (which had launched the deliberations leading to the Marshall Plan).[21]

European leaders, however, took offense. French president Georges Pompidou, for one, cryptically remarked that for France every year was the "Year of Europe."[22] Willy Brandt thought that the assumption that Europeans would simply accept the Kissinger definition of their international role "was not the way to win the future."[23] British prime minister Edward Heath later wrote, "For Kissinger to announce a Year of Europe was like for me to stand on Trafalgar Square and announce that we were embarking on a year to save America!"[24] Nor did Kissinger's subsequent effort to explain the consigning of Europeans to a "regional" role as a mere "tactical mistake" convince French foreign minister François Jobert.

When the two met in early June, Jobert accused the Americans of trying to "strengthen your mastery" in Europe and "to reinforce the U.S. position vis-à-vis the Soviets." Kissinger conceded the point but added that a strengthening of transatlantic ties "reinforces everyone's position vis-à-vis the Soviets."[25]

The Year of Europe controversy lingered on for several months, rendering Kissinger and Nixon's meetings with Brandt, Pompidou, and Edward Heath in 1973 ineffectual. To be sure, there was much discussion and debate over two prospective Atlantic declarations over the summer: one between the United States and the EEC; the other among NATO countries. But progress was slow. Still, by mid-September—a week before he was sworn in as secretary of state—Kissinger told Nixon that things were finally proceeding "very well" on the "European front."[26]

A few weeks later, however, the October War erupted in the Middle East, causing another crisis in transatlantic relations over the Organization of the Petroleum Exporting Countries (OPEC) oil embargo. In the end, it would take until June 1974—and changes in the leadership of Britain, France, and West Germany—before the Year of Europe controversy would give way to a new NATO declaration. New mechanisms were also put in place to guarantee a more formalized dialogue between Washington and Brussels. When Nixon resigned on August 9, 1974, and Gerald Ford was sworn in as the thirty-eighth president of the United States, Kissinger could feel confident that the acrimony of the previous months was giving way to transatlantic cooperation. One potential forum for strengthening Western unity further came in the form of the CSCE.

CSCE and the Rise of Human Security

The original proposal for a pan-European security conference was made by Soviet foreign minister Vyacheslav Molotov in 1954. Because the United States and Canada were not invited, the proposal was turned down by NATO countries; instead the years 1954–55 saw the creation of the Warsaw Pact and the Federal Republic of Germany joining NATO. In the 1960s, however, a number of developments increased the movement toward détente and enhanced the interest, on both sides of the Iron Curtain, in a multilateral security conference. In 1967 NATO—having been delivered a jolt by France's exit from the organization's military structure in 1966—adopted the Harmel Report, which called for a two-track policy: the alliance's traditional military security function was to be complemented by exploring the possibility of political détente with Warsaw Pact countries.

By this point, the Soviet Union had become increasingly interested in reinvigorating the idea of a pan-European security conference. This was in part because of the centrifugal tendencies within the Warsaw Pact—highlighted, for example, by Romania's increasingly independent course in the 1960s—which were only partially subdued by the crackdown of the Prague Spring in August 1968. A simultaneous attempt to reorganize the Warsaw Pact's structure by introducing a political consultative committee did not, however, prove to be a success. Decision making would simply not be shared within the Soviet-led alliance even as a cosmetic measure. Most significantly, however, in 1966–67 the Warsaw Pact advanced similar notions of détente as those adopted by NATO in its Harmel Report in late 1967. But the stress on a European security conference that, at this point, was still to exclude the United States, was not attractive to the West. It was only in the aftermath of the Prague Spring in 1968 and in the context of the Sino-Soviet border clashes that the Warsaw Pact issued, on March 17, 1969, the Budapest appeal, a call for a conference on security and cooperation in Europe. Two months later, the Finnish president Urho Kekkonen, at the USSR's urging, acted as a neutral go-between, offering Helsinki as the site for such a conference. Most significantly, he directed his invitation to all European countries as well as the United States and Canada.[27]

It took several years before the talks could get on track. Only in November 1972 did the initial multilateral preparatory talks begin at the Dipoli Conference Center, outside of Helsinki. This Stage I of the CSCE talks lasted through the summer of 1973 and concluded with a foreign ministers' meeting in Helsinki in early July. The purpose of these initial meetings was for the parties to agree on the agenda and terms of reference of the CSCE. In late August 1973 the talks moved to Geneva for Stage II, a series of negotiations during which a large number of committees and subcommittees worked on the various aspects (or "baskets") on the agenda. Stage II was the crucial stage in which the Helsinki Final Act took form. It was also a long and arduous affair, as representatives of thirty-five nations engaged in seemingly endless disputes over the various provisions to be included in the Final Act. It lasted until July 1975. Like Stage I, Stage II concluded with a foreign ministers' meeting and was then followed by the high-level three-day summit in Helsinki

(Stage III), which opened on July 30. Attended by the heads of state of the ipant countries, the Helsinki summit was a largely ceremonial affair but on to many in Europe, represented a significant turning point in East-West relations and the codification of European détente.[28]

Throughout the negotiations that led to the signing of the Helsinki Accords, most American policymakers, and particularly Henry Kissinger, treated the CSCE as a peripheral affair. Kissinger, whose lack of enthusiasm for the CSCE was notable throughout the process, at one time quipped that the CSCE Final Act might just as well have been written "in Swahili."[29]

Such missives notwithstanding, the Helsinki Final Act was a remarkable document. The four baskets dealt with virtually every aspect of pan-European security. While Basket I dealt with traditional security issues such as the inviolability of borders, Baskets II and III dealt with economic issues and, perhaps most controversially, human rights. Basket IV—rarely mentioned—was perhaps the most important of all: it outlined the follow-up steps of the CSCE process, thus making it clear that the issues identified in other parts of the document were not to become a dead letter. In other words, the signing ceremony at Helsinki's Finlandia Hall on August 1, 1975, was as much the beginning of a process as it was the closure of the multilateral negotiation marathon that had stretched far beyond the time limits anticipated in 1972.

Remarkable—and perhaps somewhat overrated—though the CSCE's final document was, it was also inherently contradictory, producing diametrically opposite interpretations. It was widely criticized in the United States as basically recognizing Soviet control over Eastern Europe. In the Soviet bloc, the provisions on human rights were basically ignored. Nevertheless, the CSCE seems to have had a major long-term significance: it signaled the emergence of human security as an important and recognized aspect of international relations, and it would later be used as a manifesto by numerous dissident and human rights groups inside the Soviet Union and its satellites. The CSCE's recognition of the possibility that borders might be changed through "peaceful means" also satisfied the minimum demands of those Germans who still held up unification as a realistic goal.[30]

In the end, the CSCE launched and marked a certain rebirth of Europe. After all, for the first time since the end of World War II, the CSCE negotiations provided a forum in which all-European negotiations could take place. In Helsinki and Geneva, under the umbrella of the CSCE, East-West contacts were fostered in a way that could hardly have been possible a decade earlier. Western Europeans, in particular, found in the CSCE a forum for putting the recommendations of the 1970 Davignon Report—the first effort to launch what today is called European Common Foreign and Security Policy—into practice for the first time. In fact, Western Europeans tended to dominate much of the negotiation process because the Americans showed but minimal interest and the Soviets (and selected Eastern European governments) tried to keep the agenda—and results—as limited as possible.[31]

Western Europeans were also able to include questions of individual freedoms and political rights on the CSCE agenda, an important—if initially mainly cosmetic—victory. As T. A. K. Elliott, the British ambassador to Finland who was deeply involved in the negotiations, put it in 1974, "One thing the Conference has already achieved: to get it accepted for the first time by Communist states that relations between peoples—and therefore the attitudes of Governments toward their citizens—should be the subject of multilateral discussion." This, he added, was important because it might "eventually be able to get the Soviet Union to lower, even a little, the barriers to human contacts and the flow of information and ideas between East and West."[32]

Herein lay the key to the long-term significance of the CSCE and of European détente. Unlike superpower détente, it did not focus on nuclear weapons or what could be considered traditional security issues. What the CSCE, one of the key products of European détente, brought clearly to the international arena was a focus on human security, on people rather than states.

Finlandia Hall

In late July 1975 Kissinger and Ford arrived in Helsinki to participate in the ceremonial final stage of the CSCE. It was an unprecedented occasion: thirty-five countries were represented (all European nations save Albania). And while Kissinger had, less than a year earlier, told his staff that the Helsinki Accords might as well be written in Swahili, the CSCE documents, particularly the provisions on human rights and freedom of expression, later became a kind of manifesto of the dissident movements throughout the Soviet bloc. As one of the highlights of European détente, the Helsinki Accords stand, in retrospect, as a milestone in the transformation and ultimate demise of the Cold War order in Europe. Moreover, the Ford administration had, by 1975, come to view the CSCE as an important tool in its efforts at mending the troubled state of transatlantic relations. In effect, European and American negotiation efforts had been coordinated to the point of Kissinger using talking points prepared by the Brits during the last stage of the negotiations in Geneva. There was, at least in the context of the CSCE, a united Western front.[33]

Ultimately, though, the basic point remains that, notwithstanding alarmist rhetoric, there had not been—during the Johnson or the Nixon presidency—a fundamental crisis in transatlantic relations. To be sure, both détente and European integration represented challenges to American foreign policy. Both—when set against the background of the Vietnam War and other divisive factors—provided a potential setting for a rupture. But even with challenges in the form of Brandt's Ostpolitik and EEC enlargement, Western unity prevailed.

Two basic factors help explain why, despite the fears of many, détente and European integration never seriously endangered U.S. policy toward Europe.

First, there remained the basic convergence between American and Western European economic interests. To be sure, as Geir Lundestad, among others, has noted, Americans were increasingly ambivalent about European integration and worried that Europe was becoming an economic competitor to the United States. Despite such obvious American ambivalence about European integration, however, there remained a basic transatlantic interdependence that was clearly evident in the high levels of trade and investment that were yet to be replicated within the context of any other transoceanic relationship.[34]

Second, there was the Cold War. As long as the Soviet Union existed, as long as the Soviet nuclear threat was present, as long as the Warsaw Pact held a numerical advantage over the Western alliance in conventional troop levels, Western Europeans were not going to throw NATO into the wastebasket. In fact, a persistent concern of Europeans was the possibility that the Americans might decide to withdraw their forces. This straightforward fact meant that the Americans had an ace in the hole whenever they were engaged in a dialogue with their European counterparts. While burden sharing remained a thorny issue, the main point was that the Europeans clearly wanted the Americans to stay. Even French president Pompidou stated so publicly. Indeed, when it came down to security policy, it was clear that in the 1960s and 1970s the Europeans wished to maintain a high degree

of unity—or integration of policy—with the United States. This, perhaps ironically, allowed the United States to act more autonomously from its European allies
when it came to negotiations with the USSR, a fact evident in the early 1970s.[35]

In retrospect, moreover, the changes that détente brought about in Europe
had far-reaching consequences. The various German treaties in the early 1970s
may have merely confirmed the status quo and could never have occurred had the
Americans and the Soviets not been willing to accept them. Yet, one cannot easily conceive of the transformation in East-West relations in Europe and the subsequent collapse of the Iron Curtain without taking into account the various
bridge-building efforts of such leaders as West German chancellor Willy Brandt.
Similarly, the multilateral CSCE may have seemed like an irrelevant talking shop
when compared with such monumental diplomatic feats as the opening to China.
But it is difficult to imagine the rise in the number of dissident movements and
human rights organizations that undermined totalitarian control throughout the
Soviet bloc without the provisions set out through the painstaking negotiations
that culminated in the Helsinki Accords of 1975.

Ultimately, Europe represented to Americans but one piece in an increasingly global puzzle. SALT, Vietnam, triangular diplomacy, war, and peace in the
Middle East took up much more of Kissinger's time and energy than dealing with
transatlantic matters. The Nixon administration engaged Europeans primarily
because, without doing so, their grander goals—such as building détente with the
Soviet Union on American terms—would have been more difficult, if not outright
impossible. Thus, cooperating with (or co-opting) West Germans on Ostpolitik,
proclaiming—ill-advised though it was—the "Year of Europe," and even participating more actively in the CSCE negotiations were ways of ensuring that the
United States remained the primary spokesperson of a "united West" vis-à-vis the
USSR. The task was made easier as the continuance of Soviet-American détente
was called increasingly into question in the mid-1970s.

CHAPTER 5

Détente Halted: Domestic Critics and Regional Crises

"I would not link foreign policy with Watergate. You will regret it for the rest of your life," Henry Kissinger told Alexander Haig in October 1973.[1] Over subsequent months it became clear that such linkage could not be avoided. Nixon's obvious political weakness emboldened congressional opponents to challenge the administration more openly. Opposition to the granting of most favored nation (MFN) status to the Soviet Union, for example, became increasingly vocal and produced roadblocks to Soviet-American détente. Full normalization with China was rendered impossible as Nixon could not fathom alienating his conservative supporters by breaking off diplomatic relations with Taiwan. The administration was also unable to prevent cutbacks in military and economic aid to South Vietnam. In short, Watergate made the task of running American foreign policy increasingly complicated.

Yet, to argue that Watergate alone killed détente would be an oversimplification. By the time Nixon resigned in August 1974, the era of negotiations had already seen its zenith. In the United States the criticism of détente focused either on its immorality or the weakening of America's position vis-à-vis the Soviet Union. The attacks on détente became more voluminous during Gerald Ford's presidency and had an impact on the outcome of the 1976 presidential elections. In early 1976 Gerald Ford even banned the use of the word "détente" in his presidential campaign—to no avail. Ronald Reagan and Jimmy Carter—the two other main contenders for the presidency—trashed détente and its principal surviving architect, Henry Kissinger, at every available opportunity. Talking about a "structure of peace" had become a political liability.

While under siege at home, détente was in trouble abroad. Neither the Soviet Union nor the United States was willing to abandon the search for unilateral advantages in the third world. After the 1973 Middle East War, Americans worked studiously—and successfully—to deny the Soviets a significant role in the subsequent peace process. In 1974–75 the Soviets (as well as the Chinese) continued to provide substantial military aid to North Vietnam, hence undermining the remote possibility that the 1973 Paris Peace Accords would prevent an eventual takeover of all Vietnam by Hanoi (as happened in late April 1975). In 1975–76 the Soviets and the Americans were involved on opposite sides in the Angolan conflict. The victory of the "Soviet side" encouraged the more interventionist tendencies—especially in the so-called third world—among Soviet foreign policy leadership exactly at the time when détente was under attack inside the United States.

By this point the central paradox is evident. In the early 1970s détente may have been an eminently reasonable policy to the great majority of Americans wishing to see their nation redeemed after the debacle of Vietnam. Its principal practitioners had worked to ensure a strong domestic backing for their policies. But with Nixon's political career over and Kissinger unable to fully comprehend the strength of the opposition on both sides of the political spectrum, the once so popularly acclaimed policy began to evaporate.

Domestic Chaos

Regardless of one's perspective, the events collectively known as Watergate were a gross misconduct of justice. The judgment, though, depends on one's perspective. To Nixon, his supporters, and his apologists, Watergate was a minor event blown way out of proportion by a left-wing press and a Democratic Party bent on bringing down the least loved but most enduring Republican politician of the Cold War era. To others, Nixon was a serial offender whose personal ambition drove him to abuse presidential power in unimaginable ways. In recent years the release of the related White House tape recordings have clearly tilted the balance of judgment in favor of the "excessive abuse of power" school. Yet, because of his impressive record in foreign policy, the historical Nixon will always be a controversial and complicated character.[2]

Nixon's downfall has been retold on so many occasions as to require no repeating here. Yet, it is worth reminding ourselves that the impact of the

Watergate crisis—because it shook one of the major political institutions of the United States—was felt way beyond the narrow confines of Nixon's inner circle or even the Republican Party. Most importantly, given the centralization of foreign policy making in the Nixon presidency, the disgraceful exit of the commander in chief called into question, not only his character and lack of respect for the fine points of domestic law, but also all the policies that he had engineered. Foreign policy may have had little to do with the break-in at the Democratic Party offices in the Watergate complex, but the collateral damage was inevitable.

In part, the impact of Watergate was structural: as Nixon began to fight for his political life, the reigns of leadership in matters of foreign policy fell increasingly into Henry Kissinger's hands. Most obviously, Nixon nominated Kissinger as secretary of state in September 1973, while allowing him to retain control of the National Security Council. In effect, Kissinger was the undisputed czar of American foreign policy during the last year of the Nixon presidency. This state of affairs continued into the first fourteen months of Gerald Ford's tenure in the White House, but by 1975 Kissinger was in the process of losing some of his "star power." Gradually, he became a whipping boy for those who either resented the substance of détente but had not been able to properly air their message earlier or were taking all possible political advantage from the long shadow of Nixon's resignation. In the so-called Halloween massacre of November 1975, Ford removed the NSC portfolio from Kissinger in a vain effort to deflect mounting criticism.

The morality of détente might well have become a serious domestic political issue without Watergate. But the abuses of power that were so publicly exposed in 1974 further enlarged the scope for and the political benefits of such criticism. As a result, in the November 1974 midterm elections Democrats made significant gains, enhancing their majorities in both houses: 61 seats in the Senate (with 38 Republicans and 1 Independent) and 291 against 144 in the House (giving them a two-thirds majority). The Democrats were thus poised for a successful challenge in the presidential election of 1976.

But not only Watergate highlighted the governmental abuses of power in the mid-1970s. In 1975 the previously untouchable Central Intelligence Agency (CIA) was suddenly under serious scrutiny by several congressional committees. The most damaging and public of them was the Senate Select Committee to Study Governmental Operations with Respect to Intelligence Activities, better known as the Church Committee, after its chairman, Frank Church (D-ID). The Church Committee took public and private testimony from hundreds of people; collected huge volumes of files from the Federal Bureau of Investigation (FBI), CIA, National Security Agency (NSA), Internal Revenue Service (IRS), and many other federal agencies; and issued fourteen reports in 1975 and 1976.[3] Among the disturbing revelations were a CIA program to open the mail of selected American citizens in a database of 1.5 million names; a half million FBI investigations of suspected "subversives" between 1960 and 1974 (resulting in no court convictions); the NSA's monitoring of all cables sent overseas from the United States or received by Americans between 1947 and 1975; the CIA's drug experiments, which had resulted in two deaths; a number of assassination plots against foreign leaders (none successful); and the manipulation of foreign elections (Chile being the most prominent case). Kissinger's comment on such a catalogue of abuse and incompetence revealed his sense of priorities. "What is happening is worse than in the days of McCarthy," he told Ford and deputy NSC adviser Brent Scowcroft on the morning of January 4, 1975. In other words, the Church Committee was conducting a domestic witch hunt that would have difficult implications for executive prerogatives.[4]

Watergate and congressional investigations into CIA activities did indeed have an impact on the Ford administration's ability to conduct an effective foreign policy. In fact, the list was remarkable: Nixon's resignation in August 1974 (preceded by Vice President Spiro Agnew's resignation over an embezzlement scandal a year earlier), significant Democratic gains in the 1974 congressional elections, a complete overhaul of the main officeholders within the executive branch (with the exception of Kissinger)—all of these augured ill for the forthcoming 1976 presidential elections. Within the context of American foreign policy, they allowed the opponents of détente to gain the necessary momentum to undermine further progress on nuclear arms control and Soviet-American trade.

SALT II vs. MFN

The 1972 SALT agreements were supposed to be but the first step toward a more comprehensive set of nuclear arms control agreements. Aside from the ABM Treaty, which was to remain in force for the remainder of the twentieth century, the two sides had agreed only to an interim five-year arrangement on offensive weapons. As part of the overall design of détente after 1972, the Americans and Soviets planned to negotiate a more comprehensive treaty—including such relatively new weapons systems as MIRVs—that would actually commit each side to a certain reduction of nuclear arms. By the time of Nixon's resignation, negotiations had been ongoing for a further two years. Finally, in November 1974 in Vladivostok it appeared that Ford and Brezhnev had reached an agreement.

In the end, no SALT II would be negotiated on Kissinger's (or Ford's) watch. To be sure, they agreed in Vladivostok on a basic formula: each side would be allowed a total of 2,200 nuclear delivery vehicles (ICBMs, SLBMs, and long-range bombers) out of which a maximum of 1,320 could have multiple warheads. But two years after the Vladivostok agreement, despite endless meetings between Soviet and American delegations in Geneva and numerous discussions between Kissinger and his various Soviet counterparts, no treaty had been signed. As Soviet ambassador Dobrynin puts it in his memoir, "Détente reached its height and began its decline" in Vladivostok.[5] A major part of the explanation for the impending decline of détente lay in American domestic politics.

While it was clear that Ford and Kissinger were keen on concluding an arms control agreement in 1975, they were swimming against a strong current of opposition in the United States. This was hardly unexpected. Already in the aftermath of the 1972 SALT agreements, congressional critics had raised objections to nuclear arms deals. At the time, the critics had focused on the fact that SALT I appeared to give the Soviets a numerical advantage in offensive nuclear weapons (although, as mentioned in chapter 3, this was not actually the case). As related earlier, in August 1972 the most outspoken critic, Senator Henry Jackson, had introduced an amendment to the SALT I Agreement that explicitly stated that the next nuclear arms treaty would not limit U.S. intercontinental strategic forces to levels "inferior . . . to the Soviet Union." The amendment thus underlined one of the major general criticisms of détente in the United States: that it put the United States, for the first time in the post–World War II era, at the risk of being in an inferior position vis-à-vis the Soviet Union.[6]

By the time Ford was sworn in as president, Jackson had emerged as the main critic of détente and, not by coincidence, the early frontrunner for the 1976 Democratic nomination. The issue that Jackson had homed in on, though, was not so much prospective U.S. "inferiority" in nuclear weapons as the more emotional one of Jewish emigration from the USSR. Basically, what Jackson and his supporters aimed to do was link the question of Jewish emigration to improvements in Soviet-American trade, especially the granting of MFN status to the USSR.

The original cause of the controversy regarding Jewish emigration had been a heavy "education tax" levied by the Kremlin in August 1972 on all Soviet citizens who wished to leave the USSR; since Jewish citizens were the only ones allowed to emigrate to Israel, they were clearly the target of such an "exit tax." Although rarely applied, the tax provided the initial impetus for the introduction of two draft bills in Congress in October 1972: one by Jackson in the Senate and the other by Representative Charles Vanik (D-OH).[7] After a congressional recess, the issue picked up again in January 1973. Jackson rounded up support from Jewish groups, labor organizations (who saw increased trade with the USSR as a threat to American jobs), many Israeli politicians with close connections to the United States, and the American-Israel Political Action Committee (AIPAC). On March 15, 1973, the Jackson-Vanik amendment—which denied MFN status to countries that denied their citizens the right to emigrate—was formally introduced as an attachment to the Nixon administration's 1973 Trade Reform Act (TRA). In practice, the Jackson-Vanik Amendment thus meant that the Soviets would need to lift restrictions on emigration if they were to be granted MFN status by the United States. The controversy, which would continue into the Ford presidency, had truly begun.[8]

The Jackson-Vanik Amendment was a scourge on détente for years. While the Nixon administration—mistakenly thinking that the issue was simply about lifting restrictions on emigration—quietly negotiated deals with the Soviets that allowed a significant increase in the number of Soviet Jews permitted to emigrate to Israel, the amendment held back the passing of the MFN status for the USSR. It drove Soviet leader Leonid Brezhnev up the wall: during his trip to the United States in the summer of 1973, after meeting with Senator Fulbright and the rest of the Senate Foreign Relations Committee, Brezhnev volunteered to the press that one of the senators had asked him about the Jackson-Vanik Amendment. "I told them any amendment can have a counter amendment," Brezhnev said.[9]

This one did not. The Jackson-Vanik Amendment was reintroduced with the 1974 TRA, causing Kissinger to fume at a staff meeting on March 18, 1974. "The Soviets are getting nothing out of détente. We are pushing them everywhere and what can I deliver in Moscow?" he complained. "God damn it," he went on. "The same sons of bitches who drove us out of Vietnam and said it would be immoral for us to tamper with the North Vietnamese internal system now try to destroy détente and assert that it's our moral obligation to change internal Soviet policies." He went on to quip that "Jackson has obviously been convinced that I am a hostile country" and to refer to the senator as the leader of "these bastards on the hill [who] ignore the fact that 400 Jews were leaving the Soviet Union in 1969 and now say that 30,000 a year is inconsequential." In summing up trade and SALT problems, Kissinger said, "What I want to give the Russians is something to start the SALT process working smoothly. I do not want to give them a final position and tell them to take it or leave it . . . [because] trade is no good, SALT can't go down the drain."[10] Nine months later, while celebrating the Vladivostok agreements with the Soviets, Kissinger further warned that if SALT II "becomes like the trade issue, I think we will see a massive reversal of the Soviet position on détente."[11]

Kissinger's concerns proved well founded. To be sure, the U.S. Congress passed resolutions supporting the Vladivostok agreement in January and February 1975, while Soviet and American delegations began meeting in Geneva to hammer out the details of the SALT II Agreement (there was no formal treaty as of yet).[12] Amid such support, however, a revolt, again spearheaded by Jackson, was brewing. The Vladivostok agreement merely legitimized "the massive continuation of Soviet arms expenditures," Jackson charged. He called Vladivostok "an arms buildup agreement" and vowed to conduct intensive hearings in Congress to convince the general public that it was necessary "to insist on strategic force reductions in a SALT II agreement." Whatever the merits of his case, Jackson's opposition ultimately helped shelve the Vladivostok agreement for the remainder of Ford's term.[13]

While SALT II was postponed, economic détente floundered further. On December 20, the 1974 TRA finally passed both houses of Congress. But rather than offering an opening for East-West trade, the law managed to single out the Soviet Union as a country that needed to clean up its domestic conduct. In particular, the much-sought-after MFN status was not only tied to Soviet compliance on observing the freedom of emigration rules embedded in the Jackson-Vanik amendment but also subject to an annual review. The first such review was to take place, as Kissinger acidly noted, in April 1976, when the presidential primary season was in full swing.[14]

The Soviets responded on January 10, 1975, a week after President Ford had reluctantly signed the TRA. Moscow refused to accept the 1974 Trade Act and abrogated the 1972 Soviet-American trade agreement. It was hardly a surprise. The Soviet press had repeatedly stated that Moscow "flatly reject[s] any attempts to interfere in internal affairs that are entirely the concern of the Soviet state and no one else." In a letter to Ford, Brezhnev had declared the new trade legislation "fundamentally unacceptable."[15]

The lack of progress in arms control and the virtual collapse of economic détente were symptoms of the stalled state of Soviet-American relations. The Watergate-weakened presidency of 1973–75 could ultimately not override growing domestic opposition to détente. But détente was by no means in trouble only because of the tensions between the executive and the legislative branches. In addition, a number of regional crises eroded the incentives for furthering détente. Between 1973 and 1976 turmoil in the Middle East, Southeast Asia, and Southern Africa lay bare the limitations of cooperation between Moscow and Washington.

October War and Unilateral Advantage

Between October 6 and 26, 1973, Israel, Egypt, and Syria fought a war that had a long-lasting impact on the conflict-ridden area and its role in superpower relations. The war began when Egyptian and Syrian troops crossed cease-fire lines to enter the Israeli-held Sinai Peninsula and Golan Heights, captured and occupied since the 1967 Six-Day War. After some initial success, the Egyptians and Syrians were thwarted by the Israelis, who drove deep into Syrian territory and crossed the Suez Canal into Egypt. Intensive negotiations and several UN Security Council resolutions eventually allowed a new cease-fire to take hold on October 26, 1973. By that time, Israeli forces were almost in sight of Damascus and Cairo. Only a day before that, Americans had put their nuclear forces on alert following Soviet threats (how serious is unclear) of unilateral military action against Israel. By this point, the conflict had prompted other global effects. Most importantly, the oil-rich Arab states—in a show of support for Egypt and Syria—had instituted an oil embargo against countries supporting Israel. Although it caused a great deal of economic turmoil, the embargo did little to stop the decisive American airlift of arms to Israel.

The October War of 1973 and its aftermath allowed the United States to claim the role as the preeminent external player in the region. Before the war, a certain balance of power had reigned: the United States had supported Israel with extensive military assistance while the Soviets had backed Egypt and Syria. But soon after, if not already during, the war, it became clear that Egypt, headed by Anwar Sadat, had lost interest in relying on Moscow's support. Following a disengagement agreement mediated by Secretary of State Henry Kissinger, Israeli troops pulled back to the Sinai Peninsula in March 1974. Two months later, Kissinger produced another shuttle success: after endless meetings between Syrians and Israelis, another disengagement accord was signed on May 31, 1974. Although there were simultaneous multilateral negotiations in Geneva, the Soviets had been sidelined in what amounted to the first public meetings between Israeli and Arab officials. The Middle East peace process—still under way almost four decades later—had begun.

For Henry Kissinger, the October War and its resolution, particularly the shuttle diplomacy that followed, were to cement his reputation as a skillful negotiator. Later on, Kissinger would take great pride in his performance of 1973–74, devoting eleven out of twenty-five chapters of the second volume of his memoir either entirely or predominantly to the October War and shuttle diplomacy. In August 2003 Kissinger published *Crisis*, a book dedicated, for the most part, to the Middle East crisis during which, Kissinger wrote, his "policy was designed to shape events in conformity with America's values and national interests."[16]

Such pride is understandable. In retrospect, the period from October 1973 until Nixon's resignation in August 1974 saw few other triumphs: in Indochina fighting continued, Chinese progress was stalled over Taiwan, and Nixon's last summit with the Soviets in the summer of 1974 did not produce substantive results. Meanwhile, Watergate continued to erode the Nixon administration's morale and effectiveness. Any foreign policy move requiring congressional support faced an uphill struggle. In fact, from the domestic perspective, solving a crisis in the Middle East—especially if it could be done while simultaneously reducing the USSR's role in the area—could even help restore some of the beleaguered president's credibility. And, by the summer of 1974 Kissinger could take heart in the fact that he had played a major role in mediating the nigh impossible: agreements between the Arabs and the Israelis. By spending a great deal of time in the region, Kissinger had managed to insert the United States as the key external player in the Middle East. In 1975 the United States would commence economic and military aid programs to Egypt. In the fall of 1978 Jimmy Carter would host Anwar Sadat and Menachem Begin as the two leaders signed the Camp David Accords. American diplomacy appeared to have borne fruit.

But the success did not come without caveats. In the regional context, Kissinger's diplomacy failed to take into account the most troubling long-term issue: the fate of the displaced Palestinians. Peace, as a result, remained a relative concept. In the broader context of American foreign policy and the pursuit of détente, moreover, Kissinger's unilateral approach proved counterproductive. While Kissinger talked of a multilateral approach and had seemingly agreed to a joint Soviet-American approach, he worked hard to sideline the Soviets and searched for unilateral advantage. Kissinger may have acted in a more evenhanded manner toward the principal regional adversaries than his predecessors had in the 1960s. But the Soviets, while acting as cosponsors of the Geneva Peace Conference on the Middle East, were effectively excluded from the day-to-day diplomacy. In sporadic meetings, Kissinger "informed" the Soviets of progress but ignored their demand for a joint approach. As Kissinger put it to Nixon in December 1973, "We are the only participant who is in close touch with all the parties, the only power that can produce progress, and the only one that each is coming to in order to make that progress."[17]

This drove the Soviets mad. Brezhnev made a habit of writing critical letters to Nixon, demanding that the Americans and Soviets plan "joint steps" in the Middle East. When Andrei Gromyko arrived in the United States on February 4, 1974—a few days after the Egyptian-Israeli disengagement agreement—the Soviet foreign minister asked Nixon and Kissinger point blank, "What happened to our agreement that the [Geneva] conference would be under the auspices of the US and the Soviet Union?" Despite repeated assurances to the contrary, the Americans had acted without consulting the Soviets. Clearly, the United States had "decided to take matters into its own hands and to act in circumvention of the agreement." Nixon was defensive. The United States was not trying to push the Soviets out of the Middle East but simply working toward peace, he insisted. The impression of a "one-man show" was incorrect. It was just a matter of tactics, the best way toward a disengagement of forces. "We have no interest in proceeding unilaterally," Kissinger added.[18]

Kissinger faced more Soviet complaints when he visited Moscow in March 1974. The Soviets vented their anger over the Middle East, correctly complaining about being purposely shut off from the Middle East peace process. On March 27 Brezhnev, in fact, demanded "that we will cooperate with one another completely as was initially agreed upon by our two sides." To drive the point home to Kissinger, Brezhnev then added, "I stress the word 'cooperate,' and by that I mean not simply inform each other. That should characterize our relationship in the Middle East." Disingenuously, Kissinger assured the Soviets that the United States was "prepared to cooperate and not seek unilateral advantage." As further assurance, he added, "I agree that we should coordinate our moves." Of course he had no intention of following up on such promises. He had already managed to place himself and the United States at the center of the process that had produced the January 1974 disengagement agreement between Israel and Egypt and would produce another one, between Israel and Syria, in late May (not to mention his efforts to lift the oil embargo in March 1974). Clearly, he was seeking unilateral advantage.[19]

At the end of the day, Kissinger's strategy was successful. America's role in the Middle East became central to the region's future while Moscow's influence was severely diminished. In a concrete sense, Kissinger made the United States into the preeminent Middle East player in 1973–74. By the summer of 1974 the press would once again idolize Kissinger—Super-K—for his Middle East successes. Most of Congress, even as they prepared for the impeachment of Richard Nixon, agreed that the secretary of state had put in another virtuoso performance. What few dared to mention, however, was the simple fact that by acting unilaterally in one region, Kissinger was making it evident that America's détente policy did not translate into Soviet-American cooperation in regional crises. So where was the Soviet incentive to act differently? Why should one have expected Moscow to restrain its search for unilateral advantage elsewhere?

Collapse in Indochina

Amid the fighting in the Middle East in October 1973, Henry Kissinger was awarded the Nobel Peace Prize for negotiating an end to the Vietnam War. He shared the much-coveted honor with his North Vietnamese interlocutor, Le Duc Tho. Together the two men had put the final touches to the January 1973 Paris Peace Accords, which brought to an end America's direct military commitment to South Vietnam. In December of the same year, however, neither Kissinger nor Tho were present at the ceremony in Oslo; the former cited an urgent NATO meeting, the latter had refused to accept the prize.

In reality, there had not been a day's worth of peace in Indochina since January 1973. Although the Americans had withdrawn their remaining troops, they had continued to provide military assistance to the South Vietnamese armed forces. In contrast, the North Vietnamese may have agreed not to support subversion in the South, but the presence of more than 100,000 North Vietnamese regulars in the territory created an untenable solution. After a series of minor skirmishes, the war flared up in full in late 1973. In this new war, the Saigon government was at a decisive disadvantage. In early January 1973 Nixon—in an effort to try and secure a peace settlement—may have made a personal promise to South Vietnam's President Thieu to continue supporting South Vietnam with airpower and military aid. But it was a promise he could not keep. In subsequent months, the U.S. Congress passed a series of resolutions that diminished presidential warmaking capabilities. The War Powers Act of June 1973 put strict limits on the length of time that the president could keep American troops abroad without congressional approval. In August a bill put an end to further military activity in Cambodia. And Nixon, facing an all-out assault on his authority as the Watergate scandal unfolded, could not prevent the cuts in military aid to South Vietnam that Congress insisted upon. At the time of Nixon's resignation in August 1974, the North Vietnamese, who could count on continued Soviet (and, to a lesser extent, Chinese) aid, were already planning the final offensive against the South. Hanoi was undoubtedly further encouraged in November 1974, when Congress cut the Ford administration's proposed military aid budget for South Vietnam in 1975 in half: from $1.5 billion to $700 million.

The final stage of the "post-American" Vietnam War was relatively quick. Beginning in early 1975 the North Vietnamese troops gradually advanced to take over a series of South Vietnam's provincial capitals. Finally, in late April, the NLF and North Vietnamese troops entered Saigon, while Americans desperately airlifted their embassy staff and selected South Vietnamese officials to safety (President

Thieu would spend most of the rest of his life in the United States; he died in 2001 in Boston). Vietnam was finally unified, and Saigon was renamed Ho Chi Minh City (Ho Chi Minh himself had died in September 1969).

The impact of the "loss of Vietnam" was made worse by the fate of neighboring countries. At roughly the same time that Hanoi's forces clinched victory in their war, the Khmer Rouge and the Pathet Lao took over in Cambodia and Laos, respectively. To some observers, this meant that the domino theory rang true after all, for with the Americans out of the way, communism was on the march. To other observers, however, it was clear that although the new ruling elites were composed of communists, the respective loyalties and interests—internal, regional, and international—of the Cambodians, the Laotians, and the Vietnamese did not indicate that a monolithic communist force had suddenly subdued a large part of Southeast Asia. National leaders in each country were influenced by nationalist sentiments as much as by communist ideology, and they were wary of external influences. Indeed, by the late 1970s self-inflicted war and genocide rather than peaceful reconstruction were the order of the day throughout much of Indochina.

In Vietnam itself, the country's forced reunification was followed by efforts to unify the nation under the Communist Party. However, Hanoi's leadership faced many obstacles. In addition to the massive human suffering previously described, the country lacked the resources for a successful reconstruction program. While there had been some hope that American aid would be offered in the immediate aftermath of the 1973 Paris Peace Accords, the continued war and unification had frozen the Vietnamese-American relationship. In the North, the Sino-Vietnamese relationship, which had begun its decline in the late 1960s, was growing worse by the day with the Chinese side cutting back on its military and economic assistance (the PRC would cancel all such aid in 1978). As a result, for external aid, the DRV depended largely on the Soviet Union. Indeed, one irony of the unification was that it made Hanoi more, rather than less, dependent on Moscow.

In Cambodia, the situation after 1975 was far worse. Under the leadership of Pol Pot, the Maoist-influenced Khmer Rouge initiated virtual genocide after it took over the country. Declaring that 1975 was "Year Zero" of the new Cambodia, the Khmer Rouge launched a homicidal effort to cleanse the country of any remaining "bourgeoisie" elements and to create a pastoral communist utopia.

Much of the urban population was forcefully transferred to rural areas. Libraries, schools, and temples were destroyed. Between 1975 and 1978 an estimated 2 million Cambodians were killed, and countless others fled the country. To guard its independence from the more populous and better-armed Vietnam, Pol Pot's regime established close ties with China, a country eager to prevent Soviet-backed Vietnamese hegemony in Indochina. However, at the same time, the Khmer Rouge provoked Vietnam by initiating a series of border incidents and persecuting ethnic Vietnamese within Cambodia. Finally, in December 1978, Vietnam's patience snapped, and it launched an invasion of Cambodia, which drove Pol Pot out of power and established a puppet government to replace the Khmer Rouge. China followed up by invading Vietnam in February 1979. In the brief nonconclusive war, 35,000 people died. Meanwhile, Pol Pot gathered his troops and fought a prolonged guerrilla warfare campaign against the new regime of the People's Republic of Kampuchea. More than 100,000 Vietnamese troops remained in the impoverished country until 1989.

These tragic histories—to which one could add the permanent impoverishment of Laos, also under Vietnamese domination—ultimately proved that American fears of the continued spread of communism had been exaggerated. In 1975, however, the shock of the collapse of Saigon was mainly seen as an ignoble end to a war no one wanted to "own." While criticizing congressional cutbacks, Gerald Ford and Henry Kissinger accepted them as the final nail in the Saigon government's coffin. They naturally attempted to shift the blame for the outcome elsewhere, to the Democrat-controlled Congress and the deceitful North Vietnamese and their allies. Yet there was a marked difference in the concerns that the two men had at the time. To Kissinger, Vietnam was a question of credibility, chiefly important in the broader context of U.S. foreign policy. As he explained to the cabinet on April 16, 1975, "The great challenge to the United States is how does the country manage its exit from this tragic situation. The answer to that will be the world's perception of the United States' foreign policy. These events have a profound impact on world leaders. They are very interested in the United States position, not only in South Vietnam, but how it relates to their specific countries all across the globe."[20]

To Gerald Ford, the chief calculation appeared to be in the domestic arena. Given that the war had been a bipartisan affair, the president decided that it was politically more expedient to ignore Vietnam rather than start playing the blame game with Congress. Thus, on April 23, 1975—a week before North Vietnamese troops entered Saigon—Ford made Vietnam the key subject of his convocation address at Tulane University in New Orleans. He declared that the war was over. After evoking images of Andrew Jackson's 1815 victory in the Battle of New Orleans, Ford noted that the former president's epic triumph had "restored America's pride." He went on to say, "Today, America can regain a sense of pride that existed before Vietnam. But it cannot be achieved by refighting a war that is finished as far as America is concerned. . . . I ask that we stop re-fighting the battles and the recriminations of the past." When Ford uttered the word "finished," his audience burst out in thunderous applause, perhaps the loudest he ever received during his political career.[21]

The trouble was not that the American domestic audience got upset when Saigon fell. In fact, most Americans appeared quite eager to ignore the fact that a long-term ally had suffered a defeat to a Soviet-sponsored rival. In 1975 few worried about the moral implications of the sudden end to American involvement in Indochina. The real concern—that had been at the heart of U.S. policy in Vietnam for at least a decade—had to do with American credibility. The events of April 1975 were sure to damage the American image in the eyes of allies and adversaries alike. Robert Tucker in the May 1975 issue of *Commentary* put it as follows: "To be militarily frustrated, and eventually defeated, by so small a state is humiliating, and nothing we say can deny this." *Time* magazine, which in 1972 had chosen Nixon and Kissinger as its men of the year, summed up the dreaded credibility crisis somewhat differently: "What was imperiled by America's performance in South Vietnam was not so much the nation's credibility as its aura of competence."[22]

The scenes surrounding the collapse of Saigon—the helicopters hectically airlifting U.S. personnel and South Vietnamese from a city under siege—illustrated America's unwillingness to employ its military power directly. In 1975 it was simply impossible for any American president to order large numbers of troops into a military campaign. The Vietnam syndrome had set in.

Frustration over Angola

Far from the killing fields of Cambodia and the reeducation camps of Vietnam, another region was boiling as a result of decolonization. In the first half of the

1970s, the long-standing Portuguese effort to hold onto its rebellious colonies of Angola, Mozambique, Portuguese Guinea (Guinea-Bissau), and Cape Verde finally failed. In March 1974 the Carnation Revolution in Lisbon brought in a government headed by young military officers keen on ending the colonial wars that had been ongoing since the early 1960s. Within a year the new revolutionary government had negotiated transitional agreements with the various independence movements in the territories. In Angola, the largest of the colonies, the Portuguese government and the three major Angolese liberation movements signed the Alvor Accord in January 1975. The agreement set up a transitional government and specified November 11, 1975, as the official date for independence. Instead of providing the context for a smooth transition and a peace process, however, the Alvor Accord prompted one of the most globalized civil wars of the Cold War era, between the Popular Movement for the Liberation of Angola (MPLA), the National Front for the Liberation of Angola (FNLA), and the National Union for the Total Independence of Angola (UNITA). The Soviet Union, Cuba, the United States, the PRC, East Germany, Great Britain, France, Romania, India, Israel, Algeria, Zaire (the former Congo), South Africa, Uganda, North Vietnam, and North Korea all played their roles in the struggle for Portugal's colonial legacy. Not since the Belgians had abruptly departed Congo some fifteen years earlier had a former European colony become a subject of this sort of magnified global interest.

In a different international context, the Ford administration might have ignored Angola. But given the collapse of the Indochinese "dominoes" and the influx of foreign troops to southern Africa, the struggle against the Soviet-supported MPLA became a virtual test case of American influence in the post-Vietnam era. Yet, it was impossible in 1975 to conceive a large-scale direct American military intervention. Thus, in July 1975 the administration commenced a large-scale covert operation, code-named IAFEATURE. Over the next three months, the CIA used $50 million recruiting mercenaries and providing material assistance to the FNLA and UNITA. The United States prompted the FNLA to cooperate with neighboring Zaire's military forces. In a move disastrous for America's overall reputation on the Continent, the Ford administration also chose to encourage apartheid South Africa's intervention in the Angolan war. Starting on October 14, 1975, roughly three thousand South African troops—

cooperating with UNITA—moved rapidly toward the Angolan capital, Luanda, in Operation Zulu.

From the U.S. perspective, things could not have ended much worse in Angola. The rapid influx of Cuban troops into Angola—flown there by Soviet aircraft—in early November (there were approximately twelve thousand Cuban troops in the country by early 1976) helped turn the tide of the war. On November 11, 1975, the leader of the MPLA, Agostinho Neto, was able to proclaim Angola's independence from Luanda. By December both the FNLA and UNITA (and their South African and Zairean allies) were on the run, and the U.S. Congress refused to grant any more money for operations in Angola. For the FNLA and UNITA, the only chance to salvage some political influence in an independent Angola was through some form of a negotiated settlement. But the key to any such deal was now largely dependent on the USSR.

Visiting Moscow in January 1976, Henry Kissinger discovered that the Soviets had no interest in obliging American interests in southern Africa. Leonid Brezhnev bluntly announced that the purpose of the meetings was to discuss SALT and refused to discuss Angola. But Kissinger persisted. "We have made it a cardinal principle of our relations that one great power must exercise restraint and not strive for unilateral advantage," he insisted, warning that "if that principle is now abandoned, the prospect is for a chain of action and reaction with the potential for disastrous results." Brezhnev was not impressed. "If we raise all sorts of extraneous matters, we will accomplish nothing," he responded. Moreover, if Kissinger was worried about the consequences of unilateral actions in Angola, then the Soviets should probably "talk of disastrous consequences for the United States in the Middle East." When Kissinger pressed the matter further with Foreign Minister Gromyko, his Soviet counterpart simply concluded that there was no reason for such "momentary events" as those in Angola "to have an adverse effect on Soviet-American relations."[23]

The Soviet leaders' recalcitrance with regard to Angola should have come as no surprise. Humiliated by Kissinger's shuttle diplomacy in the Middle East, the Soviets used Angola as an opportunity to teach the Americans a lesson about the "rules" of détente. If Ford and Kissinger worried about prestige and credibility, so did Brezhnev and Gromyko. In this narrow sense, Angola was payback time, something that Brezhnev made abundantly clear. Not that the Soviets could do much, lest they were willing to alienate the Cubans and the MPLA, both of whom often acted independently of Moscow. Although Soviet matériel was important for the success of the MPLA, Cuban engagement in Angola was not dependent on Soviet approval or, by January 1976, subject to Moscow's veto.

When it came down to maintaining the momentum of détente, however, Angola was a complication. The trouble with success is that it tends to breed inflated expectations. This is apparently what happened inside the Soviet Union's foreign policy circles in the wake of Hanoi's victory in Vietnam and the MPLA's triumph in Angola. As the historian Odd Arne Westad puts it, "The socialist offensives in the Third World gave many Soviets a renewed sense of pride in their own achievements and a conviction that the Soviet Union could contribute decisively to breakthroughs for socialism elsewhere."[24] By 1976 the Soviets—helped by their Cuban, Vietnamese, and African allies—were apparently rebounding from the disappointments of their newfound irrelevance in the Middle East. If the Americans had been successful in acting unilaterally and "stealing" Egypt from the Soviet camp, the Soviets had subsequently achieved a string of victories—none fundamentally of their own doing—that promised a bright future for international socialism. As one Soviet official put it, "The world was turning in our direction."[25]

In the United States, this prospect of a resurgent and globally active Soviet Union was disturbing. But it was also a useful political asset for those wishing to replace Gerald Ford in the White House.

The Reagan Challenge: Act I

The foreign policy context of the 1976 presidential election in the United States was fraught with doubt about America's role in the world. Somewhat unjustly, the leading contenders for the job portrayed the policy of détente in extremely negative terms. To be sure, Vietnam and Angola were important but hardly the linchpin of domestic discontent. After all, Vietnam was a heavily bipartisan "mistake," and Angola inhabited but a minor space in the collective mental map of the American electorate. In the end, the most effective critique of what Democratic candidate Jimmy Carter called the "Nixon-Ford-Kissinger" foreign policy emphasized the perceived immorality of détente and the secrecy that surrounded Kissinger's operational methods.

Aware of the forthcoming critique, Kissinger had attempted to explain the morality of détente to the American public in 1975. In a series of so-called heartland speeches, the secretary of state paid lip service to American ideals while arguing that the nuclear age demanded a more cooperative relationship with such foes as the Soviet Union. Détente, he insisted, was a moral foreign policy. With an implied reference to his own efforts at raising the levels of emigration from the USSR, he stressed that the United States' "immediate focus is on the international actions of the Soviet Union not because it is our only moral concern, but because it is the sphere of action that we can most directly and confidently affect. As a consequence of improved foreign policy relationships, we have successfully used our influence to promote human rights. But we have done so quietly, keeping in mind the delicacy of the problem and stressing results rather than public confrontation." Kissinger then issued a challenge: "The critics of détente must answer: What is the alternative that they propose? What precise policies do they want us to change? Are they prepared for a prolonged situation of dramatically increased international danger? Do they wish to return to the constant crises and high arms budgets of the cold war? Does détente encourage repression—or is it détente that has generated the ferment and the demands for openness that we are now witnessing?"[26]

As the critics continued to attack détente and the 1976 elections approached, Kissinger shifted his tack and started emphasizing the nonpartisan aspects of foreign policy making. In Detroit on November 24, 1975, amid the Angolan crisis, Kissinger intoned,

> In a world of thermonuclear weapons, shrunken distances, and widely dispersed power, we cannot afford disunity, disarray, or disruption in the conduct of our foreign affairs. Foreign policy requires authority. . . . This country cannot have a moratorium on a responsible foreign policy. . . . A great responsibility rests upon both the Congress and the Executive. Our foreign policy has been most effective when it reflected broad bipartisan support. . . . Our free debate once again must find its ultimate restraint in the recognition that we are engaged in a common enterprise.[27]

It was to no avail. For those gearing up to challenge Ford in 1976, attacking détente was a political asset. In a Gallup poll released on the same day as Kissinger spoke in Detroit, Ford and Jackson were in a dead heat (at 44 percent).[28]

While trouble from the Democrats was to be expected, the earlier challenge was issued from a future Republican president. On November 20, 1975, Ronald Reagan announced his candidacy for the Republican nomination. Within weeks he was polling 12 percentage points ahead of the president.[29] Throughout the primary season, Reagan needled Ford and, in particular, Kissinger for having conducted a defeatist foreign policy.[30] "Henry Kissinger's recent stewardship has coincided precisely with the loss of U.S. military supremacy," was one of Reagan's favorite lines in the spring of 1976. Détente, he argued, was a "one-way street." Reagan—like Ross Perot in 1992—purchased time to deliver a nationwide television address on March 31. His sharpest attacks focused on détente. "'Wandering without aim,'" Reagan argued, "describes U.S. foreign policy." He complained about American weakness in Angola. He then wondered why Ford had refused to invite the Soviet dissident Alexander Solzhenitsyn to the White House and why he and the president had traveled to Helsinki to sign the CSCE, "putting our stamp of approval on Russia's enslavement of the captive nations [of Eastern Europe]."

Reagan's anti-détente campaign was further assisted by the "revelation" of the so-called Sonnenfeldt Doctrine. On March 22 Rowland Evans and Robert Novak of the *Washington Post* reported on a memo written by Helmut Sonnenfeldt about his December 1975 briefing to U.S. ambassadors in Europe. The State Department counselor and longtime Kissinger aide had allegedly called for U.S. support for "an organic union" between the Soviet Union and Eastern Europe. His point was that the United States should strive to promote conditions that would create a less volatile situation within the Soviet bloc, one that was not based on the overwhelming presence of the Soviet military. But Sonnenfeldt had done so in easily misinterpreted prose. "It sent shivers up the spine" to read that American officials were so cynical, C. L. Sulzberger of the *New York Times* wrote. In late March and early April, a series of articles blasted the obvious moral callousness of such policies. The Romanian government issued a note of protest. And Reagan, naturally, upped the ante. The Sonnenfeldt Doctrine was further proof, if such was needed, that détente amounted, not only to appeasement, but also to a de facto call for the Soviet Union to formally incorporate Eastern Europe.

There was no such thing as the Sonnenfeldt Doctrine. But in the charged atmosphere of the day, the leaked memo gained notoriety far out of proportion to its true significance. Kissinger, initially bemused, grew restive and outraged as the notion lingered even beyond the Republican primaries, despite his denials at congressional hearings that the United States "emphatically" rejected the legitimacy of a Soviet empire in Eastern Europe. In a meeting with Ford, Secretary of Defense Donald Rumsfeld, and NSC Adviser Scowcroft, Kissinger exploded, "Reagan doesn't know what he's talking about and he's irresponsible."[31]

While Kissinger may have been right to castigate Reagan in this manner, Ford's campaign team had come to consider him and détente as severe handicaps. On March 5, in a speech in Peoria, Illinois, the president publicly banished "détente" from his vocabulary, a move that his campaign staff had urged for months. But "peace through strength"—Ford's replacement—did little to improve his defensive position vis-à-vis Reagan's straightforward rhetoric. Meanwhile, Kissinger was advised to sit back for the remainder of the campaign season; instead of continuing his heartland speeches, the secretary of state went on extended tours of Africa, Europe, and Latin America.

After suffering numerous losses in key primaries, Ford entered the August Republican Convention in Kansas City with a slight lead, but not a majority, in delegates. Much haggling followed. Finally, on August 18, 1976, Ford was nominated after the first ballot with 1,187 votes to Reagan's 1,070.[32] "Now that we've gotten rid of that son-of-a-bitch Reagan, we can just do what is right," Ford told Kissinger and Scowcroft a few weeks later. Kissinger was equally confident in the prospects. "I think Carter is vulnerable on a number of areas," he maintained.[33] They were both wrong.

Morality over Realpolitik

Reagan's formidable challenge set the stage for the unlikely success of James Earl Carter. Little in Carter's past suggested that the one-term (1970–74) Georgia governor would have had a chance to even win his party's nomination. Yet he was a far more skillful politician than many realized. Having set his sights on the presidency as early as 1972, Carter built a base for himself as chairman of the Democratic Congressional Campaign Committee in 1974. Throughout 1975, however, Carter's campaign was short of money and his name recognition remained limited. In a poll of possible Democratic candidates conducted in January 1976, Carter received only 4 percent of the prospective vote, behind

Hubert Humphrey, George Wallace, George McGovern, Henry Jackson, Edmund Muskie, and several others. But by March he was in the lead and ended up winning nineteen of the thirty-one primaries. In July, Carter officially became the Democratic Party's nominee at Madison Square Garden in New York.[34]

Carter's sudden surge is explained by a combination of factors. First, like Ronald Reagan, Carter ran a campaign as an outsider; even more than Reagan, he was a fresh face. He repeated, sometimes to the point of exasperation, a few simple messages, such as "I'm Jimmy Carter and I'm running for president. I will never lie to you." In contrast, his Democratic opponents, such as Jackson, were Beltway insiders. But, most of all, Carter ran as an unabashed Wilsonian moralist. As the historian Robert Greene puts it, "Carter planned to corner the market on morality and beat the Republicans senseless with it." In the post-Watergate era of intelligence investigations and concerns over the morality of American foreign policy, this was a fruitful political strategy.[35]

Carter's main target was often Kissinger. While faulting Ford for allowing Kissinger to run foreign policy, the presidential candidate argued that the secretary of state was "obsessed with power blocs, with spheres of influence." This sort of obsession had resulted in "a policy without focus [that] is not understood by the people or the Congress." In numerous speeches authored partly by Zbigniew Brzezinski, Kissinger's old academic competitor from Harvard and Carter's future NSC adviser, the Democratic candidate attacked "a kind of secretive, 'Lone Ranger' foreign policy, a one man policy of international adventure." In fact, Carter charged, "the president is not really in charge. Our policies are Kissinger's ideas and his goals, which are often derived in secret." Carter told the Foreign Policy Association that the heart of the problem was that "a foreign policy based on secrecy inherently has had to be closely guarded and amoral."[36]

Carter's ultimate victory in November 1976 owed much to this criticism of an immoral foreign policy. Instead of secret deals with the Soviets and the Chinese, in contrast to covert action in Chile and other places, Carter vowed to conduct a foreign policy that in its methods and goals would be guided by openness and moral principles. Carter further benefited from the simple fact that his opponent was a poor political campaigner. The low point came when, in one of the televised debates, Ford said, "There is no Soviet domination of Eastern Europe and there never will be under a Ford administration." Carter did not hesitate to demand that the president explain to those Americans of Eastern European origin what he meant by this astonishingly counterfactual statement. Ford's credibility was all but finished.

The election of a Democrat to the White House was probably inevitable in the aftermath of Watergate. Even a more skillful candidate than Gerald Ford would have had a difficult time proving to Americans that their country had not lost touch with its idealism. The ultimate morality of détente that Kissinger, for example, had preached during his heartland speeches in 1975 was no match for the call for supporting those struggling to defend their human rights and promising to end the era of secret diplomacy and covert actions. Yet, while Jimmy Carter excelled in painting the contrast between the secretive realpolitik of the Nixon-Ford years and the open idealism that was to follow, his administration would find it difficult to cut loose all the policies of the preceding years. With its principal architects gone, détente may have been halted. But it had yet to be buried.

CHAPTER 6

Reason or Morality: Carter, Human Rights, and Nuclear Peace

"Are you proud of our nation?" Jimmy Carter asked soon after he had won the 1976 presidential election. His supporters roared in the affirmative. The grinning president-elect appeared ready to restore confidence in an embattled America. He pledged to set a new course for the country's foreign policy by emphasizing issues that had, in the minds of many, been ignored by the preceding administrations. Most importantly, Carter would bring a new moral purpose to foreign relations by abandoning the immoral realpolitik that had reigned over the previous eight years. Within weeks of his election, Carter had sent a telegram of support to Soviet dissident Vladimir Slepak. In December 1976 the incoming secretary of state, Cyrus Vance, met with another dissident, Andrei Amalrik. Such overtures continued soon after the inauguration when the State Department accused the Czechoslovak government of violating human rights by persecuting members of the Group of 77, a human rights organization that counted among its leaders the future Czech president Václav Havel.[1] The Carter administration thus made it clear that it was not going to shy away from the moral agenda that had been a centerpiece of the presidential campaign.

If the new president emphasized human rights, he was also keen to move further on nuclear arms limitation. As Carter put it in his inaugural address, he wanted to go—as so many presidents after him—for zero. As he pledged: "We will move this year a step toward the ultimate goal—the elimination of all nuclear weapons from this Earth."[2] To be sure, Carter and his team were not driven simply by the prospect of a nuclear-free world, a prospect all involved thought was but a utopian pipe dream in 1977. The need to curtail military spending and to use these resources to reinvigorate the battered domestic economy was particularly important for an administration taking office at a time of growing inflation (5.75 percent in 1976 to 13.58 percent in 1980) and continued high unemployment (7.7 percent in 1976 and still 7.1 percent in 1980). Indeed, the so-called misery index (unemployment + inflation) would hit its post–World War II peak in Carter's fourth year in office and count among the major reasons for his failure to win a second term.

Further emphasis on human rights and deeper cuts in nuclear armaments—in 1977 these were noble goals for a new American foreign policy, a new kind of moral détente. Carter was not about to turn back the clock and revert to an uncompromising Cold War stance. As the historian Olav Njolstad puts it, Carter "did not want US-Soviet relations to deteriorate. Rather, he hoped to change the character of that relationship and to move beyond the Cold War framework of international politics." At the same time, however, Carter also believed that there was no need to soft-pedal on difficult issues (such as human rights). To Carter, détente could not be "selective"; it would need to be "reciprocal" and "comprehensive." Issues could not simply be dropped from the negotiation agenda because the Soviets were not comfortable discussing them. The president did not want "linkage"—tying progress in one area (e.g., arms control) to progress in another (e.g., finding a solution to a regional crisis)—in the sense that the Nixon administration wanted it. He seemed to desire much more: progress in *every* area of the relationship, from nuclear arms to human rights to superpower restraint in regional conflicts.[3]

But the world did not cooperate with Carter's vision. For one, trampling human rights was not a uniquely Soviet trait. From the southern cone of Latin America to the PRC, anticommunist military dictatorships and communist totalitarian states were unlikely to change their ways just because of an inexperienced new president's election promise. Liberation movements in Africa fought against institutionalized racial discrimination and imperial rule in such a violent manner that it was difficult to see whose human rights were being threatened most seriously. Carter may have been critical of the Nixon and Ford administrations' foreign policy, but he was not bent on reversing the course of America's long-awaited rapprochement with the PRC. Over time he—and those around him—learned that while moral rhetoric may have been a successful tool with American domestic audiences, in actual foreign policy, even if backed up by economic sanctions, such talk would have little chance of transforming the internal politics of totalitarian regimes. For another, the world still lived in the shadow of nuclear weapons, but politicians and defense intellectuals inside the United States (and the Soviet Union) were still convinced that cuts could easily translate into unacceptable vulnerabilities.

To further complicate matters, the third world was in turmoil. In the late 1970s the wrangling over various regional conflicts further eroded the basis of détente. Rather remarkably, seen from today's perspective, the 1977–78 war between Ethiopia and Somalia over the Ogaden Desert was considered, both in Washington and Moscow, as a key conflict in Cold War terms. Carter's national security adviser, Zbigniew Brzezinski, won support within the administration for viewing Soviet bloc aid to Ethiopia as a direct challenge to the United States. On the Soviet side, some leaders believed that through receiving Soviet advisers and Cuban troops, the leftist military regime in Ethiopia could become a star example of how socialism could triumph in Africa. Although no borders changed as a result of the Ethiopian victory in the war, many in Washington came to see the conflict in the Horn of Africa as a severe blow to superpower détente. Even as Carter flew to Vienna to meet with General Secretary Brezhnev and sign the SALT II Agreement in June 1979, détente was in deep trouble.

Brzezinski or Vance?

Carter's inexperience in foreign affairs was not a unique trait in American presidents. In the case of the former Georgia governor, however, it did produce a lengthy period of indecision and an ambiguous foreign policy. This ambiguity was symbolized in the rivalry and disagreements between the two most influential foreign policy makers in Carter's administration: NSC adviser Zbigniew Brzezinski and Secretary of State Cyrus Vance. Ultimately, as in the early period of the Nixon administration, the NSC adviser emerged at the top. Yet, the relationship between Carter and Brzezinski was never as close as that between Nixon and Kissinger; indeed, unlike Secretary of State William Rogers, who left office unceremoniously in 1973, Vance eventually resigned in protest—not for the first time in his career—in April 1980. The cause of Vance's resignation, though, was not the overall course of foreign policy but a specific disaster: a botched rescue attempt of American hostages in Iran.

In fact, Carter, unlike Nixon and any number of previous American presidents, was not obsessed with being his own secretary of state, of running foreign policy from the White House. Moreover, having criticized Kissinger's "Lone Ranger" foreign policy, he could hardly vest too much power in one official, let alone another Ivy League academic. Thus, unlike Nixon, Carter chose a strong personality with plenty of experience in foreign policy to head the State Department. Vance fit the bill. He was a Yale-trained New York lawyer who had held a number of executive positions prior to 1977. Although a navy officer, he had been John F. Kennedy's secretary of the army. Vance had then moved to become the deputy secretary of defense in the Johnson administration, serving directly under Robert McNamara. Disillusioned—a sentiment that seemed to haunt him throughout his career—Vance resigned in 1967 but still went to Paris as a delegate to the peace negotiations the following year. In addition to extensive diplomatic and executive experience, the new secretary of state also had an impeccable Democratic pedigree: his uncle and adoptive father was the former U.S. ambassador to Britain and the 1924 Democratic presidential candidate John W. Davis (who lost the election to Calvin Coolidge).

The contrast between Cyrus Vance and Zbigniew Brzezinski is reminiscent of the dichotomy between William Rogers and Henry Kissinger. If Vance and Rogers were WASP lawyers with distinguished government service under their belts, Brzezinski and Kissinger were naturalized American citizens who had made their careers as foreign policy intellectuals at Ivy League academic institutions. Brzezinski, a Warsaw-born son of a Polish diplomat who had migrated to the United States in 1953, had—like Kissinger—a PhD from Harvard, where he had taught in the 1950s. In 1961 Brzezinski moved to New York to become a professor of political science at Columbia. Again like Kissinger, he served as an occasional consultant to the Kennedy and Johnson administrations, acting later as the foreign policy adviser to Vice President Hubert Humphrey, the Democratic candidate in the 1968 elections. During the Nixon and Ford administrations, Brzezinski was the critical voice in waiting. In 1976 he was a key member in Carter's foreign policy team and a natural choice to a key post in the administration. In contrast to Nixon's nomination of Kissinger in 1968, few were surprised when Brzezinski was named Carter's NSC adviser.

The differences in the personal backgrounds of Vance and Brzezinski were matched by their contrasting views on how foreign policy should be organized and managed. His disillusioning experience with Vietnam had convinced Vance not only that military interventions were usually counterproductive but also that bad decisions were often results of the lack of public debate and broad reflection on foreign policy issues. Not one to mince words, Vance declared during his confirmation hearings that the intervention in Vietnam had been a "mistake," a result of a series of "misjudgments." To avoid repetition of such a disaster, the United States needed to have a "keener appreciation of the limits" of American power and a "democratic foreign policy." Vance thus promised the Senate Foreign Relations Committee to "come completely clean" with them at every step of the way. Gone were the days of Kissinger's Lone Ranger style; Vance would help Carter run a foreign policy that would reflect a new "openness of government."[4]

In contrast, Brzezinski had little appetite for the inclusion of a multitude of actors—including, it would become evident, the State Department—into serious foreign policy making. Although a strong critic of the substance of Kissinger's policies, Brzezinski later admitted that "operationally" he had no problems with how the Nixon administration's NSC adviser had grabbed hold of the foreign policy machinery. "Large bureaucracies do not produce strategies—they produce shopping lists," Brzezinski declared in a BBC radio interview in 1990, when asked about the State Department. Like Kissinger, Brzezinski would also complain about the troublesome role of Congress, especially regarding the appropriate tactics to be used to press the Soviet Union on human rights issues. "Pressure on the Soviets is justified; but it has to be measured in order to be effective," Brzezinski wrote in his journal in June 1977.[5]

The differences between Brzezinski and Vance—which owed as much to the respective positions they held within the administration as to their overall outlook on foreign policy—were no secret to Jimmy Carter. But the president believed that he could tease out the best of the two men and act as the ultimate judge on policy. As Hamilton Jordan—a key aide in the 1976 campaign who became White House chief of staff in 1979—would sum up Carter's thinking, "Zbig would be the thinker, Cy would be the doer, and Jimmy would be the decider."[6] The trouble was that neither Zbig nor Cy were entirely content with these roles, and this made it exceedingly hard for Jimmy to perform his. In an administration not blessed by happy circumstances or a clear-cut agenda, the rivalry produced indecision, incoherence, and stalemate.

Carter, Brezhnev, SALT II

Jimmy Carter seemed to believe that the United States had been, as he put it during a presidential debate in 1976, "out-traded in almost every instance" during the détente process. This applied in the field of nuclear arms limitation, an issue on which Carter thought much more could be gained through negotiation. He had criticized the Vladivostok accord of 1974 throughout the presidential campaign as a deal that would simply legitimize the continuation of the nuclear arms race. SALT II, Carter argued, should go much further than limiting the numbers of nuclear missile launchers and MIRVs to 2,400 and 1,320, respectively. Negotiating deep cuts in numbers—rather than ceilings that had yet to be reached—was the way for a true nuclear peace. In addition, Carter wished to include a set of restraints to the qualitative development of nuclear arms. In short, the new president wanted reductions rather than restraints.[7]

Wasting little time, Carter commenced a direct correspondence with Leonid Brezhnev upon taking office. In late January—while he still appeared ready to use the Vladivostok accord as the basis for negotiations—he emphasized the need to move on in the direction of additional limitations and reductions in the sphere of strategic weapons. A few weeks later, Carter emphasized that it was "necessary for us to achieve some maximum progress" in nuclear arms limitation talks. Aside from such platitudes, however, Carter also indicated a number of specifics that included, among others, a proposal to put aside any discussion of cruise missiles. Brezhnev's reactions to such proposals were not positive. Although he agreed with the ultimate goal of reducing and abolishing nuclear weapons, "[the] advancement forward toward these elevated goals will not be accelerated, but, on the contrary, will be slowed down, if we first of all do not value what we already managed to accomplish in this area over the last few years, and, second, if we abandon a responsible, realistic approach to determining further concrete steps in favor of introducing proposals which are known to be unacceptable."[8] Brezhnev simply wanted to seal the deal agreed to in Vladivostok in 1974; Carter wished to restart the talks with a far more ambitious agenda.

Knowing that he was on a mission doomed for failure, Vance flew to Moscow in late March 1977. He presented the centerpieces of the new proposals to Brezhnev: a 10 percent reduction in the limits agreed on at Vladivostok and sweeping future cuts in the arsenals of each country. There was also a call for a five-year moratorium on nuclear tests. The Soviet response was simple: no way. "If the United States wants to reopen questions that have already been solved, then the Soviet Union will again raise such problems as the American Forward-Based Systems and the transfer of American strategic weapons to its allies," Brezhnev told Vance in Moscow. The American demands were "utterly unacceptable," he helpfully added.[9]

Several explanations account for the Soviets' initial rejection and later intransigence regarding Carter's proposals. For one, it was made clear to the Soviets in the spring of 1977 that the new American administration was internally divided. In one of the many conversations between Vance and Ambassador Anatoly Dobrynin in February 1977, the secretary of state was openly frustrated with Carter's approach, telling the ambassador that the "President still approaches certain international problems lightly. . . . He doesn't pay much attention . . . on remaining contradictory questions."[10] That Carter—unlike his predecessors—chose to repeatedly publicize his proposals (at the UN General Assembly on March 17 and in a press conference a week later) before Vance arrived in Moscow in late March did not help to improve the chances of success. As Dobrynin maintains, such publicity was considered mere propaganda by the Soviet leadership; consequently the proposals themselves were thought to be less than serious. This was confirmed by the fact that Carter was proposing the deepest cuts in weapons systems—land-based ICBMs—a category in which the Soviets had a significant numerical advantage. Brezhnev's reference to U.S. forward defense strategy and transfer of technology also emphasized a broader issue that had clouded previous negotiations. In terms of the geopolitics of nuclear arms, the Soviets did not consider the United States their only adversary (although Americans were clearly the principal one). The French, British, and even Chinese nuclear forces—minor though they were in comparison to the American force—were also counted as strategic threats in Moscow. From the Soviet perspective, this ring of American allies justified higher numbers.

After his first visit to Moscow in March 1977, Vance had his work cut out for him. Over the next two years, a series of painstaking negotiations in Washington, Geneva, and Moscow focused on narrowing down the differences between two broad objectives: while the Soviets wanted an agreement that consolidated existing levels of weapons, the Carter administration pushed for reductions. Predictably, each side wanted to keep as many of its options open as possible while it sought ways to constrain the other. Gradually, differences were narrowed. In the meantime, the SALT I Agreement expired—it was an interim deal concluded in 1972 for five years—but both sides respected a tacit accord to comply with its terms while negotiations continued. Other events—such as the announcement of the normalization of Sino-American diplomatic relations in December 1978 (discussed later in the chapter)—complicated matters. Ultimately, the last remaining questions were settled between Vance and Dobrynin, who met twenty-five times between January 1 and May 7, 1979. As Raymond Garthoff writes, "The final details were ironed out only on June 14, the very eve of the [Vienna] summit meeting [between Carter and Brezhnev]."[11]

The terms of SALT II were ultimately much closer to the 1974 Vladivostok agreements than Carter's March 1977 proposals. The total number of strategic delivery vehicles of all types (land-based, submarine-based, and air-based) was capped at 2,400 for both sides, to be reduced to 2,250 by 1982. The overall limit of MIRVed missiles was 1,320 (of which a maximum of 1,200 could be based on ICBMs and SLBMs; a further maximum of 820 on ICBMs). Compromises were reached on the Backfire bombers and cruise missiles and on limits on further testing. In fact, the two sides came to an agreement that, while not ratified by the U.S. Congress, was actually observed by the United States during the Reagan years. Yet, it was a far cry from the ambition that Carter had outlined at the beginning of his presidency. Carter, upon returning to Washington, acknowledged that zero was nowhere in sight, but he also told Congress that the treaty was "the most detailed, far-reaching, comprehensive treaty in the history of arms control. Its provisions are interwoven by the give-and-take of the long negotiating process. Neither side obtained everything it sought. But the package that did emerge is a carefully balanced whole, and it will make the world a safer place for both sides."[12]

In fact, as Olav Njolstad has argued, the eventual SALT II Agreement signed in 1979 was "the best possible agreement the United States and the Soviet Union could reach at the time." The asymmetry of Soviet and American missile systems made it impossible to reach true strategic parity. Given technological innovations—from new types of missiles to more accurate and varied guidance systems—the assumptions behind MAD were being challenged by military experts in both countries. If SALT I fell short of setting limits on MIRVs, cruise missiles, or even heavy Soviet missile systems, then SALT II would leave loopholes for various counterforce and war-fighting systems (e.g., the MX, the Mark-12A warhead, the Trident II SLBM, and the Tomahawk cruise missile). Once again, the negotiations that concluded in 1979—like those in 1972—had produced a treaty that would not cap the nuclear arms race but would allow it to shift toward new types of weapons system development (most of which were already under way).[13]

SALT was not the only negotiation aimed at reaching an agreement on matters of military security. The MBFR talks between NATO and the Warsaw Pact had begun in Vienna in January 1973. During the Nixon and Ford administrations, these negotiations had become bogged in all manner of significant detail: whether troops stationed in Hungary counted (in the end, NATO agreed to exclude them and Hungary participated only as an observer); whether troop reductions should be proportional (the Warsaw Pact view, given higher numbers of Warsaw Pact troops) or asymmetrical aiming at a common ceiling (NATO position); whether only ground troops should be discussed (NATO) or air, navy, and nuclear forces as well (Warsaw Pact); and whether initial talks should focus only on U.S. and Soviet forces while others would be the subject of a second phase of discussions. Later on other complications arose, most importantly regarding the verification of numbers and how they were to be counted. Ultimately, the MBFR talks would continue, without resolution, into the late 1980s, when they would be superseded by the conventional forces in Europe (CFE) negotiations. The CFE Treaty was ultimately signed on November 19, 1990, less than a year before the formal dissolution of the Warsaw Pact.[14] Compared with the MBFR, the SALT II negotiations were, in fact, a resounding diplomatic success.

In the end, there was some "reciprocity" to the SALT II negotiations, and the fact that they actually continued showed the need that both sides felt for ongoing arms control. But that need—and the talks themselves—was probably not the overriding issue that consumed decision makers in Moscow and Washington between 1977 and 1979. The Carter administration's "comprehensive" détente agenda was not just about nuclear weapons. In fact, one could speculate that had SALT taken place in isolation from the world around it, a treaty could have easily been signed much earlier than June 1979. But the administration's agenda was dominated by questions that inevitably led to a collision with Soviet leaders. One major obstacle to a more ambitious arms reduction and control agenda was a political one: human rights.

Human Rights: From Sakharov to Belgrade and Beyond

In 1975, amid widespread criticism, Gerald Ford refused to meet with the exiled Soviet dissident author Alexander Solzhenitsyn. Many of the Ford administration's critics characterized the decision as a blunt betrayal of American values in the name of realpolitik. Jimmy Carter was bound to do no such thing. Instead he was ready to pick up the banner of Henry Jackson and other Democrats keen on demanding improvements in the USSR's human rights policies. An opportunity to do so arrived early on. On January 21, 1977, Nobel Peace Prize winner Andrei Sakharov's handwritten letter complaining about the treatment of dissidents in the Soviet Union arrived at the State Department. In a reply published two weeks later, Carter told Sahkarov to "rest assured that the American people and our government will continue our firm commitment to promote respect for human rights not only in our own country but also abroad."[15] A few days later, in his first press conference as president, Carter further insisted that human rights questions "can legitimately be severed from our inclination to work with the Soviet Union, for instance, in reducing dependence upon atomic weapons and also in seeking mutual and balanced force reductions in Europe." On February 21, *Time* magazine featured a defiant-looking Sakharov on its cover with the headline, "The Dissidents Challenge Moscow."[16]

Carter thus openly rejected the idea that by criticizing Soviet human rights abuses he might jeopardize progress in nuclear arms limitation talks. Unfortunately, the reality was that—whether Carter admitted it or not—there was a link between the two. For the Soviets, concern over internal dissidents was not a trivial matter; the Komitet Gosudarstvennoy Bezopasnosti (KGB, or Committee for State Security), headed by future general secretary Yuri Andropov, was actively monitoring dissident groups throughout the Soviet Union. The USSR reacted to any statements that expressed support for internal dissidents immediately and predictably by complaining of American interference in Soviet internal affairs. At the very beginning of the Carter administration, Soviet Ambassador Dobrynin repeatedly protested about American meddling. On March 21, 1977, Brezhnev told the Soviet Congress of Trade Unions, "Our adversaries would

have liked to find some kind of forces against socialism in our countries. . . .
Precisely for this reason a ballyhoo is being organized about the so-called 'dissidents,' a cry to the whole world about 'violations of human rights' in the countries
of socialism."[17]

Parallel developments occurred in satellite countries in Eastern Europe. In
January 1977 a group of 243 Czech intellectuals and writers—including Václav
Havel—signed a petition known as Charter 77. Published in a number of Western
newspapers and circulated widely in Czechoslovakia, the manifesto criticized the
government for failing to implement the human rights provisions in a number of
documents it had signed, including the 1968 Czechoslovak Constitution, Basket
III of the Helsinki Accords, and the UN Charter. Although the authors of the
document emphasized that Charter 77 was not a formal political organization
opposed to the official government—important because Czechoslovak law made
organized political opposition illegal—the manifesto nevertheless invited an
instant reaction. The Czech police conducted arrests, illegal searches, harsh inter-
rogations, and general harassment. Most tragically, one of the spokesmen of
Charter 77, the retired professor Jan Patocka, died after a weeklong intensive inter-
rogation. Havel was more fortunate: after four months in jail, he was released
without being charged, only to be rearrested and imprisoned in 1979 for crimes
against the Czechoslovak state. Similar developments—more open criticism of
Eastern European states' human rights policies followed by repression—were subsequently observed throughout the Soviet bloc. To be sure, Poland and Czechoslovakia were quite exceptional: in the late 1970s there was no comparable
dissident activism in, for example, Romania or Bulgaria.[18]

Indeed, one of the by-products of European détente was a steady growth of
transnational human rights advocacy. The Czechs who signed Charter 77 actively
sought contacts with both Western European peace activists and other Eastern
European dissidents. They saw the CSCE biannual follow-up meetings—the first
one in Belgrade in July 1977—as an assurance that the pledges made in Helsinki
two years earlier were not mere empty phrases but an intergovernmental guarantee of basic human and political rights. Despite police surveillance, Pole and Czech
dissidents organized border meetings and even a joint publication. And, perhaps
most important of all, the election of a Polish pope and the visit of John Paul II
to his homeland in 1979 heralded the growing hunger for political and religious

freedom in Warsaw Pact countries. "It is necessary to open borders," the pope declared in a June 1979 message that was transferred beyond Poland to the Catholic community in Eastern Europe. It was no accident that in subsequent months strike activity—a growing phenomenon since the government had raised food prices between 30 and 50 percent in 1976—among Polish workers increased further. The most famous of these strikes led to the creation of the Solidarity movement in 1980.

In the 1980s Pope John Paul II emerged as a key figure in conveying the call for human rights and religious freedoms to a growing transnational movement that would play its part in challenging totalitarian regimes throughout the Soviet bloc. When the Polish government arrested thousands of Solidarity activists in December 1981, for example, the Reagan administration consulted the Vatican consistently. More important than such attempts to coordinate a response to a specific event, however, was the pope's growing role as a symbol of resistance to totalitarian control, particularly important in such heavily Catholic nations as his native Poland.

It is ultimately impossible to evaluate the exact significance of John Paul's role in the chain of events that ultimately culminated in the Eastern European revolutions of 1989. But the important point to underline is that his remarkable pilgrimage to Poland in 1979 could hardly have taken place a decade earlier. Détente and the Helsinki process made it possible not only for intellectuals such as Václav Havel and trade union leaders such as Lech Wałesa to challenge the unjust nature of the political system in their respective countries. They had also made it possible for the public reemergence of centuries-old religious traditions that, much like the political activists, rejected the legitimacy of totalitarian regimes.[19]

While Eastern European dissidents and the Catholic Church were clear on their moral and political agenda, however, the Carter administration's approach was somewhat confused. For example, there were plenty of gestures and protests regarding human rights abuses inside the Soviet Union and in Eastern Europe. Yet, a number of other Communist countries seemed to be left off the hook, prompting the standard-bearer of the Republican right, Ronald Reagan, to point out in March 1978, "If the Carter administration 'stands with the victims of repression,' the people of Cuba, Panama, Vietnam, Cambodia, and the mainland of China have yet to hear about it."[20] Of course, Reagan had his own selective and less-than-consistent view of human rights abuses and American foreign policy, which would become evident when he entered the White House a few years later. What he, and anyone criticizing Carter, tended to overlook for political purposes was the mere fact that abusing human rights was no specific privilege of left-wing regimes.

Indeed, in much of Latin America the situation was virtually the opposite of that in Eastern Europe: the conservative anticommunists were committing the worst violations while the socialists were the human rights activists. Although a number of Latin American dictatorships—Argentina, Paraguay, and several Central American countries among them—were guilty of repression, Chile emerged as the focal point of public controversy. After the 1973 toppling of Salvador Allende's regime, the military junta headed by Augusto Pinochet launched a concerted campaign that was, if not supported, at least condoned by the Nixon and Ford administrations. Between 1973 and 1978 at least three thousand people "disappeared" or were killed by government forces. And the campaign was not limited to Chile; on September 21, 1976, a car bomb went off in Washington, killing a former Chilean diplomat and Pinochet critic, Orlando Letelier. In Latin America as a whole, one of Jimmy Carter's challenges was to develop a new policy that would, as the president himself promised, show "a high regard for the individuality and the sovereignty of each Latin American and Caribbean nation, . . . our respect for human rights, . . . [and] our desire to press forward on the great issues which affect the relations between the developed and the developing nations."[21] In other words, to appear coherent, Carter would need to uphold human rights standards in America's backyard similar to those he was demanding be applied in the Soviet bloc.

The Carter administration did make an effort. In May 1977, for example, Vice President Walter Mondale met with Eduardo Frei, a former Chilean president and a critic of the Pinochet regime. The administration produced detailed reports to Congress on human rights abuses in countries such as Argentina, Brazil, Chile, Nicaragua, Guatemala, and El Salvador. In Honduras, the Carter administration pushed for democratization by backing those within the military leadership who supported the process that culminated in free elections and a return to democracy in 1980. Yet, the campaign to promote human rights in the Western Hemisphere was an uphill struggle in the late 1970s: only three Latin American countries (Venezuela, Costa Rica, and Colombia) had democratically elected governments when Carter assumed office. By the time he left the White House, Honduras remained the only bright spot in this regard. Cutting off military aid to Guatemala and El Salvador, for example, did not prompt any significant change in the internal politics of either country. From the perspective of human rights activists, the Carter legacy was one of great promise but limited success.[22]

A major part of the explanation for the lackluster implementation of human rights standards lay in the ongoing debate about détente. In the late 1970s the shadows of Soviet and Cuban activism in the third world were felt in Latin, particularly Central, America. While the events in Nicaragua—the collapse of the regime of Anastasio Somoza in 1979—and an increasingly violent civil war in El Salvador had no direct link to Moscow (and only limited ones to Havana), the Carter administration faced a quandary. In both Central American countries, the fighting was taking place between the supporters of long-standing military dictatorships supported by previous American administrations and left-wing guerrilla movements (the Sandinista National Liberation Front in Nicaragua and the Farabundo Martí National Liberation Front in El Salvador). After decades of oppression and amid ongoing brutality, a smooth transition to electoral democracy was simply impossible. Meanwhile, Carter's domestic critics—Ronald Reagan foremost among them—made the most of the apparent failure of the president's human rights policies. By 1979 it was difficult for Carter to uphold a policy that was consistent on human rights standards because he was heavily criticized at home for siding with elements friendly to the Soviets. It was no wonder that Ronald Reagan found attacking Carter's "leftist" human rights in Latin America an equally profitable political strategy as attacking his "timid" human rights agenda vis-à-vis the Soviet bloc.

In Africa, one of the focal points of human rights issues was Rhodesia. Following its unilateral declaration of independence from Great Britain in November 1965, the landlocked southern African country had been ruled by a white minority (whites were, though, outnumbered 22 to 1). Soon after independence, the UN had imposed sanctions on Rhodesia that the United States had complied with fully until 1971, when Congress lifted bans on imports of Rhodesian chrome. In Rhodesia itself, a bloody Bush War was raging as the Zimbabwe African National Union (ZANU) fought to end the apartheid system imposed by the government of Ian Smith. Headed by Robert Mugabe and Joshua Nkomo, ZANU and its political umbrella organization, the Zimbabwe African People's Union (ZAPU), unsuccessfully sought the support of the United States and Great Britain. Mugabe forged alliances with other liberation movements in the region (such as the Liberation Front of Mozambique [FRELIMO]) and extracted aid from the Soviet Union and Cuba. After the victory of the Soviet-Cuban-backed MPLA in Angola in early 1976, however, the Ford administration became increasingly concerned about growing Soviet influence in southern Africa. Henry Kissinger thus pressed Smith to accept an agreement that would lead to black majority rule within two years. Increasingly isolated and losing even the support of neighboring South Africa, Smith agreed. Ultimately, years of bitter fighting ensued before the country—to be named Zimbabwe—became fully independent in 1980. Yet, as later events testified, the victory of Mugabe's ZANU did not solve all the country's problems; in particular, racial tensions clouded Zimbabwean politics well into the twenty-first century.[23]

Addressing the Rhodesia/Zimbabwe conflict should have been a straightforward task in terms of Carter's human rights policies. But nothing was uncomplicated. In 1977 Carter, following up on his human rights campaign pledges, persuaded the U.S. Congress to restore full sanctions. American ambassador to the UN Andrew Young and Vice President Walter Mondale, however, came under fire from Republican senators such as Jesse Helms for their critical comments about white minority rule. As the Rhodesian Bush War continued and Secretary of State Vance's effort to mediate between Smith and Mugabe failed, the Rhodesian prime minister announced an "internal settlement" in early 1978. The deal established a new government that incorporated moderate black Zimbabweans but not representatives of the combined Patriotic Front of ZAPU/ZANU. The Carter administration split. Vance thought that Smith's plan was a simple subterfuge for hanging on to white minority rule, while Brzezinski—concerned about reports of Soviet military aid to ZAPU guerrillas in Zambia and the presence of Cuban military instructors at training camps—thought it was a promising avenue for gradual transition. Ultimately, Carter cave in to the twin pressures from conservative senators and his own NSC adviser and sought what he may have thought was an easy way out: he designated Young to abstain voting on a UN resolution banning Smith's plan. It solved nothing. To the supporters of a rapid transformation to black majority rule,

Carter appeared to have betrayed his own pledges to uphold human rights; to the likes of Jesse Helms, Carter's determination not to lift sanctions amounted to hostility toward Smith. Perhaps most of all, however, Carter was seen as indecisive, lacking in clear-cut direction and commitment, unable to maintain a coherent line of policy. In 1979, when he denounced the first multiracial elections in Rhodesia as flawed because the Patriotic Front had boycotted them, Carter added further to this image of vacillating and confused leadership. Although the Rhodesian question was ultimately solved through negotiations under the auspices of Margaret Thatcher's new conservative government in December 1979, followed by Mugabe's sweeping electoral victory in 1980, the result was hardly "the greatest reverse the Russians have suffered in Africa for years," as U.S. assistant secretary of state Richard Moose described it.[24]

Promoting human rights was, in fact, far from a simple guide for foreign policy. In a world filled with victims of regimes of various political persuasions, it was not simple to define whose abuses deserved priority. Within a context of trying to implement a foreign policy based on at least some form of accommodation with a consistent violator of human rights, the challenge was doubly difficult. When one adds to this the critics at home who found fault in both consistency and inconsistency, it is even easier to grasp that the task Carter had set for himself was particularly vexing, if not downright impossible. The great political beneficiary of Carter's imperfections, Ronald Reagan, was ultimately not far off the mark when he pointed out in March 1978 that "the administration means to do good by espousing a human rights doctrine it cannot define, much less implement. In the process, this policy has met with scorn from our enemies and alarm from our friends."[25]

In terms of détente, Carter's human rights policy was counterproductive. Linkage was not explicit. But open American support for dissidents raised doubts about the usefulness of détente—or at least the costs of détente for the Soviets. The CSCE's human rights provisions may have been cast away as mere window dressing by a number of Soviet leaders. Yet, the growing advocacy for and eminent popularity of democratic reform within several Warsaw Pact countries also drove up the cost of maintaining totalitarian control. The Soviets were still "masters of this house" as Yuri Andropov, KGB chief and future general secretary, had pointed out during Politburo debates about whether or not to accept the CSCE's Basket

III with its human rights provisions (in 1975). But repression of dissidence—closely monitored by such groups as the U.S. Helsinki Watch Committee (founded in 1979)—grew in the late 1970s with negative effects on economic and intellectual life inside the Soviet bloc. Indeed, while Carter's policies had little immediate or direct effect, the emergence of a Soviet human rights movement in the 1970s created "the fertile soil for Gorbachev's perestroika after 1985."[26] Human rights advocacy may have had limited—even negative—short-term impact for Soviet-American détente. But its long-term consequences were far more significant.

China: Going All the Way with Triangulation

During the 1976 presidential campaign, Carter and Brzezinski may have been critical of the Nixon-Kissinger foreign policy. Yet one aspect that they rarely touched upon was China. Indeed, during the second debate between Carter and Ford—famous for Ford's gaffe about the "lack of Soviet domination of Poland"—the People's Republic of China came up only once and mainly in connection with the impact that a full normalization of relations between Washington and Beijing would have on the long-standing military alliance between the United States and Taiwan. Carter's comments echoed the essential unanimity between the two candidates: "In the Far East I think we need to continue to be strong, and I would certainly pursue the normalization of relationships with the People's Republic of China. We opened up a great opportunity in 1972—which has pretty well been frittered away under Mr. Ford—that ought to be a constant inclination toward friendship." After his victory and inauguration, Carter continued in the same vein. In a speech in May 1977, the president described Sino-American relations as "a central element of our global policy" and the post-Mao China "a key force for global peace." In August 1977 Secretary of State Vance visited Beijing for what Carter later described as an "exploratory" mission aimed at measuring the possibilities for rapprochement.[27]

There was much irony in this. The opening to China, with its secret trips and clandestine maneuverings was a perfect example of the Lone Ranger foreign policy that Carter—and Reagan—had so much criticized. When Carter took office, the PRC—the country he was keen to become friends with—was among the worst violators of human rights. For a decade since 1966, the Cultural Revolution had

wreaked havoc throughout the world's most populous nation, already unfairly pun-
ished during Mao's disastrous Great Leap Forward. In the late 1960s the red guards
had done their best to destroy as much of China's rich cultural legacy as possible,
while the cancelling of university entrance exams had effectively brought the
nation's higher education system to a halt. We will never know how many Chinese
perished, but historians Roderick MacFarquhar and Michael Schoenhals assert that
as many as 35 million were persecuted and up to 1.5 million may have been killed.[28]

At the time of Carter's inauguration, the Cultural Revolution was, to be
sure, over. Mao's death in September 1976 was followed by a lengthy power struggle that ultimately confirmed the leadership position of Deng Xiaoping over that
of Hua Guofeng, the Great Helmsman's designated successor. In December 1978
Deng's victory was heralded at the Chinese Communist Party's Central
Committee meeting in Beijing. Most significantly for China's future development,
Deng unveiled a radical departure by calling for "reform and opening" instead of
"class struggle" and "continuous revolution." China's rapid transformation began
almost immediately. At home and abroad, economic growth trumped political
orthodoxy as the leitmotif of the PRC. In terms of its foreign policy, China started
pulling back from its commitments to various liberation movements and
Communist regimes. The initial signs of improvement in Sino-Soviet relations—
a treaty on navigation in the channel connecting the Ussuri and Amur Rivers was
signed in October 1977—gave way to continued coolness as Deng confirmed his
leadership position.

While tensions in Sino-Soviet relations augured well for the relations between
Washington and Beijing, plenty of controversial issues hampered full normalization.
Within the Carter administration, one of the main concerns was the perplexing
question of Taiwan; essentially, the State Department wanted to maintain an official consulate there, while the NSC was ready to cut off all diplomatic ties in order
to smooth the way toward full normalization with the PRC. Deng's angry retort
during Cyrus Vance's visit to China in August 1977 about the impossibility of having a "flagless [American] embassy" in Taipei was enough to cause a delay on the
road to rapprochement. The Chinese also cultivated senior Republicans more sympathetic to their views: when former ambassador and CIA director George H. W.
Bush visited China in the fall of 1977, he was given red carpet treatment. Bush
returned the favor by writing a positive article in *Time* magazine about China's

development policies in Tibet and the supposedly negative views many Tibetans held about the exiled Dalai Lama.[29]

In the end, Brzezinski's push for playing the China card vis-à-vis the Soviets and Beijing's need to open avenues for economic growth combined to make full recognition possible. In May 1978 Brzezinski flew to Beijing with a portfolio of inducements. The United States was ready to help China obtain—not directly from the United States but from its NATO allies—advanced technology items previously withheld as part of the strategic embargo. A Pentagon official gave the Chinese a detailed briefing on Soviet troop deployments on the Chinese border, while an NSC expert, Benjamin Huberman, suggested joint intelligence gathering against the USSR. Perhaps most importantly, Brzezinski said that the United States was ready to withdraw all official U.S. representation in Taiwan. Indeed, as the NSC adviser kept repeating throughout his visit, President Carter had "made up his mind" on the question of full normalization. The Chinese, being offered almost everything they were asking for, could only try to press home what was clearly an advantageous negotiating position from Beijing's perspective.[30]

The final agreement on full normalization was reached in December 1978, after several months of negotiations in Beijing by Ambassador Leonard Woodcock and by Brzezinski and the head of China's liaison office in Washington, Chai Zemin. On the evening of December 15, Carter announced the full normalization of Sino-American diplomatic relations, which would take effect on January 1, 1979. In his televised address to the nation—reminiscent of Nixon's announcement of Kissinger's secret trip to China some eight years earlier—Carter outlined what was definitely bad news for Taiwan and its supporters: the United States would terminate formal diplomatic relations with Taiwan, cancel the 1954 mutual defense treaty that committed the United States to guaranteeing Taiwan's military security, and withdraw the seven hundred U.S. troops stationed on the island. On March 1, 1979, the United States and Beijing would formally exchange ambassadors. Deng—who would soon be named *Time*'s Man of the Year—would visit Washington at the end of January for a series of summit talks.

Following Carter's announcement, a new phase in Sino-American relations opened with a gradual—eventually staggering—growth of economic and military cooperation. What Nixon and Kissinger had commenced in the early 1970s was thus concluded by their most ardent critics by the end of the decade. To be sure,

Brzezinski's secret negotiations and Carter's willingness to move ahead were not the real story; the true movers behind full normalization were ultimately the Chinese. With Deng at the helm, Beijing was pursuing what was dubbed the Great Leap Outward. When the Chinese leader arrived in the United States, American politicians and businessmen were falling over each other to meet with him and members of his delegation. Deals were made over trade and over Chinese students coming to the United States. Intelligence sharing was strengthened. And Carter— at Brzezinski's urging—even gave tacit support to China's pending military invasion of Vietnam (which would occur on February 1, 1979). It had been a decade in the making, but the reversal of Sino-American relations was finally complete.[31]

There were a number of other consequences to normalization. One had to do with bureaucratic infighting. Much as the opening to China had confirmed Kissinger's predominance over foreign policy making in the Nixon years, normalization signaled a clear pendulum shift from the State Department to the NSC. Brzezinski had not only gotten his wish on a substantial level, but he had also managed to outmaneuver Vance. Domestically, normalization caused a brief uproar among senior Republicans—Ronald Reagan and Barry Goldwater among them—who criticized the "betrayal" of Taiwan. The abandonment, Reagan admonished, "diminished American credibility in the world." As a result, the bill that "normalized" the new relationship with Taiwan was rewritten by Congress. The Taiwan Relations Act essentially amounted to a slightly modified version of the cancelled Mutual Defense Treaty. It passed overwhelmingly in both houses, and Carter, whose veto could not have been sustained should he have used it, signed the bill into law on April 1, 1979. The Chinese protested but did not retaliate. To them, the Taiwan Relations Act was ultimately a small price to pay for the benefits of normalization.[32]

But a paradox that would plague Sino-American relations for decades to come was evident. Critics may have pointed to the betrayal of trust and the abandonment of Taiwan, but normalization also confirmed that Americans, both politicians and the greater public, did not care about—or did not clearly recognize—the immorality of having a love fest with a country that remained one of the worst violators of human rights on the globe. To be sure, the worst days of the Great Leap Forward and the Cultural Revolution were in the past. In fact, Deng Xiaoping had appeared to be supportive of basic democratic freedoms: he had not yet cracked down on the Democracy Wall movement that had spread throughout major Chinese cities in December 1978. The movement got its name from the wall posters that criticized China's political system and became the rallying points of the budding pro-democracy movement. In Shanghai, up to ten thousand Chinese attended one such rally. But the movement was cut short soon after normalization. Starting in late March 1979, key leaders of the Democracy Wall movement were arrested; by the end of the year, a full crackdown, complete with trials behind closed doors, was evident. Wei Jingsheng, one of the leaders, received a fifteen-year prison sentence. While the State Department put out a statement critical of the "severity" of the ruling, the Carter administration did nothing. Nor did it feel the pressure of an outraged public opinion. When it came down to China, promoting human rights was not much of a policy doctrine.[33]

Sino-American normalization would have far-reaching effects echoing into the twenty-first century. But for the immediate term, as Deng Xiaoping toured the United States triumphantly in early 1979, the consequences were less than happy for Soviet-American détente. As *Time* magazine put it, "[Deng's] visit also holds potentially grave risks. Moscow's Americanologists are geared up to scrutinize every public statement . . . for evidence of an anti-Soviet thrust to his visit. . . . Some Soviet officials have warned that if the visit proves to be an extravaganza of bearbaiting, they may further delay a strategic arms limitation treaty or scuttle it altogether."[34] Although SALT II was eventually signed, the normalization of Sino-American relations had done little to improve the chances of détente's longevity.

No Waltz in—or after—Vienna

Notwithstanding all the seeming difficulties, détente was still a fact of life in the summer of 1979 when Carter and Brezhnev met in Vienna face to face for the first and only time. However, much like the previous superpower summit in the Austrian capital—between Kennedy and Khrushchev in 1961—this one was far from harmonious. To be sure, there was a marked difference: in 1961 the Soviet leader's assertiveness, bordering on bullying, had made a mark on the meeting. This time, the impatient interlocutor was the American president, and the aging general secretary found himself on the defensive. While the two leaders did sign the SALT II Agreement on June 18, 1979, Brezhnev later complained to East German leader Erich Honecker about "dark moments" in Soviet relations with the United States. The Vienna talks had been "very difficult" as they had touched upon the whole panoply of difficulties in Soviet-American relations: "the Middle East, Southeast Asia, the situation in Southern Africa, the relationship between the United States and China." Brezhnev was also pessimistic about the ratification of SALT II by the U.S. Senate, yet he took some solace in the belief that such failure "would be an extremely severe blow to the international prestige of the United States."[35]

Carter was fully aware of the difficulties he was bound to face at home. "SALT II will undoubtedly become the most exhaustively discussed and debated treaty of our time, perhaps of all times," he told a joint session of Congress upon returning from Vienna. But, sounding upbeat, he vowed to do his best to explain the treaty and its significance. "This treaty will withstand the most severe scrutiny because it is so clearly in the interest of American security and of world peace," Carter said. But he faced plenty of opposition as even the Democrats were split over the treaty. "If the U.S. Senate fails to ratify the SALT treaty, history will judge it harshly," declared Senator Edward Kennedy (D-MA). But Senator Henry Jackson remained consistent in his critique of arms control. "The U.S. would be better off with no agreement than [with] this one."[36] As it happened, Jackson got his wish as ratification of SALT II would never take place. Brezhnev, already recognizing the likelihood in July 1979, told Honecker that this was not necessarily bad news for the USSR. The Soviet Union, he added, "will not lose politically [from the U.S. failure to ratify SALT II] because the entire world will recognize who is consistently seeking disarmament and who is working in the opposite direction."[37] Brezhnev's judgment was, of course, somewhat biased. In fact, neither the United States nor the Soviet Union won too many points around the world on the conclusion of SALT II; nor would the fate of the treaty ultimately tip the balance of world public opinion or the superpower rivalry.

Moreover, the tensions surrounding nuclear weapons were not limited to discussions about intercontinental missiles. Already in 1976 the Soviets had decided to start deploying their new generation of medium-range missiles (SS-20s) in Europe. By the time of the Vienna summit, the failure to include these theater missiles in Soviet-American discussions and the onset of Soviet deployments had heightened concerns among NATO countries about a growing Soviet military threat. In simple terms, Western Europeans feared that MAD no longer applied to Europe; the Warsaw Pact was about to enjoy both nuclear and conventional military superiority over NATO. As the ratification of SALT II was stalled in the U.S. Senate, NATO leaders agreed to the so-called double-track decision on December 12, 1979. In essence, they offered a deal of sorts to the Warsaw Pact member states: either the two sides would agree to limit their intermediate nuclear forces or NATO would proceed with the modernization of its intermediate nuclear forces in order to provide a counterweight to the new Soviet missiles. While peace activists took to the streets of Europe to protest the decision, the Soviet leaders were preoccupied with something else.

Indeed, in retrospect, the significance of the double-track decision and the U.S. Congress's failure to ratify SALT II seems somewhat mundane. The real issues of concern of the day, affecting real lives and shifting allegiances around the globe, did not revolve around counting Soviet or American nuclear missiles. Nor did the fate of détente ultimately depend on how many strategic delivery vehicles or MIRVs were under the Pentagon's command. Of course, psychologically it mattered to those who had grown up with the Cold War, who instinctively worried about the possibility that "the other side" was gearing up to annihilate "us." But whether one side held a slight advantage—numerical or tactical—at a particular point in time in the nuclear arms race was ultimately of limited practical consequence. What truly mattered was the series of upheavals in areas that, up to the 1960s, had been virtually ignored as arenas of Cold War competition. As the Cold War had gone global in the 1960s and 1970s, the potential for a serious clash between the United States and the Soviet Union in disparate regions of the world had dramatically increased. Up to this point, a direct clash had been avoided, although many areas—in Indochina, parts of Africa—had already seen proxy conflicts cause senseless suffering despite the relative insignificance of East-West ideological allegiances and power alignments to the native inhabitants. In the late 1970s, however, these proxy conflicts touched a region that had become known as the graveyard of empires. This time around, it would be the graveyard of détente.

Enter the arc of crisis.

CHAPTER 7

CRISIS AND COLLAPSE: IRAN, AFGHANISTAN, AND THE CARTER DOCTRINE

IT WAS AN UNPRECEDENTED AGREEMENT. On September 17, 1978, Israeli prime minister Menachem Begin and Egyptian president Anwar Sadat signed the Camp David Accords, the outcome of twelve days of secret negotiations at the American president's compound in Maryland. The accords consisted of two separate agreements: the Framework for Peace in the Middle East and the Framework for the Conclusion of a Peace Treaty between Egypt and Israel. The latter would be followed up within six months by the conclusion of the 1979 Israeli-Egyptian peace agreement, which ended decades of hostilities between these two adversaries. The framework for a regional settlement created the backdrop for future negotiations and raised hopes for a sustainable solution to the many conflicts in the Middle East. In front of the U.S. Congress the day after the signing of the accords, President Carter sounded optimistic: "For many years the Middle East has been a textbook for pessimism, a demonstration that diplomatic ingenuity was no match for intractable human conflicts. Today we are privileged to see the chance for one of the sometimes rare, bright moments in human history—a chance that may offer the way to peace."[1]

Some three decades later, the Camp David Accords appear but a momentary bright spot. To be sure, Begin and Sadat shared the 1978 Nobel Peace Prize for their efforts, and the agreements were clearly a milestone in Arab-Israeli relations. But Egypt found itself isolated within the Muslim world and was suspended from the Arab League for two decades (1979–99). Worse, in 1981 Sadat was assassinated by a Muslim extremist for his "betrayal." Also, the Accords failed to solve the Palestine question or prevent future hostilities between Israel and its other neighbors. Camp David might have signaled a chance for something other than continued conflict. When Sadat signed the accords he might have "put Egypt firmly and inalterably in the American orbit in the Middle East," as Patrick Tyler puts it.[2] But deeply ingrained hostilities that had been stoked by decades of conflict made further progress virtually impossible.

Nor could a successful Israeli-Egyptian agreement rescue the declining fortunes of détente. To an extent, Carter's personal role in bringing about the Camp David Accords only confirmed Soviet suspicions of American unilateralism in the Middle East, which had become neuralgic since the 1973 October War and Kissinger's shuttle diplomacy. There was nothing surprising about this: in the 1970s the United States had clearly managed to position itself as the only indispensable external actor in the Arab-Israeli peace process. The idea of comprehensive, multilateral conflict resolution had no more room in the Carter administration's foreign policy than it had during the previous Republican administrations. Indeed, as Anatoly Dobrynin acidly pointed out, "In general, the Americans wanted to talk with us about the Middle East only when they had problems in the region."[3]

Ironically, in 1978–79 the region—broadly conceived—burst with problems that consumed the remainder of Carter's presidency and brought down the façade of détente. The Somali-Ethiopian conflict in the Horn of Africa, the collapse of the shah's regime in Iran, and the Soviet invasion of Afghanistan caused a shift in American foreign policy toward an increasingly aggressive stand vis-à-vis the USSR. The key proponent of such a stand was Brzezinski, who had already expressed concern in December 1978 over an "arc of crisis" extending from northeast Africa to Southeast Asia, an area where the Soviets appeared to take advantage of local circumstances to bring much of the region—including its oil-rich countries—under its dominion. In January 1979 a *Time* magazine article quoted Brzezinski as saying, "An arc of crisis stretches along the shores of the Indian Ocean, with fragile social and political structures in a region of vital importance to us threatened with fragmentation. The resulting political chaos could well be filled by elements hostile to our values and sympathetic to our adversaries."[4] A few months later Berkeley professor George Lenczowski wrote that the "central core" of the arc of crisis was the Middle East, "the last major region of the Free World directly adjacent to the Soviet Union [which] holds in its subsoil about three-fourths of the proven and estimated world oil reserves, and it is the locus of one of the most intractable conflicts of the twentieth century: that of Zionism versus Arab nationalism." But that was not all. In the Middle East, Lenczowski continued, "national, economic and territorial conflicts are aggravated by the intrusion of religious passions in an area which was the birthplace of Judaism, Christianity and Islam, and by the exposure, in the twentieth century, to two competing appeals of secular modernization: Western and communist."[5]

By 1980 the events that had unfolded in the arc of crisis helped to bring down détente and the Carter presidency. The geopolitics of the region looked dismal from the American perspective; the loss of an ally (Iran) and the introduction of a large number of Soviet troops outside Warsaw Pact borders (Afghanistan) were enough to cause severe headaches in the White House. Carter's reaction to these developments was understandable: he adopted Brzezinski's anti-Soviet outlook and unleashed a series measures to "punish" Moscow. But by harking back on the idea that all that was evil in the world ultimately emanated from the Soviet Union, Carter not only proved himself unable to grasp the significance of the rise of Islamic fundamentalism but further played into the hands of those who had long criticized the administration's foreign policy.

Aided further by the continuous economic malaise in the United States (itself a by-product of the Iranian Revolution, which produced a dramatic rise in oil prices), Ronald Reagan's promise to restore America's strength dashed Carter's hopes for a second term.

Trouble in the Horn

On July 23, 1977, Somali troops invaded the Ogaden Desert, sparking an eight-month war with Ethiopia. By September the Somalis had conquered most of the Ogaden, but the war drew to a stalemate. In early December Cuban troops, airlifted by Soviet planes, began to arrive in Ethiopia; they numbered twelve thousand by March 1978. Somali troops were gradually forced back, and on March 9 President Carter announced that they were withdrawing from the Ogaden completely. He also called for an end to the Cuban and Soviet military presence in Ethiopia but to no avail. Meanwhile, a spin-off war in Eritrea continued. The region was mired in a series of deadly conflicts that would persist into the twenty-first century.[6]

The fighting in the Horn of Africa was closely tied to the currents of the Cold War and the unraveling of détente. Following the 1974 overthrow of Emperor

Haile Selassie of Ethiopia, Maj. Mengistu Haile Mariam had gradually established himself as the unchallenged leader of the country. He purged rivals and eventually took complete control after a coup on February 3, 1977. But Mengistu was not just a military man, he was an ideologue who actively courted—and was courted by— the Soviet embassy in Addis Ababa. Ethiopia moved toward "scientific socialism," a new kind of African Marxist society with strong links to the Soviet Union, Cuba, and Eastern Europe. Mengistu launched his own red terror within Ethiopia and billed himself as the latest embodiment of the global anti-imperialist struggle. In a letter to the East German leader Erich Honecker, Mengistu pleaded for support in the "final but desperate assault" of imperialism against "the oppressed people of Ethiopia." When Mengistu visited Moscow in May 1977, his ambitions were stoked by promises of significant military aid from the USSR. In 1977–78, for example, the Soviets would send an estimated $1 billion worth of weapons to Ethiopia, while Soviet, Cuban, and East European military experts provided train- ing to Mengistu's army. Mengistu sent the remaining Americans packing. An American base in Asmara was ordered closed soon after the February coup. According to a Soviet embassy report, Ethiopia was seeing "the deepening of the revolutionary process . . . and the intensification of the struggle against internal reaction supported by imperialism."[7]

In 1977 Mengistu was not the only leader in the Horn of Africa claiming to be a devotee of scientific socialism. In neighboring Somalia another military man, Mohammad Siad Barre, had taken power in 1969. Like his predecessors, Barre had turned to the USSR for military support. In return, under a 1972 agreement, the Soviets gained control of a naval and missile base in Berbera, an ancient port on the Gulf of Aden. In 1974 the Soviet Union and Somalia signed the Treaty of Friendship and Cooperation, which increased the number of Soviet military advisers and arms deliveries. Prompted in part by the increasingly close cooperation between Moscow and the Mengistu regime, however, Barre terminated this treaty in 1977 and expelled all Soviet advisers from the country. Ironically, although Somalia turned to other sources of military aid—Arab states (most prominently Egypt) as well as the United States, Great Britain, France, and China—much of the initial fighting in the Ogaden Desert by both the Ethiopians and Somalis was conducted with Soviet weapons.

Convoluted though the situation in the Horn was, the Carter administra- tion could not ignore the broader issues at stake. From Washington's perspective, the developments in the Horn were but the latest manifestation of a troubling phenomenon of Soviet-Cuban military activity in Africa. The 1976 victory of the MPLA in Angola had been abetted by thousands of Cubans airlifted to the region by Soviet aircraft. The People's Democratic Republic of Yemen (PDRY), a former British colony at the mouth of the Gulf of Aden (with a potential stranglehold on the Red Sea), had become a recipient of Soviet military and economic aid in the early 1970s. Even if Carter and his advisers could have seen the folly of trying to build a socialist society in a deeply religious area, the fact was that growing Soviet influence—direct or indirect—in the Middle East and Africa was a potential threat to the West's access to the region's precious raw materials, most notably oil. In the aftermath of the 1973 oil crisis, this was no idle problem. Particularly to NSC Adviser Brzezinski, the fluctuating allegiances of Ethiopia and Somalia appeared intricately linked to Soviet efforts to undermine America's position in the Middle East. As Brzezinski put it, "The expansion of Soviet influence . . . represented a serious setback in our attempts to develop with the Soviets *some rules of the game* in dealing with turbulence in the Third World [emphasis added]."[8]

Brzezinski's views were not shared by all in the Carter administration. To Secretary of State Vance, the war between Somalia and Ethiopia was best treated as a regional conflict in which the United States should not be too closely involved. The ominous presence of twelve thousand Cuban troops in Ethiopia and evidence of growing Soviet involvement led Carter, in contrast, to conclude that something broader than the fate of a desert was at stake. Yet, the president—still keen to pursue SALT II and unwilling to risk the collapse of détente—was reluctant to issue an open challenge. The administration openly protested and criticized Soviet and Cuban involvement but preferred to work via proxies (such as the Organization for African Unity) to contain the conflict. When the Ethiopian armies—victorious in the Ogaden War—did not invade Somalia proper, the policy appeared to have been successful.[9]

The crisis in the Horn of Africa was evidence of the further globalization of the Cold War in the 1970s. Within the Carter administration, it certainly raised questions about the USSR's global and regional ambitions; the Horn was one part of Bzezinski's arc of crisis. In fact, the United States could not forge a solution because the situation was hopelessly convoluted. As one scholar points out, "Brzezinski was right: doing nothing in the Horn made the United States look and feel weak. But Vance was also right: supporting Somalia—a country of some 3 million people that had no political, economic, cultural, or historical ties to the United States and that had launched a war of aggression—was not worth derailing SALT." In fact, as far as Moscow and Washington were concerned, there was hardly a clear-cut winner. After all, the Soviets lost a base in Somalia (Berbera) and gained a needy client state in Ethiopia. Americans lost, or felt they lost, prestige and looked weak, which "during the Cold War was tantamount to being weak."[10] In isolation, however, the Ethiopian-Somali squabbles—even with Cuban troops and Soviet involvement—would hardly have invited much prolonged interest in Washington. But the crises multiplied.

Stability Lost

In retrospect, it was the most unfortunate of presidential toasts. "Iran, because of the great leadership of the Shah, is an island of stability in one of the more troubled areas of the world," Jimmy Carter told the audience gathered for a state dinner in Tehran on December 31, 1977. He closed by affirming, "We have no other nation on Earth who is closer to us in planning for our mutual military security. We have no other nation with whom we have closer consultation on regional problems." Shah Mohammed Reza Pahlavi had earlier addressed his American guests with similar hyperbolic ingenuity; he had even referred to the American-Iranian "special relationship made all the closer by a wide community of mutual interests." To have Carter as the first official guest of the New Year was, the shah maintained, "a most excellent omen."[11]

In 1978 that "island of stability" was hit by a tsunami-like wave of Islamic fundamentalism and anti-Americanism that transformed Iran into a place very different from what Carter had described. Only weeks after the U.S. president's visit, anti-shah riots broke out in Tehran. The Islamic Republic, founded in 1979, would have no interest in military cooperation with the United States or in helping Washington solve the vexing problems of the Middle East. The Iranian Revolution of 1978–79 was, in fact, the first manifestation of a series of collisions between political Islam and the West. Yet this crisis accelerated the death of détente. The fall of the shah and the success of the deeply anti-American Iranian Revolution came at a time when doubts about the course of American foreign policy had already been expressed owing to the events in Angola in the mid-1970s and in the Horn of Africa more recently. While the role of the Soviet Union in Iran was virtually nonexistent, the loss of a strong regional ally—a cornerstone of U.S. policy in the Persian Gulf region—was an unexpected blow to the Carter administration's foreign policy and, ultimately, to the president's political future.

The irony was that Carter's policy toward Iran was an example of continuity. Since the Americans and British had assisted the overthrow of Prime Minister Mohammad Mosaddeq in 1953, the shah had received generous support from Washington. In the 1960s the United States had celebrated Iran's "remarkable" success; 10 percent economic growth rates during the second half of the decade appeared to validate the shah's authoritarian leadership. Meanwhile, Iran emerged as an important strategic ally, providing the United States with transit access to Southeast Asia and intelligence facilities for monitoring the Soviet Union. The final British withdrawal from East of Suez in 1971 further strengthened the importance of having a strong Iran as an American ally. In May 1972 Nixon and Kissinger visited Tehran and promised the shah that the United States would sell him any nonnuclear weapons systems. The shah took full advantage by investing much of Iran's burgeoning oil revenues into increasing the defense budget sevenfold in 1972–77. When Carter took office, he simply chose to continue his predecessors' policies and repeatedly made clear that, as long as he paid for them, the shah's defense requirements would be met. For example, agreements on the sale of F-16 aircraft and sophisticated radar systems went ahead in 1977 and 1978.[12]

Carter's public support for the shah, however, was also a reflection of the president's wish to counter the Iranian leader's growing domestic weakness. The means of his ascendancy—British and American covert support—had made him a "Western lackey" in the minds of many Iranians. The shah's methods of consolidating his power via the banning of political parties and the use of his secret police, the Organization of Intelligence and National Security (SAVAK), to repress any dissent further added to domestic discontent. His effort to modernize Iran through the so-called White Revolution bred turmoil among those who were either economically dislocated or viewed the Americanization of Iran as a threat to pure Islam. In the 1970s much of the anti-shah sentiment came from followers of the exiled conservative Shi'a Muslim cleric, Ayatollah Ruhollah Khomeini, whose 1971 book *Islamic Government* advocated an end to the shah's rule and the establishment of an Islamist republic. By the time of Carter's visit in late 1977, Khomeini and his writings had become a focal point of the Iranian opposition.[13]

Following a series of violent antigovernment riots in the first months of 1978, the shah pressured the Iraqi government to deport Khomeini in June. The move backfired. Establishing himself in Paris, with full access to media outlets and, paradoxically, enjoying easier communication lines to his allies in Iran, Khomeini upped the ante. He became an international celebrity and openly called for the abdication of the shah. As opposition gained strength inside Iran, Carter was faced with conflicting advice: Brzezinski told the president to urge the shah to use his military to retain power, while Vance proposed restraint and secret contact with the opposition to facilitate communication with a potential new government. When the shah declared martial law in November, Carter finally made up his mind and advised the course suggested by Brzezinski. But with millions of people joining the demonstrations throughout Iran, it was too late to stop the tide of revolution. In January 1979 the shah fled the country, having first appointed a member of the opposition, Shapour Bakhtiar, as the prime minister. But Bakhtiar found his career short-lived. Upon his return to Tehran on February 1, 1979, Khomeini appointed his own prime minister, Mehdi Bazargan. Over the next few years, under Khomeini's leadership, the Islamic Republic of Iran—a unique mixture of Islamic theocracy and populist democracy—replaced Pahlavi Iran.[14]

The fall of the shah was a severe setback to the Carter administration's foreign policy in the region and beyond. As Brzezinski put it, the loss of Iran as an ally was the "most massive American defeat since the beginning of the Cold War, overshadowing in its real consequences the setback in Vietnam." Not only was Iran geopolitically at the heart of the arc of crisis, but its transformation from ally to enemy translated into the loss of significant military and intelligence facilities. Iran's oil was an important energy resource for the West, particularly America's NATO allies. And, ultimately, the turmoil in Iran seemed to offer the Soviet Union an opportunity to reverse the setbacks it had suffered in the Middle East since the late 1960s. Indeed, already in the spring of 1979, the Iranian crisis caused a thorough reassessment of U.S. policy that would ultimately surface as the so-called Carter Doctrine. As Brzezinski wrote in a memorandum in March 1979, the state of affairs in the Middle East after the Iranian Revolution was akin to the situation in Europe after World War II. "Then too," Brzezinski maintained, "a strategically vital region faced external threat, intra-regional conflicts, socio-economic privation, and local radicalism for which U.S. power, wealth and leadership toward unity were the remedy." The United States was facing another "Truman Doctrine moment" and Brzezinski had cast himself in the role of George Kennan. The remedy he proposed was a new security framework, complete with additional U.S. bases and security guarantees to remaining regional allies.[15]

Indeed, while the administration attempted to build a diplomatic dialogue with the new Iranian regime in 1979, it also began transferring military aid to North Yemen, tilting more clearly toward Somalia against Ethiopia, and supplying aid to the antigovernment fighters in Afghanistan. The common denominator of these three situations was clear: concern over growing Soviet influence. While North Yemen faced a threat from the Soviet-supported South (or the Democratic Republic of Yemen, DRY), Ethiopia continued to build its scientific socialism with Moscow's help and Afghanistan was ruled by a Communist regime loyal to the USSR. As one scholar puts it, "The entire Southwest Asian region had become linked to the Iranian crisis and to the [American] perception of a looming Soviet threat."[16]

In November 1979 all hope for anything resembling a normal relationship between the United States and the new Islamic Republic of Iran vanished. Carter's decision to admit the exiled shah into the United States so that he could receive treatment for cancer (diagnosed in 1974) was viewed as a major provocation by Khomeini's followers. On November 4 Iranian militants stormed the U.S. embassy in Tehran and took sixty-six Americans hostage. In subsequent days, similar attacks against U.S. embassies—confirming a deep reservoir of anti-Americanism throughout the arc of crisis—took place in Pakistan and Libya. Carter's failed attempts to solve the hostage crisis through economic and diplomatic pressure ultimately led him to break off diplomatic relations with Iran and to order a military rescue mission in April 1980. But Operation Eagle Claw was a complete failure. It added further fuel to Khomeini's rants against the Great Satan and caused the chief advocate for diplomacy, Secretary of State Cyrus Vance, to resign. In little over two years after his infamous toast in Tehran, Carter had to face one of the most difficult foreign policy debacles of the Cold War era with a foreign policy team in utter disarray and a presidential election looming. To add insult to injury, the Iranians would not free the remaining fifty-three hostages until early 1981.

To be sure, the impact of the Iranian Revolution on détente and American foreign policy was evident months before Khomeini's supporters stormed the American embassy. The loss of this regional ally was a massive blow to both American prestige—far outweighing the impact of any embarrassment in the Horn of Africa—and strategy in a region identified as a key and growing concern by successive administrations in the 1970s. By exposing American vulnerability in the Middle East, the departure of the shah and the emergence of a hostile new regime in Tehran accelerated the process that saw its culmination in the Carter Doctrine and the subsequent death of détente.

Afghanistan and the Carter Doctrine

While the Carter administration contemplated the unwelcome turn of events in Iran, the Soviet Union faced its own debacle in the arc of crisis. In April 1978—as the shah's regime began to crack under waves of protest—the Afghan Communist Party (the People's Democratic Party of Afghanistan, PDPA) launched a successful coup d'état against the government of President Mohammed Daoud. In power since 1973, when he had deposed his cousin, King Zahir, Daoud had tried to establish cordial relations with the United States and its two key regional allies, Pakistan and Iran. In domestic policy, Daoud adopted a path toward modernization—by using a centralized state to develop the economy, build communication networks, and boost agricultural output—similar to that of the shah in Iran. Much like the shah, Daoud lacked broad-based support at home in a country with deep-seated ethnic divisions that far outweighed any loyalty to an Afghan state. Although Daoud considered his connection to the royal family an assurance against serious rural opposition, he worried more about the urban-based Communists and Islamists. Considering the Communists more dangerous opponents, Daoud commenced a series of purges against the PDPA in 1977. The following year, the "founder, president, and prime minister of the Republic" paid the ultimate price for these often brutal acts.[17]

The bloody coup of April 27, 1978, was apparently planned without the direct participation of the USSR. In fact, Soviet ambassador Aleksandr Puzanov's immediate assessment of the coup and the killing of Daoud and many of his family members hardly amounted to a ringing endorsement. Puzanov worried that the new government would be riddled with infighting between two rival factions—

the Khalq (Masses) and the Parcham (Banner)—but vowed to "take steps to over-come the differences" within the new Afghan leadership. It proved a task beyond anything he may have expected as Babrak Karmal (leader of the Parcham) vied for power with Khalq leaders Noor Mohammad Taraki and Hafizullah Amin. In the first few months after the coup, the Khalqis managed to outmaneuver the Parchamis, and in July, in what amounted to exile, Karmal was sent to Prague as the ambassador of the People's Democratic Republic of Afghanistan (PDRA). Apparently, only Soviet interference saved him—and several other Parchami leaders—from being killed.[18]

While the Khalqis may have won control over the government, they soon faced a serious challenge from a growing Islamist movement supported by Pakistan. Doubts about the viability of the Khalqi regime began to swell after a seemingly spontaneous uprising in the western provincial capital of Herat in March 1979 resulted in the deaths of Afghan officials, Soviet advisers, and their families. However, throughout most of 1979 the Soviets responded to appeals by increasing military, economic, and adviser assistance but refusing to send in combat troops. When Amin engineered another internal coup in September and had his former partner, President Taraki, killed in October, the relationship between Kabul and Moscow deteriorated rapidly. The Soviets began to seriously consider a full-scale military intervention. By November 1979 chaos reigned. As Amin approached the United States and sought a cease-fire with the Islamists, the new Soviet ambassador, Fikrat Tabeev, concluded that the only way to save the PDRA and contain the spread of radical Islam to the neighboring Soviet Central Asian republics was by outright intervention. In early December Defense Minister Dmitri Ustinov and KGB Chief Yuri Andropov agreed on a plan: the Soviet army should intervene, and Amin should be eliminated and replaced by the exiled Karmal. Citing both the dangers of Islamism and the possibility that the United States would take advantage of the demise of the PDRA under Amin, they convinced General Secretary Brezhnev to support their plans for invasion. On December 12 the Politburo gave its approval. What Brezhnev, for one, believed would be "a limited operation over in a few weeks time" commenced on Christmas Day 1979. When he died in November 1982, no end was in sight; the initial 80,000 Soviet invasion force had swelled to 130,000.[19]

Brezhnev was probably more surprised than anyone about the strong U.S. reaction to the Soviet invasion. For members of the Carter administration, however, the Soviet invasion of Afghanistan represented a confirmation of their worst fears: an expansionist move beyond the Warsaw Pact that amounted to a significant step in a global communist third world challenge. That the Soviets conceived the invasion as essentially a defensive preemptive strike on their southern border was inconceivable to Carter and Brzezinski, who were reeling with the repercussions of the loss of Iran and the ongoing hostage crisis, concerned with the Soviet role in the Horn of Africa, and challenged by the aggressive criticism at home regarding their "weak" foreign policy vis-à-vis the USSR. Thus, in his address to the nation on January 4, 1980, Carter called the Soviet occupation of Afghanistan an "extremely serious threat to peace because of the threat of further Soviet expansion into neighboring countries in Southwest Asia." He went on to explain, "We must recognize the strategic importance of Afghanistan to stability and peace. A Soviet-occupied Afghanistan threatens both Iran and Pakistan and is a steppingstone to possible control over much of the world's oil supplies." Carter went on to paint a frightening scenario that was reminiscent of the warnings about Soviet totalitarianism in the 1940s and 1950s:

> If the Soviets are encouraged in this invasion by eventual success, and if they maintain their dominance over Afghanistan and then extend their control to adjacent countries, the stable, strategic, and peaceful balance of the entire world will be changed. This would threaten the security of all nations including, of course, the United States, our allies, and our friends. Therefore, the world simply cannot stand by and permit the Soviet Union to commit this act with impunity. . . . History teaches, perhaps, very few clear lessons. But surely one such lesson learned by the world at great cost is that aggression, unopposed, becomes a contagious disease.[20]

As befitted this public reiteration of the containment doctrine, the Carter administration cut trade links with the Soviet Union and boycotted the 1980 Moscow Olympics. The administration intensified a renewed military buildup, which had already begun the year before. The SALT II Agreement, ratification of which was already deadlocked, was withdrawn from consideration in the U.S. Senate. Hopes for Soviet-American détente were, in essence, declared dead. In their place was a nightmarish, but somewhat delusional, scenario of an aggressive Soviet Union, "executing a grand strategy to reach the warm waters of the Persian Gulf and encircle Western oil supplies." That the Soviets were acting from a position of weakness to counter a growing Islamist threat at their borders was lost on almost everyone in Washington.[21]

A few weeks later, Carter spelled out what became known as the Carter Doctrine in more detail. In his January 23, 1980, State of the Union Address, the president explained the implications of the Soviet occupation:

> The Soviet effort to dominate Afghanistan has brought Soviet military forces to within 300 miles of the Indian Ocean and close to the Straits of Hormuz, a waterway through which most of the world's oil must flow. The Soviet Union is now attempting to consolidate a strategic position, therefore, that poses a grave threat to the free movement of Middle East oil.
>
> This situation demands careful thought, steady nerves, and resolute action, not only for this year but for many years to come. It demands collective efforts to meet this new threat to security in the Persian Gulf and in Southwest Asia. It demands the participation of all those who rely on oil from the Middle East and who are concerned with global peace and stability. And it demands consultation and close cooperation with countries in the area which might be threatened.

Most famously, Carter then vowed, "Let our position be absolutely clear: An attempt by any outside force to gain control of the Persian Gulf region will be regarded as an assault on the vital interests of the United States of America, and such an assault will be repelled by any means necessary, including military force."[22]

One of the consequences of this tough stance was that the United States renewed its alliance with Pakistan, a country viewed as a frontline state in the struggle against a seemingly aggressive Soviet Union. Sanctions—imposed because of Pakistan's poor human rights record under the dictatorship of General Zia ul-Haq— were dropped and the Carter administration offered the country $400 million in military and economic aid. Gradually the CIA began to coordinate the Afghan resistance movement with its Pakistani counterpart, the Inter-Services Intelligence

(ISI). Although this cooperation would grow exponentially during the Reagan presidency, the Carter administration gave the initial push to the counterintervention strategy that linked the United States, Pakistan, and the anti-Soviet mujahideen guerrillas in Afghanistan. Part of the strategy was the establishment of Islamic schools for Afghan refugees in Pakistan that would, in time, evolve into training centers for radicals. Another successful effort was the active recruiting of young jihadists from various parts of the arc of crisis for the anti-Soviet struggle in Afghanistan. One of those who joined this holy war was a rich young Saudi, Osama bin Laden.[23] Talk about a backfire effect.

The combined impact of the events in Iran and Afghanistan brought détente to a grinding halt. The Carter Doctrine ultimately changed the priorities of American foreign policy for decades to come. Although envisioned as a punishment for Soviet aggression, the investment of American prestige and resources brought the United States into constant contact with various proponents of radical Islam, one of the most potent phenomena of the late twentieth and early twenty-first centuries. The irony was that in the late 1970s one of the Soviet Union's key concerns was the rise and spread of American-supported anti-Soviet fundamentalist Islam to the southern belly of the USSR. In the end, both Moscow and Washington reacted to the various forms of Islamism in ways that betrayed the narrowness and ultimately outdated nature of their global outlook. Cold War doctrines were, simply put, a poor guide for understanding the turmoil in the arc of crisis. But, as the 1980 U.S. presidential election showed, nuance and complexity were not in vogue.

Enter Skipper: The 1980 Election

The great political beneficiary of Carter's difficulties was Ronald Reagan. After his narrow defeat to Gerald Ford in 1976, the former California governor had established himself as the front-runner for the Republican nomination four years later. Announcing his candidacy in November 1979, Reagan struck an optimistic note. He referred to America's "rendezvous with destiny" and disparaged the Carter administration for its lackluster foreign policy. "Too often in recent times we have just drifted along with events, responding as if we thought of ourselves as a nation in decline," Reagan complained. He added, "During a time when the Soviet Union may enjoy nuclear superiority over this country, we must never waiver in our commitment to our allies nor accept any negotiation which is not clearly in the national interest. . . . Though we should leave no initiative untried in our pursuit of peace, we must be clear voiced in our resolve to resist any unpeaceful act wherever it may occur. Negotiations with the Soviet Union must never become appeasement."[24]

It was a masterful start for a campaign that would sweep "Skipper" into the White House. Although he was the last Republican to officially enter the race and suffered an unexpected defeat in the Iowa caucuses in January 1980, Reagan ultimately defeated his closest challenger, George H. W. Bush, by a wide margin. After a brief flirtation with the possibility of teaming up with former President Gerald Ford, Reagan chose Bush as his vice presidential running mate. In his acceptance speech at the Joe Louis Arena in Detroit on July 17, 1980, he vowed to work for smaller government and lower taxes. But he reserved some of his toughest rhetoric for castigating the Carter administration's foreign policy, a "sorry chapter in the record of the present Administration." According to Reagan,

> Adversaries large and small test our will and seek to confound our resolve, but the Carter Administration gives us weakness when we need strength; vacillation when the times demand firmness. Why? Because the Carter Administration lives in the world of make-believe. Every day, it dreams up a response to that day's troubles, regardless of what happened yesterday and what will happen tomorrow. The Administration lives in a world where mistakes, even very big ones, have no consequence. The rest of us, however, live in the real world. It is here that disasters are overtaking our nation without any real response from the White House.[25]

But was Reagan planning a dramatic shift in policy? Not quite. In a televised address innovatively titled "A Strategy for Peace in the '80s," Reagan outlined a nine-point program that he would follow if elected:

1. An improved policy-making structure;
2. A clear approach to East-West relations;
3. A realistic policy toward our own Hemisphere;

4. A plan to assist African and Third World development;

5. A plan to send our message abroad;

6. A realistic strategic arms reduction policy;

7. A determined effort to strengthen the quality of our armed services;

8. Combating international terrorism;

9. Restoration of a margin of safety in our defense planning.[26]

There was not much here that was specifically "Republican" or "Reaganite." Yet, as in most elections, perception and circumstances mattered more than substance. And in this regard Carter had little going for him. In foreign policy he appeared weak and, as Reagan never failed to point out, as if he were only reacting to such events as the hostage crisis and the Soviet occupation of Afghanistan. When Carter had taken bold action—as in ordering a military rescue of the hostages in Iran—he was humiliated. Worse, the American economy was underperforming with high inflation, high interest rates, and unemployment at 7.8 percent in the summer of 1980. Ted Kennedy's unsuccessful primary challenge had further weakened Carter's core support base among Democrats. Still, owing in part to a series of gaffes by Reagan, polls showed that by mid-October 1980 Carter had closed the gap among likely voters. In a fateful move, the president agreed to a televised debate with his Republican challenger.

The ninety-minute session on October 28, 1980—only a week before Election Day—turned the momentum decisively in Reagan's favor. Carter did not make a serious error akin to that committed by Gerald Ford during the 1976 presidential debate; if anything, he showed that he had mastered the issues, and he projected an air of calm and deliberation. But Reagan came out ahead—way ahead—in terms of style and image. He made his killer stroke toward the end, when he asked the voters, simply, effectively, and memorably, "Are you better off than you were four years ago?" The election, Reagan pointed out, was essentially a referendum on Carter. A week later voters responded: Reagan received 51 percent of the popular vote to Carter's 41 (independent candidate John Anderson got 7 percent). In the Electoral College, Reagan dominated even more clearly with a margin of 489 to 49.[27]

Carter's resounding defeat ushered in what has been called the Reagan Revolution, a realignment in favor of political conservatism and free markets over liberalism and government intervention. But its impact on American foreign policy was not as obvious or immediate as has sometimes been argued. Most specifically, Reagan's election did not kill détente. The period characterized by ongoing negotiations between the two superpowers had already been irreparably damaged by the American and Soviet reactions to the series of confrontations in the Middle East in the late 1970s. SALT II, which Reagan rejected as a poor deal for the American people, had already been shelved a year before the new president was sworn in. The Carter Doctrine was the basis on which Reagan built his foreign policy of renewed global containment.

"A Dangerous Path"

Ultimately, Reagan's victory meant less in terms of the substance of American foreign policy than many have argued. But the rhetorical impact was significant. Anyone searching for an olive branch, a gesture aimed at restarting the "era of negotiation" that Nixon had begun some twelve years earlier in his inaugural address, was disappointed on hearing Reagan's uncompromising rhetoric on January 20, 1981:

> As for the enemies of freedom, those who are potential adversaries, they will be reminded that peace is the highest aspiration of the American people. We will not negotiate for it, sacrifice for it; we will not surrender for it, now or ever.
>
> Our forbearance should never be misunderstood. Our reluctance for conflict should not be misjudged as a failure of will. When action is required to preserve our national security, we will act. We will maintain sufficient strength to prevail if need be, knowing that if we do so we have the best chance of never having to use that strength.[28]

In the years to come, Reagan, with his formidable abilities as a communicator, would repeatedly reach back to something many Americans had felt their country had lost in the turmoil of the 1960s and 1970s: a sense of moral certainty. By doing so, he galvanized opinions and cast aside complexity.

For better or worse, the time of détente was over. In the Soviet Union, KGB Chief Yuri Andropov began to worry that the new "administration in Washington is attempting to push the whole development of international relations on to a dangerous path."[29] The irony was that this was exactly what the Carter administration had worried about when the Soviets supported Ethiopia and sent their troops to Afghanistan. By the time of Reagan's inauguration, mutual suspicion had already replaced the search for common ground. Keen on restoring optimism about America's future with his larger-than-life rhetoric and by extending further support to those engaged in conflicts against the Soviet Union or its allies and clients, Reagan would amply confirm the worst fears of the aging leadership in the Kremlin.

CHAPTER 8

COLD WAR TRANSFORMED:
THE PARADOX OF DÉTENTE

As president, Ronald Reagan made no effort to hide his sentiments about the Soviet Union and its leadership. "I know of no leader of the Soviet Union since the revolution, and including the present leadership, that has not more than once repeated in the various Communist congresses they hold their determination that their goal must be the promotion of world revolution and a one-world Socialist or Communist state, whichever word you want to use," Reagan said in response to a question posed by Sam Donaldson of ABC News during the first press conference after his inauguration. "The only morality they recognize," Reagan added, "is what will further their cause, meaning they reserve unto themselves the right to commit any crime, to lie, to cheat, in order to attain that."[1]

The statement prompted much speculation regarding the possible resumption of nuclear arms limitation talks. Thus, in early March Walter Cronkite of CBS News pressed Reagan on his views about future superpower negotiations. Although he did not unequivocally reject the possibility of such talks, Reagan made it clear that he would not sit down with Brezhnev unless there was some evidence that the Soviets were ready to modify their foreign policy. "I think it would help bring about such a meeting if the Soviet Union revealed that it is willing to moderate its imperialism, its aggression—Afghanistan would be an example," Reagan said. "We could talk a lot better if there was some indication that they truly wanted to be a member of the peace-loving nations of the world, the free world," he added.[2]

Yet even Reagan, his strong rhetoric notwithstanding, could not kill détente. NATO's double-track decision of December 1979 provided the backdrop against which the Intermediate-Range Nuclear Forces Treaty (INF) negotiations began in September 1981. There were problems and diversions; the Soviets suspended these talks in November 1983, and the Americans began deploying medium-range missiles in Europe in 1984, despite widespread public protests. However, in November 1985 Reagan, the resurgent cold warrior who had been calling the Soviet Union the "evil empire" only two years earlier and overseen a new military buildup, met with Mikhail Gorbachev, the new Soviet leader, in Geneva. In 1987 the two leaders signed the INF, agreeing, for the first time, to actually cut down their nuclear arsenals. By the time Reagan left office in January 1989, the Soviet withdrawal from Afghanistan was under way, the revolutions that would lead to the dissolution of the Soviet empire in Eastern Europe were about to begin, and the USSR itself was starting to crumble. The Cold War itself, for all intents and purposes, was no more. The impact of the "long 1970s," the era that had witnessed the most profound series of transformations in American foreign policy during the Cold War era, could not be simply wished away by moralizing rhetoric harking back to an earlier era of bipolar certainties.

Of course, the first half of the 1980s was full of international tension that caused some analysts, such as Fred Halliday, to talk about the commencement of a new, or second, cold war. At the root of this resurrection was the Reagan Doctrine, a simple call to, as conservative columnist Charles Krauthammer put it, "overt and unashamed American support for anti-Communist revolution."[3] Most obviously, the United States supported anti-Soviet "freedom fighters" around the globe. Whether it was the mujahideen in Afghanistan, the UNITA in Angola, or the contras in Nicaragua, the Reagan administration challenged the Soviet Union and its allies and proxies on a global scale. But the aid was, for the most part, indirect, and the actual impact difficult to measure. American assistance certainly contributed to Soviet difficulties in Afghanistan and made it difficult for the Sandinistas to cement control in Nicaragua. But whether the Reagan offensive—such as it was—helped bring the Soviet Union to the brink of collapse remains a matter of heavily partisan debate.

Indeed, since the collapse of the Soviet Union, much ink has been spilled arguing about the reasons for the Cold War's sudden—and on the whole unexpected—demise. In such debates, the respective roles of Reagan and Gorbachev tend to hold center stage. Economic factors (the ineffectiveness and ultimate bankruptcy of the socialist model) and imperial overreach (Soviet rather than American) count as some of the key factors (alongside technology, human rights, and numerous others) employed when explaining why (as the question is usually put) the West "won." Depending on one's perspective, détente, as far as American foreign policy is concerned, is seen either as a misconstrued policy that unnecessarily prolonged the Cold War or as a clever ploy to bring the Soviet empire down. The argument made by those who believe the policy prolonged the war is basically that via a series of high-level summits and agreements, détente accorded the Soviets unearned international legitimacy at a time when the USSR's internal contradictions were already undermining its ability to survive intact. The counterargument is that the détente process effectively destroyed the legitimacy of the Soviet Union by planting a time bomb—in the form of human rights provisions of the CSCE—within the Soviet bloc.[4]

It is difficult to prove either argument. Negotiating with the United States—dealing with the devil as it were—may have simultaneously added to Moscow's international legitimacy and undermined the USSR's role as the leading force of global revolution, hence eating away at the very raison d'être of the Soviet state. At the same time, it takes a certain leap of faith to accept the idea that the human rights provisions of Basket III of the 1975 CSCE spurred an unstoppable transnational movement that tore down a host of repressive regimes possessing well-tested tools of internal oppression. In fact, the emphasis on villains and heroes, losers and winners, is nonsensical. Détente, whatever its medium- and long-term outcomes, was hardly about good guys and bad guys.

For its American practitioners, détente was a conservative project that fit well with the previous decades' foreign policy. It was a policy aimed at stabilizing a seemingly precarious situation in which (particularly owing to the Vietnam War, the escalation of the nuclear arms race, and the breakdown of the domestic consensus over U.S. foreign policy) American foreign policy had lost its focus. Indeed, the "new beginning" that Nixon promised in his inaugural address in January 1969—not unlike the many other "new beginnings" offered by other presidents before and after—was hardly a complete and irrevocable break with the past.

To be sure, Henry Kissinger and Richard Nixon displayed an understandably sentimental and positive view of their time in office in their respective memoirs. They had grabbed history by the horns and moved it in a desirable direction.

Nixon, for example, argued that he offered a radically different foreign policy from that of his predecessor. If Johnson and the Democrats had waged war and intervened (in Vietnam, in the Dominican Republic), Nixon and the Republicans were going to make peace and negotiate. Nixon even shifted into the truly hyperbolic when, once elected, he vowed to build a new structure of peace. Even before that, he had sounded like a prophet of a forthcoming new age. But ultimately the rhetoric, as is often the case, was designed to trumpet the key theme that all candidates for office use and abuse: change.

It was meant to be largely a change of means rather than goals. As Kissinger puts it in *Diplomacy*, the "era of negotiations served as a strategy for enabling America to regain the diplomatic initiative while the war in Vietnam was still in progress."[5] There was no fundamentally new structure. Neither Nixon nor Kissinger saw détente as a policy that in its ultimate goals differed fundamentally from the principles of containment adopted in the 1940s. In fact, the basic goal for Nixon and Kissinger in 1969 was straightforward: to sustain America's position as the key power broker in the global arena. The situation they faced, though, was substantially different both domestically and internationally from the one that had existed when Dean Acheson was "present at the creation" of containment. Yet, as John Gaddis has noted, "the Nixon-Kissinger strategy returned, in its underlying assumptions, to many of the ideas upon which George Kennan had based his original strategy of containment more than two decades before."[6]

The basic idea that Nixon and Kissinger shared with Kennan—as well as with Truman, Eisenhower, Kennedy, Johnson, Carter, Reagan, and their advisers—was simple: the Soviet Union was the greatest threat to America's national security interests. From this premise it followed that containing Soviet power was the United States' key foreign policy goal. Thus, although Nixon, as early as 1967, ascertained that there could in fact be détente with the USSR, he immediately qualified such suggestions by emphasizing the incompatibility of the American and Soviet ways of thinking. As he put it, "We seek peace as an end in itself. They seek victory with peace being at this time a means toward that end. . . . We can live in peace with the Soviet Union but until they give up their goal for world conquest it will be for them a peace of necessity and not of choice." The sentiments expressed in the Truman Doctrine of 1947 or the comments made by Reagan in 1981 were not so dissimilar from these references to Soviet behavior in the international arena.[7]

Broadly speaking, the Nixon-Kissinger strategy of détente—the search for a structure of peace—basically amounted to a new method of fighting the ultimately irreconcilable struggle against Moscow. Acknowledging that they could not—in the domestic and international circumstances of the late 1960s—seriously contemplate the large-scale use of American military force to pursue such goals, the American architects of détente gravitated toward a different set of methods. They would pursue containment mainly through creative diplomacy and—when deemed necessary—via economic means and covert action. There surely had been "new approaches to friend and foe" in American foreign policy, as *Time* magazine announced in February 1969,[8] but a series of novel tactics did not mean a fundamental change in objectives; containing the Soviet Union remained the central goal of U.S. foreign policy.

This fact notwithstanding, a series of important shifts occurred in American foreign policy in the "long" 1970s. Détente's immediate results were, if anything, spectacular. Amid great secrecy, Henry Kissinger's globetrotting diplomacy did bring about some major breakthroughs. By the time Nixon began his second, Watergate-truncated presidential term, a structure of peace appeared within reach. There had been the opening to China, Nixon had traveled to Moscow to sign the SALT agreements with the Soviet Union, and Kissinger had negotiated (an ill-fated) Paris settlement that brought back American troops from the Vietnam War.

Of the three major issues that the first Nixon administration had tackled, the impact of the opening to China was by far the most enduring. It was a long overdue move that four decades later stands as the most significant achievement of the Nixon administration's foreign policy. With its secret trips and back channels, the opening to China also cemented Kissinger's position as the superstar of the Nixon administration, and indeed of American diplomacy writ large. Nicknames like "Modern Metternich" and "Superkraut" were common following press reports on Kissinger's July 1971 trip to China. Nixon's visit in February 1972 was carefully choreographed to highlight the drama of the new direction that the president's "journey of peace" represented. It was ultimately followed up by the Carter administration's full normalization of Sino-American relations. In terms of Sino-American relations, however, substance was fleeting: the 1972 Shanghai communiqué that was billed as the new blueprint for the bilateral relationship simply stated that on most key issues—especially on Taiwan—the two agreed to disagree. When Nixon told his cabinet that there was "a profound new relationship between the PRC and the United States," he was correct.[9] There was a new relationship. But its substance remained limited and did not become obvious until the 1980s, when the Sino-American economic relationship started to blossom.

The opening to China, however, was important for American foreign policy in another way. As had been the case throughout the post–World War II era, managing the competitive relationship with the Soviet Union shaped almost every aspect of U.S. foreign policy in the Nixon presidency. Even as he plotted the intricate web of moves and countermoves that brought Nixon and Mao together, Kissinger as national security adviser (and later as secretary of state) was most concerned with the USSR. The same applied—even in a more transparent way—to the machinations of Zbigniew Brzezinski in 1978–79. The Kremlin's likely reactions and existing policies affected the settlement in Vietnam, the opening to China, the relationship with America's allies, and the U.S. approach to regional conflicts in the Middle East, Africa, and elsewhere. In Soviet-American relations the Nixon administration's public record is, of course, well known. Via back-channel diplomacy between Kissinger and Soviet ambassador Anatoly Dobrynin, a number of agreements that made Nixon's promise of an era of negotiations a reality were reached in the early 1970s. Most significantly, the United States and the Soviet Union were able to move ahead on nuclear arms limitations. The SALT agreements of May 1972 represented the first serious outcome of Soviet-American negotiations. They were followed by the 1973 Prevention of Nuclear War (PNW) Agreement and the Vladivostok agreements in 1974. Jimmy Carter's moralistic rhetoric and criticism of the USSR's human rights record notwithstanding, the era of summitry continued, leading to the finalization of SALT II in 1979.

Indeed, the era of negotiations became a reality; the 1970s saw the de facto "institutionalization" of summitry as part of the Soviet-American relationship. For the remainder of the Cold War, regular high-level meetings were part of the generally accepted norm of international relations. But such summits also served as a reminder that as long as the Cold War continued, there were, ultimately, only two superpowers. In contrast to bilateral Soviet-American summitry, for example, such significant events as the 1975 CSCE Final Meeting in Helsinki appeared to be "less serious" talking shops. While superpower summits almost always produced concrete treaties and agreements, the multilateral CSCE was quickly castigated as a mere statement of principles, lacking in concrete and easily measurable achievements.

While the superpowers negotiated, they also competed. Remarkable though the development of détente in Soviet-American relations appeared, it did not change one fundamental fact: even as they talked about relaxation of tensions and signed nuclear arms agreements, the United States and the Soviet Union continued to vie for unilateral advantages around the globe. While the Soviets supported North Vietnam's quest for ultimate victory over South Vietnam even after the 1973 Paris Peace Accords, the Americans worked hard to exclude the USSR from the Middle East peace process following the 1973 Arab-Israeli War. Both Moscow and Washington got engaged in various parts of Africa (Angola, the Horn); both saw their interests best served by undermining each other's policies in Central Asia (Afghanistan and Iran). For all the breakthroughs that emerged during the golden years of détente, there was no sign that confrontation and competition were outdated within the context of the Soviet-American relationship.

Perhaps more significantly, the catchphrases of détente—"structure of peace," "era of negotiations"—failed to capture the imagination of the American public. Opponents from both parties became increasingly vocal, arguing that détente implied a de facto acceptance of the legitimacy of the Soviet Union and the socialist system. Some, like Jimmy Carter, focused on what they perceived as the immorality of détente. Others, like Henry Jackson and Ronald Reagan, maintained that détente translated into the acceptance of American weakness. While most critics accepted certain aspects of Nixon's diplomacy—such as the opening to China—they clamored for a more assertive and ideologically driven American foreign policy. Indeed, the idea that America was "just another country" did not sit well with domestic audiences who cast their votes in favor of détente's Democratic and Republican critics in 1976 and 1980. In 1957 Kissinger had written that the "acid test of a policy is its ability to obtain domestic support."[10] Détente ultimately failed to pass that acid test.

Détente as conceived in the late 1960s and early 1970s did not last. But it did introduce into the international system elements (for example, human rights via the CSCE process), that, if often unintentionally, worked to undermine the Cold War international system. That is, détente ultimately and ironically discredited the system it was meant to stabilize.

At times lost in debates about the onset of détente is the impact that the process had on subsequent developments. This is hardly surprising. Despite the sometimes larger than life rhetoric, the various aspects of détente—from the SALT negotiations and the opening to China to the CSCE and MBFR talks—tended to be specific strategies with limited, often short-term, goals. For example, détente served a number of purposes for the Nixon administration (helping to end the Vietnam War, reducing the costs of America's overseas commitments, boosting Nixon's domestic standing by emphasizing his "statesman's" qualities, and so on).

Yet, I would argue that the consequences of détente were more far-reaching and fundamental than its principal architects and practitioners thought at the time. Détente changed the international system and unleashed many of the processes that in the 1980s helped bring an end to the Cold War. That this was not, I would also argue, a conscious goal of those implementing détente is equally important. It shows that what historians like to refer to as turning points often, as the key American architect of détente would later put it, "pass unnoticed by contemporaries."[11] In fact, there were plenty of intended and unintended consequences that with the benefit of hindsight can be said to translate into something of a revolutionary legacy.

First, with the institutionalization of summitry at the superpower level, détente created an expectation that Soviet and American leaders could, should, and would meet each other on a more or less regular basis to discuss ways of reducing the danger of nuclear war and developing other formal links. Even as tensions mounted in the 1980s, there would be no dramatic walkouts as in the case of Khrushchev during the 1960 Paris summit. As a result, both sides accepted a certain responsibility for the stability of the international system; even as defense intellectuals and protesters fretted over the placement of new missile systems (as in Europe in 1984), détente had introduced a set of fundamental rules and assumptions that guided bilateral superpower relations. However, while such stability may have been a desired goal for several policymakers in Washington and Moscow, détente unleashed some forces of change that fundamentally altered the very system détente was supposed to codify. East-West interaction became not only possible but, for the most part, irreversible. Whether it was increased but still limited East-West trade; whether it was the promise, if not always the reality, of freedom of movement; or whether it was added cultural interaction, détente made it possible—in a more fundamental sense than before—for people to see how the other side lived. Europe in particular experienced a gradual growth of transnationalism as a result of détente. This was, I would argue, particularly significant if we are to grasp the growing discontent within Eastern Europe in the 1980s, which eventually climaxed in the events of 1989.

Détente further introduced the notion of human security as an important element of European (if not necessarily global) security. The importance of the CSCE in this regard is fundamental. The Soviet leaders who agreed to a document that recognized such concepts as freedom of ideas were, in the mid-1970s, comforted by guarantees that there would be no interference in their internal affairs ("we are masters in our own house," Andrei Gromyko maintained).[12] And yet, despite increased efforts to control their populations, Soviet bloc political establishments ultimately failed to maintain their hold on power. Détente may not have caused the dissident movements to emerge, but it ultimately gave the various groups important tools to advance their cause and undermine the totalitarian controls that, in the end, were at the heart of the bipolar Cold War structure. There was, as one scholar dubs it, something of a "Helsinki effect" embedded in the post-1975 European system, giving tools to those wishing to challenge totalitarian rule.[13]

Beyond Europe, of course, the Cold War continued, even intensified. As Odd Arne Westad has pointed out, "By the 1970s the conditions in the Third World and the capabilities of both superpowers had reached a stage that made events in Africa, Asia, and Latin America central to international affairs."[14] By the 1970s, the remnants of European colonial empires had been erased, the United States was caught in a period characterized by domestic political upheaval and doubt about its Cold War policies, and the Soviet Union was faced with a choice of either going global by supporting third world revolutions or accepting a new role as a guardian of the stability of the existing situation. The American retreat from Vietnam, the apparent stagnation of the West (in part because of recurrent oil crises), the seeming triumph of the Soviet-supported MPLA in Angola, and a sudden rise in oil revenues for the USSR were among the factors that made many inside the Soviet policy apparatus assume that they were riding the tide of history.[15] Ironically, the USSR that was ruled by a generation of geriatric technocrats was also the USSR that went out to support the youthful revolutionaries in the Horn of Africa and elsewhere.

This, again, had unexpected consequences. By the mid-1980s, however, it was clear that the Soviets could not manage a situation in which they were simultaneously on the offensive (supporting revolutionary movements throughout the third world) and defensive (faced with rising discontent throughout the Soviet bloc). If détente had amounted to the recognition of the Soviet Union's superpower status, it also prompted the overextension of Soviet power that proved detrimental to the USSR's survival. Add to this the rise of new international phenomena that did not fit into the dichotomies of the Cold War—political Islam chief among them—and the Soviet Union that had seemed to be on the rise to globalism in the 1970s suddenly faded away in the early 1990s.

Moreover, without détente it is difficult to envisage the emergence of the PRC as an increasingly significant player in international affairs. Yet, the Nixon administration's decision to push for the opening to China was motivated mainly by the impact that it could have on America's effort to end its involvement in Vietnam and as a means of pressuring the Soviet Union. In the end, the opening to China was far more significant than such short-term goals implied: while the week that Richard Nixon spent in China in February 1972 may not have changed the world immediately, it is hard to imagine a more far-reaching development than the gradual integration of the PRC into the international system over subsequent decades.

Three key points are worth underlining further. First, détente was not conceived as a revolutionary policy that would change the world. This is certainly the case when exploring the goals of those I have chosen to emphasize in this book: the key U.S. policymakers. Neither Kissinger nor Nixon saw détente as much more than a tactical move in a policy conceived two decades earlier. Theirs was a shift in method brought about by the circumstances of the Vietnam War. With the discrediting of American power abroad and the massive resistance to the use of force as a tool of foreign policy at home, the administration that was sworn in at the end of January 1969 had to operate in a context that was not their making. They saw détente as an attractive option not because it could end the Cold War but because it would allow them to fight it with a new toolkit in hand. Second, the results were quite newsworthy. The opening to China was—there is no getting around it—particularly spectacular. But it was equaled by the successful conclusion of SALT I in 1972 and the all-European summit in Helsinki in 1975. Third, amid such diplomatic maneuvering, however, the world was hardly a more peaceful place. Throughout Africa, the Middle East, and the Far East, conflicts festered and often flared up in violent clashes that, if they attracted the attention of one superpower, were bound to suck in the other one as well. International reconciliation clearly had its limits. And, equally important, the American body politic—a famously temperamental entity—would tolerate a policy of relative retreat only as long as it was accompanied by dazzling achievements, pomp, and circumstance.

Ultimately détente, rather than stabilizing the international situation as many of its architects had hoped it would, set in motion numerous processes that fundamentally altered the Cold War international system. Détente did not end the Cold War nor provide a clear road map toward 1989 or 1991. But, as previously stated, by bringing about an era of East-West engagement, détente was instrumental in setting in motion the many processes that ultimately caused the collapse of the international system that it was supposed to stabilize. In retrospect, this remains the central paradox of détente.

Within this paradox, one can detect themes that resonate in the twenty-first century. The process of détente brought to the fore many issues that, more than three decades after Ronald Reagan entered the White House, continue to resonate in American foreign policy and beyond. Some of these were very specific: Afghanistan and Iran, for example, emerged as key concerns of the Carter and Reagan administrations and have remained that way ever since. Others are more general: détente emerged, triumphed, and collapsed amid relative stability in the first world and concurrent instability in the third world. Small- and large-scale military interventions—from Vietnam to Afghanistan, the Dominican Republic to the Horn of Africa—were part of the era of détente; indeed, they shaped its origins and brought about its demise.

Our world today is different in many ways from that of the 1960s and 1970s. But there are many, perhaps uncomfortable, similarities. The contrast between a relatively stable "North" and a correspondingly tumultuous "global

South" remains a feature of the early twenty-first century. Military interventions—whether in Iraq, Afghanistan, Georgia, or Libya—remain commonplace and are conducted mainly by the countries of the "North" in the regions of the "South." Likewise, the unintended consequences of détente—the undermining of the stability of the Cold War international system—remind us of the similarly unintended consequences of the so-called Global War on Terror (GWT) today. If détente encouraged Soviet activism in the third world, the 9/11 attacks in the United States prompted the Bush administration to embark on a costly global effort to combat international terrorism (including the invasions of Afghanistan and Iraq). The Soviets found themselves ultimately overextended and bankrupt. More than a decade into the GWT, the United States finds its once impressive global dominance much diminished (though not solely because of excess military interventionism). Moreover, the connection between foreign and domestic policy is as present today—whether in the debates about the war in Iraq or the need to recalibrate American policy vis-à-vis China—as it was when Nixon and Kissinger set out to end the war in Vietnam or open a relationship with Beijing.

This is not to suggest that all policies, regardless of the historical context in which they were conceived, will produce only consequences that are wholly different from those intended. But it does suggest that policymakers seeking to control the world around them and shape it to their liking will always find themselves surprised by the outcomes. Indeed, if there is an enduring lesson to be learned from the rise and fall of détente in American foreign policy, it has less to do with whether the policy itself was the proper response (or series of responses) to the ways in which the U.S. global position and standing changed in the 1960s. Rather, the contours of détente, much like the more recent episodes linked to the GWT, remind us of the iron law of unexpected consequences.

Appendix of Documents

1. Khrushchev on the Need for Relaxation of Tensions, October 30, 1962

In the aftermath of the Cuban missile crisis of October 1962, both Soviet and American leaders seriously reconsidered the nuclear arms race. A few days after the agreement that ended the confrontation was reached, Soviet leader Nikita Khrushchev wrote to President Kennedy about the need to reduce superpower tensions.

Source: Document 120, in *Cuban Missile Crisis and Aftermath*, vol. 11 of *Foreign Relations of the United States, 1961–1963* (Washington, DC: U.S. Government Printing Office, 1996), 104–6.

My colleagues and I consider that both sides have displayed restraint and wisdom in liquidating the military conflict which might have resulted in a world thermonuclear war. I take the liberty to think that you evidently held to a restraining position with regard to those forces which suffered from militaristic itching. . . . I don't know, perhaps I am wrong, but in this letter I am making the conclusion on the basis that in your country the situation is such that the decisive word rests with the President and if he took an extreme stand there would be no one to restrain him and war would be unleashed. . . .

 . . . We have now conditions ripe for finalizing the agreement on signing a treaty on cessation of tests of thermonuclear weapons. We fully agree with regard to three types of tests or, so to say, tests in three environments. This is banning of tests in atmosphere, in outer space and under water. In this respect we are of the same opinion and we are ready to sign an agreement. . . .

But there are still some differences with regard to underground explosions. Therefore it would be good if you gave instructions to find a compromise in the decision on the underground test ban, but without inspection. We shall not accept inspection, this I say to you unequivocally and frankly. . . . We do not carry on underground tests, we did it but once and we are not going to do it anymore. Maybe such a necessity will arise sometime in [the] future, but in any case I do not envisage it. . . .

We appreciate it very much that you took the initiative and in such a moment of crisis stated your readiness to conduct negotiations with the purpose of signing a non-aggression treaty between the two military blocs. We responded and supported it. We are prepared to come to an agreement on this question confidentially or through diplomatic channels and then make it public and start negotiations. This also would contribute to lessening tension. The world public would learn with satisfaction that in the moment of crisis not only declarative statements were made but certain commitments with signatures affixed were taken as well. . . .

We have eliminated a serious crisis. But in order to foresee and forestall appearance of a new crisis in [the] future which might be impossible to cope with everything in our relations capable of generating a new crisis should be erased now. It would seem that now when we possess thermonuclear weapons, rocket weapons, submarine fleet and other means the situation obliges all states, every state to adhere to such norms of conduct which would not generate conflicts, to say nothing of wars. . . .

These, in effect, are my considerations after the crisis situation. I want to tell you that in this crisis, as our saying goes, there is no evil without good. . . . The good is that now people have felt more tangibly the breathing of the burning flames of thermonuclear war and have a more clear realization of the threat looming over them if [the] arms race is not stopped. And I would say that what has just happened will serve especially [well] the American people. . . .

Mr. President, you lived through this crisis yourself. For us too, it presented the Rubicon: whether to agree to a compromise, whether to make concessions. Indeed, from the point of view of the legal standards your claims had no grounds whatsoever. Therefore there was a great trial and there were hesitations. . . . Having eliminated this crisis we gave each other mutual satisfaction: you promised not to attack and not to permit attack against Cuba on the part of others, and we moved forward to make the USA feel confident that we do not contemplate anything bad against it and that there is no threat against the USA on our part. You certainly possess means of destruction. But you know that we also have these means and they are of a different nature than those that were in Cuba. Those were trifles there. Our means were brought to the state of combat readiness, they were of a more serious nature and they were pointed at the USA and your allies. . . .

2. President John F. Kennedy's Commencement Address at American University, June 10, 1963

Like Khrushchev, John F. Kennedy flirted with détente. Perhaps the most famous of Kennedy's public efforts was his commencement address at American University, delivered five months before his assassination in November 1963.

Source: John T. Woolley and Gerhard Peters, eds., *The American Presidency Project*, http://www.presidency.ucsb.edu/ws/index.php?pid=9266.

Some say that it is useless to speak of world peace or world law or world disarmament—and that it will be useless until the leaders of the Soviet Union adopt a more enlightened attitude. I hope they do. I believe we can help them to do it. But I also believe that we must reexamine our own attitude. . . .

First: Let us examine our attitude toward peace itself. Too many of us think it is impossible. Too many think it unreal. But that is a dangerous, defeatist belief. It leads to the conclusion that war is inevitable—that mankind is doomed—that we are gripped by forces we cannot control.

We need not accept this view. Our problems are manmade—therefore, they can be solved by man. . . . There is no single, simple key to this peace—no grand magic formula to be adopted by one or two powers. Genuine peace must be the product of many nations, the sum of many acts. It must be dynamic, not static, changing to meet the challenge of each new generation. For peace is a process— a way of solving problems. . . .

With such a peace, there will still be quarrels and conflicting interests, as there are with families and nations. World peace, like community peace, does not require that each man love his neighbor—it requires only that they live together in mutual tolerance, submitting their disputes to a just and peaceful settlement. And history teaches us that enmities between nations, as between individuals, do not last forever. . . .

Second: Let us reexamine our attitude toward the Soviet Union. It is discouraging to think that their leaders may actually believe what their propagandists write. It is discouraging to read a recent authoritative Soviet text on Military Strategy and find, on page after page, wholly baseless and incredible claims—such as the allegation that "American imperialist circles are preparing to unleash different types of wars . . . [and that] the political aims of the American imperialists are to enslave economically and politically the European and other capitalist countries . . . [and] to achieve world domination . . . by means of aggressive wars." . . . It is sad to read these Soviet statements—to realize the extent of the gulf between us. But it is also a warning—a warning to the American people not to fall into the same trap as the Soviets, not to see only a distorted and desperate view of the other side, not to see conflict as inevitable, accommodation as impossible, and communication as nothing more than an exchange of threats.

No government or social system is so evil that its people must be considered as lacking in virtue. As Americans, we find communism profoundly repugnant as a negation of personal freedom and dignity. But we can still hail the Russian people for their many achievements—in science and space, in economic and industrial growth, in culture and in acts of courage.

Among the many traits the peoples of our two countries have in common, none is stronger than our mutual abhorrence of war. Almost unique among the major world powers, we have never been at war with each other. And no nation in the history of battle ever suffered more than the Soviet Union suffered in the course of the Second World War. At least 20 million lost their lives. Countless millions of homes and farms were burned or sacked. A third of the nation's territory, including nearly two thirds of its industrial base, was turned into a wasteland—a loss equivalent to the devastation of this country east of Chicago.

Today, should total war ever break out again—no matter how—our two countries would become the primary targets. It is an ironic but accurate fact that the two strongest powers are the two in the most danger of devastation. All we have built, all we have worked for, would be destroyed in the first 24 hours. And even in the Cold War, which brings burdens and dangers to so many countries, including this Nation's closest allies—our two countries bear the heaviest burdens. For we are both devoting massive sums of money to weapons that could be better devoted to combating ignorance, poverty, and disease. We are both caught up in a vicious and dangerous cycle in which suspicion on one side breeds suspicion on the other, and new weapons beget counterweapons.

In short, both the United States and its allies, and the Soviet Union and its allies, have a mutually deep interest in a just and genuine peace and in halting the arms race. Agreements to this end are in the interests of the Soviet Union as well as ours. . . .

Third: Let us reexamine our attitude toward the Cold War, remembering that we are not engaged in a debate, seeking to pile up debating points. We are not here distributing blame or pointing the finger of judgment. We must deal with the world as it is, and not as it might have been had the history of the last 18 years been different. . . .

We must conduct our affairs in such a way that it becomes in the Communists' interest to agree on a genuine peace. Above all, while defending our own vital interests, nuclear powers must avert those confrontations which bring an adversary to a choice of either a humiliating retreat or a nuclear war. To adopt that kind of course in the nuclear age would be evidence only of the bankruptcy of our policy—or of a collective death wish for the world.

To secure these ends, America's weapons are nonprovocative, carefully controlled, designed to deter, and capable of selective use. Our military forces are committed to peace and disciplined in self-restraint. Our diplomats are instructed to avoid unnecessary irritants and purely rhetorical hostility.

For we can seek a relaxation of tensions without relaxing our guard. And, for our part, we do not need to use threats to prove that we are resolute. We do not need to jam foreign broadcasts out of fear our faith will be eroded. We are unwilling to impose our system on any unwilling people—but we are willing and able to engage in peaceful competition with any people on earth. . . .

Speaking of other nations, I wish to make one point clear. We are bound to many nations by alliances. Those alliances exist because our concern and theirs substantially overlap. . . . The United States will make no deal with the Soviet Union at the expense of other nations and other peoples, not merely because they are our partners, but also because their interests and ours converge.

Our interests converge, however, not only in defending the frontiers of free-dom, but in pursuing the paths of peace. It is our hope—and the purpose of allied policies—to convince the Soviet Union that she, too, should let each nation choose its own future, so long as that choice does not interfere with the choices of others. The Communist drive to impose their political and economic system on others is the primary cause of world tension today. For there can be no doubt that, if all nations could refrain from interfering in the self-determination of others, the peace would be much more assured.

This will require a new effort to achieve world law—a new context for world discussions. It will require increased understanding between the Soviets and our-selves. And increased understanding will require increased contact and commu-nication. One step in this direction is the proposed arrangement for a direct line between Moscow and Washington, to avoid on each side the dangerous delays, misunderstandings, and misreadings of the other's actions which might occur at a time of crisis.

We have also been talking in Geneva about other first-step measures of arms control, designed to limit the intensity of the arms race and to reduce the risks of accidental war. Our primary long-range interest in Geneva, however, is general and complete disarmament designed to take place by stages, permitting parallel political developments to build the new institutions of peace which would take the place of arms. . . . The one major area of these negotiations where the end is in sight, yet where a fresh start is badly needed, is in a treaty to outlaw nuclear tests. The conclusion of such a treaty, so near and yet so far, would check the spiraling arms race in one of its most dangerous areas. It would place the nuclear powers in a position to deal more effectively with one of the greatest hazards which man faces in 1963, the further spread of nuclear arms.

3. Memorandum of Understanding between the United States of America and the Union of Soviet Socialist Republics Regarding the Establishment of a Direct Communications Link, June 20, 1963

In June 1963 the United States and the Soviet Union agreed to establish the so-called hot link, a direct communication line between the White House and the Kremlin to be used in times of emergency. The purpose was to avoid another situation like the Cuban missile crisis, when the two sides had communicated via telegraph or official and unofficial personal channels.

Source: 20th Century Documents, Avalon Project at Yale Law School, http://www.yale .edu/lawweb/avalon/diplomacy/soviet/sov003.htm.

For use in time of emergency the Government of the United States of America and the Government of the Union of Soviet Socialist Republics have agreed to establish as soon as technically feasible a direct communications link between the two Governments.

Each Government shall be responsible for the arrangements for the link on its own territory. Each Government shall take the necessary steps to ensure continuous functioning of the link and prompt delivery to its head of government of any communications received by means of the link from the head of government of the other party.

Arrangements for establishing and operating the link are set forth in the Annex which is attached hereto and forms an integral part hereof.

The direct communications link between Washington and Moscow established in accordance with the Memorandum, and the operation of such link, shall be governed by the following provisions:

1. The direct communications link shall consist of:
   a. Two terminal points with telegraph-teleprinter equipment between which communications shall be directly exchanged;
   b. One full-time duplex wire telegraph circuit, routed Washington-London-Copenhagen- Stockholm-Helsinki-Moscow, which shall be used for the transmission of messages;

c. One full-time duplex radiotelegraph circuit, routed Washington-Tangier-Moscow, which shall be used for service communications and for coordination of operations between the two terminal points.

If experience in operating the direct communications link should demonstrate that the establishment of an additional wire telegraph circuit is advisable, such circuit may be established by mutual agreement between authorized representatives of both Governments.

2. In case of interruption of the wire circuit, transmission of messages shall be effected via the radio circuit, and for this purpose provision shall be made at the terminal points for the capability of prompt switching of all necessary equipment from one circuit to another.

3. The terminal points of the link shall be so equipped as to provide for the transmission and reception of messages from Moscow to Washington in the Russian language and from Washington to Moscow in the English language. In this connection, the USSR shall furnish the United States four sets of telegraph terminal equipment, including page printers, transmitters, and reperforators, with one year's supply of spare parts and all necessary special tools, test equipment, operating instructions, and other technical literature, to provide for transmission and reception of messages in the Russian language.

The United States shall furnish the Soviet Union four sets of telegraph terminal equipment, including page printers, transmitters, and reperforators, with one year's supply of spare parts and all necessary special tools, test equipment, operating instructions and other technical literature, to provide for transmission and reception of messages in the English language.

The equipment described in this paragraph shall be exchanged directly between the parties without any payment being required therefor.

4. The terminal points of the direct communications link shall be provided with encoding equipment. For the terminal point in the USSR, four sets of such equipment (each capable of simplex operation), with one year's supply of spare parts, with all necessary special tools, test equipment, operating instructions and other technical literature, and with all

necessary blank tape, shall be furnished by the United States to the USSR against payment of the cost thereof by the USSR.

The USSR shall provide for preparation and delivery of keying tapes to the terminal point of the link in the United States for reception of messages from the USSR. The United States shall provide for the preparation and delivery of keying tapes to the terminal point of the link in the USSR for reception of messages from the United States. Delivery of prepared keying tapes to the terminal points of the link shall be effected through the Embassy of the USSR in Washington (for the terminal of the link in the USSR) and through the Embassy of the United States in Moscow (for the terminal of the link in the United States).

5. The United States and the USSR shall designate the agencies responsible for the arrangements regarding the direct communications link, for its technical maintenance, continuity and reliability, and for the timely transmission of messages.

Such agencies may, by mutual agreement, decide matters and develop instructions relating to the technical maintenance and operation of the direct communications link and effect arrangements to improve the operation of the link.

6. The technical parameters of the telegraph circuits of the link and of the terminal equipment, as well as the maintenance of such circuits and equipment, shall be in accordance with CCITT and CCIR recommendations.

Transmission and reception of messages over the direct communications link shall be effected in accordance with applicable recommendations of international telegraph and radio communications regulations, as well as with mutually agreed instructions.

7. The costs of the direct communications link shall be borne as follows:

   a. The USSR shall pay the full cost of leasing the portion of the telegraph circuit from Moscow to Helsinki and 50 percent of the cost of leasing the portion of the telegraph circuit from Helsinki to London. The United States shall pay the full cost of leasing the portion of the telegraph circuit from Washington to London and 50 percent of the cost of leasing the portion of the telegraph circuit from London to Helsinki.

b. Payment of the cost of leasing the radio telegraph circuit between Washington and Moscow shall be effected without any transfer of payments between the parties. The USSR shall bear the expenses relating to the transmission of messages from Moscow to Washington. The United States shall bear the expenses relating to the transmission of messages from Washington to Moscow.

4. Test Ban Treaty between the United States, Great Britain, and the Soviet Union, August 5, 1963

In August 1963 the three existing nuclear powers signed a treaty banning nuclear weapon tests in the atmosphere, in space, and underwater. Many observers saw the treaty as an important step toward lessening tension after the Cuban missile crisis and as the first major step toward serious nuclear arms control.

Source: U.S. Department of State, Limited Test Ban Treaty, http://www.state.gov /www/global/arms/treaties/ltbt1.html#2.

The [parties] . . . proclaiming as their principal aim the speediest possible achievement of an agreement on national control in accordance with the objectives of the United Nations which would put an end to the armaments race and eliminate the incentive to the production and testing of all kinds of weapons, including nuclear weapons.

Seeking to achieve the discontinuance of all test explosions of nuclear weapons for all time, determined to continue negotiations to this end, and desiring to put an end to the contamination of man's environment by radioactive substances.

Have agreed as follows:

Article I

Each of the Parties to this Treaty undertakes to prohibit, to prevent, and not to carry out any nuclear weapon test explosion, or any other nuclear explosion, at any place under its jurisdiction or control:

In the atmosphere; beyond its limits, including outer space; or under water, including territorial waters or high seas; or

In any other environment if such explosion causes radioactive debris to be present outside the territorial limits of the State under whose jurisdiction or control such explosion is conducted. It is understood in this connection that the provisions of this subparagraph are without prejudice to the conclusion of a treaty resulting in the permanent banning of all nuclear test explosions, including all such explosions underground, the conclusion of which, as the Parties have stated in the Preamble to this Treaty, they seek to achieve.

Each of the Parties to this Treaty undertakes furthermore to refrain from causing, encouraging, or in any way participating in, the carrying out of any nuclear weapon test explosion, or any other nuclear explosion anywhere which would take place in any of the environments described, or have the effect referred to, in paragraph 1 of this Article. . . .

5. Debriefing by the President on His Talks with Chairman Kosygin, June 23, 1967

The only meeting between President Lyndon Johnson and a top Soviet leader took place in Glassboro, New Jersey, in June 1967. Although the American administration was keen on improving the bilateral relationship and moving toward nuclear arms talks, the wars in Vietnam and the Middle East cast a shadow over the meeting and limited its results.

Source: Document 230, in *Soviet Union*, vol. 14 of *Foreign Relations of the United States, 1964–1968*, http://history.state.gov/historicaldocuments/frus1964-68v14/d230.

The talks were not denunciatory or argumentative. Kosygin was reserved, contained, but jolly.

Kosygin pointed out that he had an 18-year-old grandson and granddaughter and was the senior grandfather present. They both had a duty to protect them by maintaining peace between their countries of 200 million.

The President said they had a responsibility not only to the 200 million but to the whole world of 3 billion. He hoped their grandsons would grow up to know each other. They had lived through the horrors of two wars and they did not wish their grandchildren to share that kind of experience.

Kosygin said that during the Second World War he had responsibility in Leningrad. He would never forget American help at that time. He said he wanted peace, but you don't. The President said, I believe you are sincere but I am also. At which Kosygin appeared a bit chagrined at his first ploy.

The President explained that in the 3 years he had been in office, we had made no new treaties. He had wished to make progress in relations with the Soviet Union. He began with a letter to Khrushchev urging that they both cut back their nuclear production, and they did. He urged they both cut back their levels of defense expenditure, and they did. Things then changed. There were hard words about Viet Nam.

In these 3 years, despite their stopping Mary Martin's going to Moscow, they had concluded the cultural agreement and civil [air] agreement, Consular Agreement. Working hard on non-proliferation, ready next week to start discussions on ABM's [anti-ballistic missiles) and ICBM's [intercontinental ballistic missiles]. He was awaiting [an] answer which had been delayed 3 months. (President made this point three times and never got a reply.)

The President said that on the Middle East he had presented his 5 points but got no comment from Kosygin. Kosygin said that the President before the war had talked about territorial integrity, asserted this on hot line, but wound up protecting aggression. Kosygin said that he had been Stalin's deputy for 12 years. He had served in Leningrad. He would never forget the time when arm in arm we resisted Fascism. He wished we could agree on some of these moves now. Kosygin then said we must bring back the troops to the original armistice lines, and put the question of Aqaba into International Court of Justice. Then we could discuss other problems. Then came the nearest thing to a threat. He said, unless you do this there will be a war, a very great war. I'm against it. They will fight with arms if they have them; if not, with fists. All troops must be withdrawn at once. They will fight with their bare hands, if necessary. (The President said it was not clear in this passage whether the Soviets would supply the arms for this blow up or engage themselves.) The President then leaned forward and said very slowly and quietly, let us understand one another. I hope there will be no war. If there is a war, I hope it will not be a big war. If they fight, I hope they fight with fists and not with guns. I hope you and we will keep out of this matter because, if we do get into it, it will be a "most serious" matter. The President's judgment was that this was not an ultimatum and he backed away from the implication that the Soviet Union might itself become involved.

On the NPT [Non-Proliferation Treaty], the President asked Kosygin to set a date and let us table the agreement.

On ABM's and ICBM's, he said let us go to work. Sec. McNamara can go to Moscow. We can meet in Washington or some neutral point.

On Viet Nam, the President drew a map and urged the separation of North Viet Nam from South Viet Nam. Kosygin attacked corruption of the regime in Saigon. The President did not engage in the quality of our allies.

President said some think we should invade North Viet Nam—not Sec. McNamara, but some do urge that. We think bombing North Viet Nam is better than invading it. If you could get them to stop invading the South, you could say to us don't invade North Viet Nam. But they must get their people out of South Viet Nam. The UK, ICC (International Control Commission) or anyone could have free elections. They could have any kind of government they want.

Kosygin said Sec. McNamara couldn't wait three days in February before he started bombing the North. The President said, well you didn't have any influence in Hanoi. The Chinese had taken over. You couldn't deliver them.

Kosygin said that Fawzi had given Sec. Rusk important proposals. Kosygin complained about Amb. Goldberg's position at the UN.

The President pressed him on sending arms to the Middle East. Said he hoped we both could avoid doing that. By working the hot line, they had achieved a cease-fire. The U.S. knew nothing of the attack. Had no knowledge of the Israeli attack. They thought they had commitments from both parties. He said he assumed the Soviet Union did not know of the closure of the Gulf of Aqaba before it took place.

The President repeated he hoped both of us would stay outside the area with our armed forces. If we engaged, it would be quite serious.

At one point Kosygin complained about our bombing Hanoi when he was there. The President explained that our bombing had nothing to do with his presence. Sec. Rusk was bombed when at Saigon. This was a problem of travelers going into war areas. In fact, we made clear in our Tonkin resolution we would not take such attacks. When they killed 60 of our men asleep at Pleiku, we had to take action. Totally unrelated to Kosygin's visit.

President pressed on Middle East, Viet Nam, non-proliferation, ABM's.

He got no positive reaction in the first talks. But he found Kosygin friendly.

6. Nixon's Address at the Bohemian Club in San Francisco, July 29, 1967

In 1967 Richard Nixon was gearing up for his return to high office. The former vice president was portraying himself as someone who would restore sense and stability to America's foreign policy in a time of crisis. In a speech to the Bohemian Club in July 1967, Nixon touched upon a number of the key points that would characterize his approach to the Soviet Union as president.

Source: Document 2, in *Foundations of Foreign Policy, 1969–1972*, vol. 1 of *Foreign Relations of the United States, 1969–1976*, http://history.state.gov/historicaldocuments /frus1969-76v01/d2.

We live in a new world. Never in human history have more changes taken place in the world in one generation.

It is a world of new leaders. True, De Gaulle, Mao Tse-tung and Chiang Kai-shek are still with us; but Churchill, Adenauer, Stalin, Khrushchev, Nehru, Sukarno—the other giants of the post-war period have all left the world stage.

It is a world of new people. One-half of the people now living in the world were born since World War II. This presents at once a problem and an opportunity for peace. Because, as one Asian Prime Minister puts it, the new generation has neither the old fears nor the old guilts of the old generation.

It is a world of new ideas. Communism, Marxism, Socialism, anti-colonialism—the great ideas which stirred men to revolution after World War II have lost their pulling power. As the Shah of Iran says—"the new generation is not imprisoned by any ism." The young people in all countries on both sides of the Iron Curtain are groping for a new cause—a new religion. If any idea "turns them on" it is a new sense of pragmatism—"what will work."

Because we live in a new world, many of the old institutions are obsolete and inadequate. The UN, NATO, foreign aid, USIA were set up to deal with the world of twenty years ago. A quick trip around the world will show how different the problems are today.

Twenty years ago Western Europe was weak economically and dependent on the United States. It was united by a common fear of the threat of Communist aggression. Today Western Europe is strong economically and economic independence has inevitably led to more political independence. The winds of détente have blown so strongly from East to West that except for Germany most Europeans no longer fear the threat from the East. The consequences of this change are enormous as far as NATO is concerned. As Harold Macmillan puts it, "Alliances are kept together by fear, not by love." Even without De Gaulle, the European Alliance would be in deep trouble.

Let us look at the Communist world: Twenty years ago the Soviet Union dominated a monolithic Communist empire. Today, the Soviet Union and Communist China are in a bitter struggle for leadership of the Communist world. Eastern Europe turns West, though we must recognize that the differences in Eastern Europe still cause less trouble to the Soviet Union than the differences in Western Europe cause to the United States. The Soviet economic system is turning away from the enforced equality of Marxism to the incentives of capitalism.

Let us look at Latin America: Twenty years ago Castro was a nobody. Cuba and all the other Latin republics were considered to be solidly, permanently, and docilely on the side of the United States. Today Castro has the strongest military force in the Western Hemisphere next to the United States and he is exporting revolution all over the continent. But even if Castro did not exist, Latin America would have to be considered a major trouble spot. Despite the Alliance for Progress, Latin America is barely holding its own in the race between production and population. As it continues to fall further behind the rest of the world, it becomes a tinder box for revolution.

Let us turn to Africa: Just ten years ago Ethiopia and Liberia were the only independent countries in Black Africa. Today there are thirty independent countries in Black Africa. Fifteen of these countries have populations less than the State of Maryland, and each has a vote in the UN Assembly equal to that of the United States. There were twelve coups in Black Africa in the last year. No one of the thirty countries has a representative government by our standards and the prospects that any will have such a government in a generation or even a half-century are remote.

Ironically, non-Communist Asia, except for Vietnam, is the area which has experienced the most hopeful change. Japan has recovered from the devastation of World War II to the point that its one hundred million people produce as much as Communist China's seven hundred million. Korea, Taiwan, Singapore, Malaysia, and Thailand are all dramatic economic success stories.

There are grey areas: As General Romulo might put it, the Philippines suffer from too much American style democracy. Indonesia is recovering from too much Sukarno. India suffers from too many people and a host of other problems too numerous to enumerate. But over-all, it can be said without fear of contradiction that the prospects for progress in non-Communist Asia are better than those in Communist Asia.

Let us look at the balance of power in the world: Twenty years ago the United States had a monopoly on the atomic bomb and our military superiority was unquestioned. Even five years ago our advantage was still decisive. Today the Soviet Union may be ahead of us in megaton capacity and will have missile parity with the United States by 1970. Communist China within five years will have a significant deliverable nuclear capability.

Finally, let us look at American prestige: Twenty years ago, after our great World War II victory, we were respected throughout the world. Today, hardly a day goes by when our flag is not spit upon, a library burned, an embassy stoned some place in the world. In fact, you don't have to leave the United States to find examples.

This is a gloomy picture; but there is a much brighter side as well.

Communism is losing the ideological battle with freedom in Asia, Africa, Latin America as well as in Europe. In Africa, the Communist appeal was against colonialism. Now that the colonialists are gone, they must base their case on being for Communism. But African tribalism and rebellious individualism are simply incompatible with the rigid discipline a Communist system imposes.

In Latin America, the utter failure of Communism in Cuba has drastically weakened the appeal of the Communist ideology in the rest of Latin America.

In Asia, the remarkable success of private enterprise oriented economies in Japan, Korea, Taiwan, Malaysia and Thailand, as contrasted to the failure of Communism in China and the failure of socialism in Burma and Indonesia, makes it possible to state unequivocally that the only way for the Communists to win in

Vietnam, or anywhere else in Asia, is by force and terror; they will never win by persuasion.

All over the world, whether from East Germany to West, from Communist China to free China, from Communist Cuba to the free American republics, the traffic is all one way—from Communism to freedom.

Let us reappraise U.S. policy in the light of the new world in which we live.

In Western Europe we must recognize that clearly apart from De Gaulle's actions the new economic independence of European countries and the lack of fear of Soviet aggression have contributed to a situation where it is not possible to keep the old alliance together on its former basis.

Yet, whatever changes may have occurred as far as the Soviet threat is concerned, one factor has not changed: A major reason for setting up the alliance was to provide a military, political and economic home for the most powerful people in Europe—the Germans. If the alliance is allowed to continue to disintegrate, Germany, denied the right to develop nuclear weapons, will be left defenseless in the heart of Europe and the Soviet Union, holding the pawn of East Germany, will have a tempting diplomatic target.

The highest priority American foreign policy objective must be to set up a new alliance, multilateral, if possible, bilateral, if necessary, which will keep Germany solidly on the Western side. . . .

Let us turn now to subject A, the Soviet Union.

This Spring a great debate raged in the chanceries of Europe and among foreign policy experts in the United States as to how much Soviet policy had changed under its new leaders. Some Soviet experts on both sides of the Atlantic saw the new Soviet leaders turning 180 degrees from past policies and seeking permanent peace with the United States and Europe as well as using their influence to end the war in Vietnam.

The record of the Soviets in the Middle East war has caused a sober reassessment of this point of view. At a time that they were talking peace and détente in Europe, the Soviet leaders were spending 4 billion dollars arming Nasser and his colleagues. They encouraged the Arab leaders in their aggressive actions. They blocked diplomatic moves to avoid the war. They supported a cease-fire only when it became necessary for them to do so to save their Arab clients from further losses.

Then came the Glassboro conference. Kosygin was a gentleman. He did not bang his shoe on the table at the United Nations. Many hoped that the Soviet leaders had learned their lesson and the spirit of Hollybush swept over the land. But it soon became apparent that, while the music was different, the words were the same.

More revealing have been the actions of the Soviet leaders since Glassboro. Kosygin stopped to see Castro on his way back to Moscow. The Soviet Union is sending millions of dollars in arms to build the shattered Arab armies. The Soviet Union is still providing 100 per cent of the oil and 85 per cent of all sophisticated military equipment for the armies of North Vietnam. The Soviet line against West Germany has perceptively hardened. The Soviet Union continues to build both offensive and defensive missiles.

This does not mean that the Soviet leaders have not changed. But what we must recognize is that the change is one of the head and not of the heart—of necessity, not choice.

These are some of the facts which forced the change: Communist China is a threat in the East; the Soviet Union needs friends in the West. The military and economic strength of Western Europe thwarted their progressive designs on that area. They faced increased demand for consumer goods from the Russian people. They looked down the nuclear gunbarrel in the Cuban confrontation.

The Soviet leaders today have three major foreign policy objectives: They are still Communists and they are committed to the goal of a Communist world; they are battling the Chinese for leadership of that world. They want to achieve that goal without war. At the same time they want more economic progress at home. They will work with us only when doing so serves one or more of these three objectives.

In the light of this analysis, the policy America should follow becomes clear.

Militarily, we must recognize that we have not had a world war for twenty years because of America's clear military superiority. That superiority is now threatened, both because of Soviet progress in missile development and because of an attitude in U.S. policy circles that nuclear parity with the Soviets is enough. Because the primary Soviet goal is still victory rather than peace, we must never let the day come in a confrontation like Cuba and the Mid-East where they, rather than we, have military superiority. The cost of maintaining that superiority, including the development of an ABM capability, is a necessary investment in peace.

Economically, we should have a policy which encourages more trade with the Soviet Union and Eastern European countries. We must recognize, however, that to them trade is a political weapon. I believe in building bridges but we should build only our end of the bridge. For example, there should be no extension of long term credits or trade in strategic items with any nation, including the Soviet Union, which aids the enemy in North Vietnam.

Diplomatically we should have discussions with the Soviet leaders at all levels to reduce the possibility of miscalculation and to explore the areas where bilateral agreements would reduce tensions. But we must always remember in such negotiations that our goal is different from theirs: We seek peace as an end in itself. They seek victory with peace being at this time a means toward that end.

In sum, we can live in peace with the Soviet Union but until they give up their goal for world conquest it will be for them a peace of necessity and not of choice.

7. NATO Council on Future Relations with the Warsaw Pact Members (the Harmel Report), December 13–14, 1967

The sudden departure of France from NATO's integrated military structure in 1966 and French president Charles de Gaulle's independent diplomacy toward the Soviet Union played a significant role in increasing American concerns about NATO's cohesion. In December 1967, partly in response to such worries, NATO adopted the Harmel Report (named after Belgian foreign minister Pierre Harmel), which stressed the alliance's political role and called for efforts to promote détente with the Warsaw Pact countries.

Source: NATO, "Official Text: The Future Tasks of the Alliance," http://www.nato.int/cps/en/natolive/official_texts_26700.htm.

Since the North Atlantic Treaty was signed in 1949 the international situation has changed significantly and the political tasks of the Alliance have assumed a new dimension. Amongst other developments, the Alliance has played a major part in stopping Communist expansion in Europe; the USSR has become one of the two world super powers but the Communist world is no longer monolithic; the Soviet doctrine of *"peaceful co-existence"* has changed the nature of the confrontation with the West but not the basic problems. Although the disparity between the power of the United States and that of the European states remains, Europe has recovered and is on its way towards unity. The process of decolonisation has transformed European relations with the rest of the world; at the same time, major problems have arisen in the relations between developed and developing countries.

The Atlantic Alliance has two main functions. Its first function is to maintain adequate military strength and political solidarity to deter aggression and other forms of pressure and to defend the territory of member countries if aggression should occur. Since its inception, the Alliance has successfully fulfilled this task. But the possibility of a crisis cannot be excluded as long as the central political issues in Europe, first and foremost the German question, remain unsolved. Moreover, the situation of instability and uncertainty still precludes a balanced reduction of military forces. Under these conditions, the Allies will maintain as necessary, a suitable military capability to assure the balance of forces, thereby creating a climate of stability, security and confidence.

In this climate the Alliance can carry out its second function, to pursue the search for progress towards a more stable relationship in which the underlying political issues can be solved. Military security and a policy of détente are not contradictory but complementary. Collective defence is a stabilizing factor in world politics. It is the necessary condition for effective policies directed towards a greater relaxation of tensions. The way to peace and stability in Europe rests in particular on the use of the Alliance constructively in the interest of détente. The participation of the USSR and the USA will be necessary to achieve a settlement of the political problems in Europe.

From the beginning the Atlantic Alliance has been a co-operative grouping of states sharing the same ideals and with a high degree of common interest. Their cohesion and solidarity provide an element of stability within the Atlantic area.

As sovereign states the Allies are not obliged to subordinate their policies to collective decision. The Alliance affords an effective forum and clearing house for the exchange of information and views; thus, each of the Allies can decide its policy in the light of close knowledge of the problems and objectives of the others. To this end the practice of frank and timely consultations needs to be deepened and improved. Each Ally should play its full part in promoting an improvement in relations with the Soviet Union and the countries of Eastern Europe, bearing in mind that the pursuit of détente must not be allowed to split the Alliance. The chances of success will clearly be greatest if the Allies remain on parallel courses, especially in matters of close concern to them all; their actions will thus be all the more effective.

No peaceful order in Europe is possible without a major effort by all concerned. The evolution of Soviet and East European policies gives ground for hope that those governments may eventually come to recognize the advantages to them of collaborating in working towards a peaceful settlement. But no final and stable settlement in Europe is possible without a solution of the German question which lies at the heart of present tensions in Europe. Any such settlement must end the unnatural barriers between Eastern and Western Europe, which are most clearly and cruelly manifested in the division of Germany.

Accordingly the Allies are resolved to direct their energies to this purpose by realistic measures designed to further a détente in East-West relations. The relaxation of tensions is not the final goal but is part of a long-term process to promote better relations and to foster a European settlement. The ultimate political purpose of the Alliance is to achieve a just and lasting peaceful order in Europe accompanied by appropriate security guarantees.

Currently, the development of contacts between the countries of Western and Eastern Europe is mainly on a bilateral basis. Certain subjects, of course, require by their very nature a multilateral solution.

The problem of German reunification and its relationship to a European settlement has normally been dealt with in exchanges between the Soviet Union and the three Western powers having special responsibilities in this field. In the preparation of such exchanges the Federal Republic of Germany has regularly joined the three Western powers in order to reach a common position. The other Allies will continue to have their views considered in timely discussions among the Allies about Western policy on this subject, without in any way impairing the special responsibilities in question.

The Allies will examine and review suitable policies designed to achieve a just and stable order in Europe, to overcome the division of Germany and to foster European security. This will be part of a process of active and constant preparation for the time when fruitful discussions of these complex questions may be possible bilaterally or multilaterally between Eastern and Western nations.

The Allies are studying disarmament and practical arm control measures, including the possibility of balanced force reductions. These studies will be intensified. Their active pursuit reflects the will of the Allies to work for an effective détente with the East.

The Allies will examine with particular attention the defence problems of the exposed areas e.g. the South-Eastern flank. In this respect the present situation in the Mediterranean presents special problems, bearing in mind that the current crisis in the Middle East falls within the responsibilities of the United Nations.

The North Atlantic Treaty area cannot be treated in isolation from the rest of the world. Crises and conflicts arising outside the area may impair its security either directly or by affecting the global balance. Allied countries contribute individually within the United Nations and other international organizations to the maintenance of international peace and security and to the solution of important international problems. In accordance with established usage the Allies or such of them as wish to do so will also continue to consult on such problems without commitment and as the case may demand...

8. Nixon's Inaugural Address, January 20, 1969

After a hard-fought campaign, Richard Nixon was elected in November 1968. During the transition period, he recruited a foreign policy team that would ultimately be dominated by National Security Adviser and Harvard professor Henry Kissinger. Nixon and Kissinger identified détente as the cornerstone of the new administration's approach. And, while the actual implementation of Nixon's foreign policy would often be shrouded in secrecy, the message was publicized actively, starting with the inaugural address.

Source: John T. Woolley and Gerhard Peters, eds., *The American Presidency Project*, http://www.presidency.ucsb.edu/ws/index.php?pid=1941&st=&st1=.

As we learn to go forward together at home, let us also seek to go forward together with all mankind.

Let us take as our goal: Where peace is unknown, make it welcome; where peace is fragile, make it strong; where peace is temporary, make it permanent.

After a period of confrontation, we are entering an era of negotiation.

Let all nations know that during this administration our lines of communication will be open.

We seek an open world—open to ideas, open to the exchange of goods and people—a world in which no people, great or small, will live in angry isolation.

We cannot expect to make everyone our friend, but we can try to make no one our enemy.

Those who would be our adversaries, we invite to a peaceful competition—not in conquering territory or extending dominion, but in enriching the life of man.

As we explore the reaches of space, let us go to the new worlds together—not as new worlds to be conquered, but as a new adventure to be shared.

With those who are willing to join, let us cooperate to reduce the burden of arms, to strengthen the structure of peace, to lift up the poor and the hungry.

But to all those who would be tempted by weakness, let us leave no doubt that we will be as strong as we need to be for as long as we need to be.

Over the past [20] years, since I first came to this Capital as a freshman Congressman, I have visited most of the nations of the world. I have come to know the leaders of the world and the great forces, the hatreds, the fears that divide the world.

I know that peace does not come through wishing for it—that there is no substitute for days and even years of patient and prolonged diplomacy. I also know the people of the world.

I have seen the hunger of a homeless child, the pain of a man wounded in battle, the grief of a mother who has lost her son. I know these have no ideology, no race.

I know America. I know the heart of America is good.

I speak from my own heart, and the heart of my country, the deep concern we have for those who suffer and those who sorrow.

I have taken an oath today in the presence of God and my countrymen to uphold and defend the Constitution of the United States. To that oath I now add this sacred commitment: I shall consecrate my Office, my energies, and all the wisdom I can summon to the cause of peace among nations.

Let this message be heard by strong and weak alike:

The peace we seek to win—is not victory over any other people, but the peace that comes "with healing in its wings"; with compassion for those who have suffered; with understanding for those who have opposed us; with the opportunity for all the peoples of this earth to choose their own destiny.

Only a few short weeks ago we shared the glory of man's first sight of the world as God sees it, as a single sphere reflecting light in the darkness.

As the Apollo astronauts flew over the moon's gray surface on Christmas Eve, they spoke to us of the beauty of earth—and in that voice so clear across the lunar distance, we heard them invoke God's blessing on its goodness.

In that moment, their view from the moon moved poet Archibald MacLeish to write: "To see the earth as it truly is, small and blue and beautiful in that eternal silence where it floats, is to see ourselves as riders on the earth together, brothers on that bright loveliness in the eternal cold—brothers who know now they are truly brothers."

In that moment of surpassing technological triumph, men turned their thoughts toward home and humanity—seeing in that far perspective that man's destiny on earth is not divisible; telling us that however far we reach into the cosmos, our destiny lies not in the stars but on earth itself, in our own hands, in our own hearts.

We have endured a long night of the American spirit. But as our eyes catch the dimness of the first rays of dawn, let us not curse the remaining dark. Let us gather the light.

9. Willy Brandt and Henry Kissinger on West German Ostpolitik, 1969–70

During the chancellorship of the Social Democrat, Willy Brandt, the FRG began earnestly building bridges to the Soviet Union and Eastern Europe (including East Germany). While the ultimate goal of this Ostpolitik was German unification, its immediate results produced various agreements between the FRG and the Soviet Union, Poland (on postwar borders), and most dramatically, with the GDR. As the Brandt government moved to build links to the Soviet bloc, however, the Nixon administra-

tion in the United States worried over the broader implications of Ostpolitik. In these two documents, Brandt explains the rationale of Ostpolitik to the West German Bundestag and Henry Kissinger speculates over its impact.

Sources: Document 9A is from *Documents on Germany 1944–1985*, Department of State Publication 9446 (Washington, DC: U.S. Department of State, 1985); and Document 9B is from *Germany and Berlin, 1969–1972*, vol. 40 of *Foreign Relations of the United States, 1969–1976*, http://history.state.gov/historicaldocuments /frus1969-76v40/d55.

9A. Brandt at the Bundestag on Ostpolitik, October 1969

This Government works on the assumption that the questions which have arisen for the German people out of the Second World War and from the national treachery committed by the Hitler regime can find their ultimate answer only in a European peace arrangement. However, no one can dissuade us from our conviction that the Germans have a right to self-determination just as has any other nation.

The object of our political work in the years ahead is to preserve the unity of the nation by deconcentrating the relationship between the two parts of Germany. . . . We still have common tasks and a common responsibility: to ensure peace among us and in Europe.

Twenty years after the establishment of the Federal Republic of Germany and of the GDR we must prevent any further alienation of the two parts of the German nation, that is, arrive at a regular modus vivendi and from there proceed to cooperation.

This is not just a German interest, for it is of importance also for peace in Europe and for East-West relations. . . . The Federal Government . . . again offers the Council of Ministers of the GDR negotiations at government level without discrimination on either side, which should lead to contractually agreed cooperation. International recognition of the GDR by the Federal Republic is out of the question. Even if there exist two States in Germany, they are not foreign countries to each other: their relations with each other can only be of special nature.

. . . The Federal Government declares that its readiness for binding agreements on the reciprocal renunciation of the use or threat of force applies equally with regard to the GDR . . . [and that it] will advise the United States, Great Britain, and France to continue energetically the talks begun with the Soviet Union on easing and improving the situation of Berlin. . . . West Berlin must be placed in a position to assist in improving the political, economic and cultural relations between the two parts of Germany.

We welcome the renewed increase of intra-German trade. . . .

The German people needs peace in the full sense of that word also with the peoples of the Soviet Union and all peoples of the European East. We are prepared to make an honest attempt at understanding, in order to help overcome the aftermath of the disaster brought on Europe by a criminal clique. . . .

We are not deluding ourselves to believe that reconciliation will be easy or quick to achieve. It is a process; but it is time now to push ahead that process.

9B. Kissinger to Nixon on Ostpolitik, February 16, 1970

The German Chancellor has stated the goals of his "Ostpolitik" in rather sober and realistic terms: he wants to normalize relations with the Communist countries and move from "confrontation to co-operation"; he is prepared in this context to accept the GDR as a separate state and to accommodate the Poles, within certain limits, on the question of the Oder-Neisse Line. He hopes in this way to reduce the antagonism toward West Germany in the USSR and Eastern Europe and to make the division of Germany less severe. He rejects the idea that Germany should be free-floating between East and West and he remains strongly committed to NATO and West European integration. Indeed he believes his Eastern policy can be successful only if Germany is firmly anchored in the West. He has in effect renounced formal reunification as the aim of German policy but hopes over the long run to achieve special ties between the two German states. . . . Although Brandt has stressed that his Western policy has priority, German attention is currently heavily focused on the East. . . .

Much of the opposition within Germany and the concern among its allies stems not so much from the broad purposes which Brandt wants to achieve but from suspicions or fear that Eastern policy is acquiring its own momentum and will lead Brandt into dangerous concessions. . . . Much of the worry . . . focuses on the danger that as Brandt pursues the quest for normalization, his advisors and supporters will eventually succeed in leading him to jeopardize Germany's entire international position. This fear has already embittered domestic debate in Germany and could in time produce the type of emotional and doctrinaire political argument that has paralyzed political life in Germany and some other West European countries in the past. It is this possibility that we must obviously be troubled about ourselves. . . .

The most worrisome aspects of Ostpolitik are long-range. . . . Assuming that Brandt achieves a degree of normalization, he or his successor may discover before long that the hoped-for benefits fail to develop. Instead of ameliorating the division of Germany, recognition of the GDR may boost its status and strengthen the Communist regime. . . . More fundamentally . . . the Soviets having achieved their first set of objectives may then confront the FRG with the proposition that a real and lasting improvement in the FRG's relations with the GDR and other Eastern countries can only be achieved if Bonn loosens its Western ties. . . .

It should be stressed that men like Brandt, Wehner and Defense Minister Schmidt undoubtedly see themselves as conducting responsible policy of reconciliation with the East and intend not to have this policy come into conflict with Germany's Western association. . . . Their problem is to control a process which, if it results in failure could jeopardize their political lives and if it succeeds could create a momentum that may shake Germany's domestic stability and unhinge its international position.

10. White House Background Press Briefing by the President's Assistant for National Security Affairs (Kissinger), February 16, 1970

After a year in office, Henry Kissinger had established himself as the key adviser to Richard Nixon and the major interlocutor—through the back channel with Soviet ambassador Anatoly Dobrynin—with the Soviet Union. Kissinger's staff also authored a series of extensive foreign policy reports for the U.S. Congress, which outlined the major goals, achievements, and shifts of policy. The first report was released in early 1970 and laid out a strategy for engaging the USSR. In the excerpt below, Kissinger explains to the White House press corps the significance of the report.

Source: Document 58, in *Foundations of American Foreign Policy, 1969–1972*, vol. 1 of *Foreign Relations of the United States, 1969–1976*, http://history.state.gov /historicaldocuments/frus1969-76v01/d58.

Q. Dr. Kissinger, the President used the word "watershed" in introducing this briefing this afternoon. In his remarks to the reporters, President Nixon characterized the report to Congress, which ran to some 40,000 words, as "the most comprehensive statement on foreign and defense policy ever made in this country." As such, he styled it "a watershed in American foreign policy." If I understand watershed correctly, it means a separation, division, going in a new direction. I have not had a chance to read this. What are the watershed points in this foreign policy statement?

Dr. Kissinger: What the President meant is the fact that there now exists a comprehensive, philosophical statement of American foreign policy. It makes it clear that for better or worse our policies are not simply tactical responses to immediate situations, but that there exists a coherent picture of the world; that we are taking our action in relation to this picture; and that this document outlines his experience in foreign policy, national security policy and his expectations for the future.

So whatever debate is generated by this would have to be in terms of a general concept of foreign policy and not simply in terms of tactical responses to immediate situations.

Secondly, it is his belief and it is the Administration's belief that we are reaching the end of the post-war era, the end of the post-war era in the sense that in the immediate period after World War II the United States, among the non-Communist countries, was the only one that had emerged from the war with its society and its economy relatively intact. Therefore, it was natural that the United States would assume a predominant role anyplace where it felt that security of the non-Communist world was threatened.

This, in turn, imposed on us the requirement that we were trying to remedy immediate crisis situations rather than deal with the overall structure of peace, or, rather, we identified the overall structure of peace with the solution of immediate crisis.

This is ending now for a number of reasons. It is ending, according to this document and our convictions, because many other parts of the world have now regained a degree of cohesion, have grown into independence, which was, of course, not the case at the end of World War II, and are capable of assuming a greater responsibility, both for their security and for their problems.

In these conditions, the United States should not be the fireman running from one conflagration to the other, but can address itself to the longer-term problems of a peaceful international structure and leave to local responsibilities the immediate task of construction.

In other words, the United States will participate where it can make a difference. It will attempt to contribute to the creation of regional organization where that is appropriate, but the United States in this new era will have to change its position from one of predominance to one of partnership.

Now, we recognize—and to pick up a point that the President made in introducing this report—that there is a danger that in moving from predominance to partnership some people may believe that we are moving towards disengagement or returning to isolation. This is not the philosophy of this Administration.

The philosophy of this Administration is to find a basis for a long-term engagement in the world, one that is consistent with the realities of the contemporary world, one that we can sustain over an indefinite period of time, and one that will give an impetus to our foreign policy of the same order that the Marshall Plan conception did to the conditions of 1947. Those conceptions were appropriate to the realities of the '40s and '50s and early '60s and we are attempting to find conceptions that are appropriate to the realities of the '70s.

Q. Dr. Kissinger, I am not sure from all of this whether you think the Cold War is increasing or lessening. Do you think it is increasing or lessening from this broad philosophical statement?

Dr. Kissinger: The Cold War, as it came to be known in the immediate post-war period, we would say has in that forum lessened. At that time, there was a belief in a monolithic communism, and that no longer exists in this forum.

At that time, there was a belief in the notion of irreconcilable hostility. On the other hand, we believe that there are objective causes for the tension that has existed over this period. We believe that we are doing no one a service by pretending that these tensions do not exist or that they can be removed by mere atmospherics.

We are prepared to negotiate seriously, either individually or comprehensively, on these issues with either of the great Communist countries. And, therefore, the foreign policy that was appropriate to the period that was called the Cold War is not appropriate to the period into which we believe we are now entering.

But we make this statement without under-estimating that there are still serious causes of tension, that ideology is not dead, even though it has changed some of its character, and that large areas of potential discord and of hostility remain. But we are prepared to work seriously, and as energetically as we can.

11. Telegram from Ambassador Dobrynin to the Soviet Foreign Ministry, July 17, 1971

A key element—and arguably the greatest achievement—of the Nixon administration's foreign policy strategy was triangular diplomacy: the idea that the United States could use the hostile relationship between the Soviet Union and the PRC to its advantage. After months and years of contacts, Kissinger visited Beijing in secrecy in July 1971 and reached an agreement for a forthcoming trip by Nixon. The Soviet reaction to these events is captured in a cable by Soviet ambassador Dobrynin, written shortly after Kissinger's trip.

Source: David C. Geyer and Douglas E. Selvage, eds., *Soviet-American Relations: The Détente Years, 1969–1972* (Washington, DC: U.S. Government Printing Office, 2007), 401–4.

The agreement reached between Peking and Washington on President Nixon's trip to Peking is unquestionably of major international significance, with potentially broad consequences for regions such as Southeast Asia and the Far East, as well as for relationships within the USSR-PRC-U.S. triangle. The Chinese leadership has clearly demonstrated that it is even more unprincipled in its policy than Nixon himself. As practically everyone here believes, this abrupt about-face by the

Chinese is based on the anti-Soviet thrust of Peking's policy, its aspiration to play a global role, and its obstinate pursuit of its nationalistic objectives above all else—objectives it places much higher than ideological considerations.

Several factors underlie Nixon's approach to relations with the PRC. One factor that is constantly at work is his desire to exploit Soviet-Chinese differences to the maximum and to deepen and intensify them whenever possible; he is not particularly scrupulous in his choice of ways and means to accomplish this goal. It is now becoming clear that for a long period of time Nixon conducted parallel talks regarding personal meetings not only with the Soviet leaders but also with the leaders in Peking. No sooner did Mao Tse-tung and Chou En-lai show willingness for such a meeting and, most important, agree to announce it well in advance, than the U.S. President straightaway seized this opportunity.

There is no doubt he would act the same way if there were a similar turn of events with respect to his Moscow trip.

In the U.S. the President now wields so much authority—this being a trend that began after the Second World War—that he is effectively able to use all means to carry public opinion along with him, while having made a decision like this essentially on his own.

Another important factor currently influencing Nixon's behavior is his tremendous desire to be re-elected president in 1972. In this regard he is prepared to pay a high price for anything that can advance this paramount goal of his. He now views a trip to Peking or Moscow primarily in this electoral context.

There is yet one more significant factor: an agreement on a meeting with the Chinese leadership is also important to Nixon in terms of the most pressing domestic issue he now faces—finding a way out of the Vietnam War. There are two aspects to this. In terms of public relations, an agreement now enables Nixon to greatly reduce pressure from his own public opinion for a prompt solution of the Vietnam issue and withdrawal of U.S. troops, and for a favorable response to the latest PRG proposals in Paris. Thanks to the Chinese, Nixon has now gained a considerable respite in this regard. But alongside this public relations aspect, we know the White House now genuinely hopes that an acceptable peace settlement can be reached in Vietnam with the help of the Peking leadership. Success in this endeavor would almost certainly guarantee Nixon's re-election for a second term. Of course, as a consequence of the agreement on Nixon's Peking trip, we should anticipate that the Americans and the Chinese will intensify their game in the international arena. The rather clear subtext is that this game will be played out primarily within the invisible U.S.-PRC-USSR triangle.

There now arises the question of our possible response. It seems to us that also in the present circumstances one of our principal tasks should be to continue our efforts, in accordance with previously adopted directives, to counteract any U.S.-Chinese rapprochement that has an anti-Soviet basis. Judging by the conduct of the Chinese leadership, which considers the Soviet Union to be the number one enemy, we do not currently appear to have sizeable capabilities to directly influence the Chinese side in this respect. In our view, such capabilities are somewhat better with respect to the U.S. side. It seems to us that we should continue to focus the aforementioned efforts on utilizing all the objective and subjective factors determining U.S. interest in development of relations with the USSR so as to check possible sliding into anti-Sovietism by the U.S. in building its relations with Peking.

Nixon's personal interest in maintaining such relations with us, which continues to be of no small importance for him in light of the 1972 presidential election campaign, is one such factor; also, the desire of the American public to avoid anything that might lead to a confrontation with the USSR, whose consequences are feared immeasurably more here than a conflict with China; and growing sentiment in the business community in favor of developing stronger ties with us, etc. For many reasons, primarily having to do with the elections, the possibility of a "summit" conference with the Soviet leaders continues to play an essential role with Nixon—although this is now somewhat less of an immediate issue for him.

We should also fully take this important factor into account: despite the U.S.-Chinese agreement on Nixon's visit to Peking, the profound objective differences that have divided the U.S. and the PRC for all these many years still remain; and the anti-China aspect of the Nixon doctrine continues to be valid. No less ballyhoo preceded Kennedy's meeting with Khrushchev, and we all know how that turned out.

With the enormous sensational ballyhoo in the U.S. and the entire world that surrounds Nixon's upcoming visit to China, and in the heat of predictions now being made here about the rosy future of U.S.-Chinese relations, there is clearly a desire to read considerably more into the President's action than it

[margin handwritten note: Potential for escalation]

seems to promise for the U.S. in reality. This ballyhoo also reflects, to a certain degree, the mutual interest of the U.S. and the PRC in deliberately exaggerating and exploiting the factor of U.S.-Chinese relations in order to exert pressure on us. . . .

In general, what we should do is continue our current policy towards the U.S., as reflected in decisions of the CC CPSU, while paying greater attention to the U.S.-Chinese flirtation in light of the most recent developments. In the final analysis presidents—with all their manipulation and swings from one extreme to the other—come and go. But our relations with the U.S., the leading country of the Western world, will remain of major importance to us.

12. Basic Principles: The United States and the Soviet Union Agree on the "Rules" of Détente, May 1972

At the May 1972 Moscow summit—the culmination of the early road toward Soviet-American détente—the American and Soviet delegations signed a series of bilateral agreements. Perhaps the most significant of these were the ABM Treaty and the Interim Agreement on Offensive Weapons (SALT I). In addition, however, the two sides released a document titled "Basic Principles of Soviet-American Relations." Many of the principles—some of which are extracted below—would be tested in the years following the first Soviet-American summit.

Source: *Department of State Bulletin*, June 26, 1972, 898–99.

The United States of America and the Union of Soviet Socialist Republics . . . have agreed as follows:

First: They will proceed from the common determination that in the nuclear age there is no alternative to conducting their mutual relations on the basis of peaceful coexistence. . . .

Second: The USA and the USSR attach major importance to preventing the development of situations capable of causing a dangerous exacerbation of their relations. Therefore, they will do their utmost to avoid military confrontations and to prevent the outbreak of nuclear war. They will always exercise restraint in their mutual relations, and will be prepared to negotiate and settle differences by peaceful means. . . . Both sides recognize that efforts to obtain unilateral advantages at the expense of the other . . . are inconsistent with these objectives. . . .

Third: The USA and the USSR have a special responsibility . . . to do everything in their power so that conflicts or situations will not arise which would serve to increase international tensions. Accordingly, they will seek to promote conditions in which all countries will live in peace and security and will not be subject to outside interference in their internal affairs.

Fourth: The USA and the USSR intend to widen the juridical basis of their mutual relations. . . .

Fifth: The USA and the USSR reaffirm their readiness to continue the practice of exchanging views on problems of mutual interest. . . .

Sixth: The parties will continue their efforts to limit armaments on a bilateral as well as on a multilateral basis. They will make special efforts to limit strategic armaments. . . .

Seventh: The USA and the USSR regard commercial and economic ties as an important and necessary element in the strengthening of their bilateral relations and thus will actively promote the growth of such ties. . . .

The development of US-Soviet relations is not directed against third countries and . . . do not affect any obligations with respect to other countries earlier assumed by the USA and the USSR.

13. Jackson-Vanik Amendment to the
1974 Trade Law, January 3, 1975

The opposition to détente was constant in the United States. One key issue for congressional Democrats, headed by Henry Jackson, was the lack of respect for fundamental human rights in the Soviet bloc, including the right of religious minorities—mainly Jews—to freely emigrate from the USSR. After a long campaign, Congress unanimously adopted the Jackson-Vanik Amendment, which essentially tied the granting of MFN status to freedom of emigration. The amendment is contained in Title IV of the 1974 Trade Act, signed into law by President Ford on January 3, 1975.

Source: Legal Information Institute, Cornell University Law School, http://www.law.cornell.edu/uscode/text/19/2432.

19 USC § 2432. Freedom of Emigration in East-West Trade

(a) Actions of nonmarket economy countries making them ineligible for normal trade relations, programs of credits, credit guarantees, or investment guarantees, or commercial agreements

To assure the continued dedication of the United States to fundamental human rights, and notwithstanding any other provision of law, on or after January 3, 1975, products from any nonmarket economy country shall not be eligible to receive nondiscriminatory treatment (normal trade relations), such country shall not participate in any program of the Government of the United States which extends credits or credit guarantees or investment guarantees, directly or indirectly, and the President of the United States shall not conclude any commercial agreement with any such country, during the period beginning with the date on which the President determines that such country—

(1) denies its citizens the right or opportunity to emigrate;

(2) imposes more than a nominal tax on emigration or on the visas or other documents required for emigration, for any purpose or cause whatsoever; or

(3) imposes more than a nominal tax, levy, fine, fee, or other charge on any citizen as a consequence of the desire of such citizen to emigrate to the country of his choice, and ending on the date on which the President determines that such country is no longer in violation of paragraph (1), (2), or (3).

(b) Presidential determination and report to Congress that nation is not violating freedom of emigration

After January 3, 1975,

(A) products of a nonmarket economy country may be eligible to receive nondiscriminatory treatment (normal trade relations),

(B) such country may participate in any program of the Government of the United States which extends credits or credit guarantees or investment guarantees, and

(C) the President may conclude a commercial agreement with such country, only after the President has submitted to the Congress a report indicating that such country is not in violation of paragraph (1), (2), or (3) of subsection (a) of this section. Such report with respect to such country shall include information as to the nature and implementation of emigration laws and policies and restrictions or discrimination applied to or against persons wishing to emigrate. The report required by this subsection shall be submitted initially as provided herein and, with current information, on or before each June 30 and December 31 thereafter so long as such treatment is received, such credits or guarantees are extended, or such agreement is in effect.

(c) Waiver authority of President

(1) During the 18-month period beginning on January 3, 1975, the President is authorized to waive by Executive order the application of subsections (a) and (b) of this section with respect to any country, if he reports to the Congress that—

(A) he has determined that such waiver will substantially promote the objectives of this section; and

(B) he has received assurances that the emigration practices of that country will henceforth lead substantially to the achievement of the objectives of this section.

(2) During any period subsequent to the 18-month period referred to in paragraph (1), the President is authorized to waive by Executive order the application of subsections (a) and (b) of this section with respect to any country, if the waiver authority granted by this subsection continues to apply to such country pursuant to subsection (d) of this section, and if he reports to the Congress that—

(A) he has determined that such waiver will substantially promote the objectives of this section; and

(B) he has received assurances that the emigration practices of that country will henceforth lead substantially to the achievement of the objectives of this section.

(3) A waiver with respect to any country shall terminate on the day after the waiver authority granted by this subsection ceases to be effective with respect to such country pursuant to subsection (d) of this section. The President may, at any time, terminate by Executive order any waiver granted under this subsection.

14. Memorandum from the President's Assistant for National Security Affairs (Kissinger) to President Ford, July 1975 (undated)

The CSCE process concluded with the Helsinki summit in July–August 1975. Attended by thirty-five countries—all European nations save Albania, plus the United States and Canada—the highlight of the meeting was the Helsinki Accords. Watergate having forced Nixon's resignation, the chief American representative at Helsinki was Gerald Ford. Below are Henry Kissinger's analysis and instructions for the president.

Source: Document 323, in *European Security*, vol. 39 of *Foreign Relations of the United States, 1969–1976*, http://history.state.gov/historicaldocuments/frus1969 -76v39/d323.

I. Purpose

The *United States, Canada* and 33 European states will participate in the third and concluding summit phase of the Conference on Security and Cooperation in Europe. You and each of the other political heads of state or government will sign the CSCE's final act, and each leader will address the Conference.

Through your presence at the Conference, you will demonstrate that the United States retains a vital interest in Europe, and that the security of the United States is tied through our participation in the Atlantic Alliance, to the stability of the European continent.

Your address to the Conference is scheduled for the morning of August 1, 1975. (Speaking order for the 35 participants was drawn by lot: Prime Minister Wilson is first, General Secretary Brezhnev 13th and you are 26th.) *Your speech, which will command worldwide attention, and your bilateral meetings during the conference will provide you with the very valuable opportunity to place the CSCE results in correct perspective.*

Your purpose will be to:

—evaluate the results of CSCE by stating that its declarations are not legally binding but, instead, represent political and moral commitments to lessen East-West tensions and increase contacts and cooperation;

—stress that while CSCE is a step forward, it is not the culmination of the process of détente, that large standing armies still oppose each other and that major differences between East and West remain to be resolved;

—urge concrete implementation of the promises contained in the declarations, noting the importance the United States attaches to the humanitarian provisions and stating that Europe's military security problems still must be dealt with in MBFR and that SALT II must still be concluded.

II. Background, Participants and Press Arrangements

A. *Background*: The Conference on Security and Cooperation in Europe is the product of a long-standing Soviet proposal first raised in 1954 and resurrected in the aftermath of the Czech invasion in 1968. The Western governments recognized the proposal for what it was—a vehicle by which the Soviet Union hoped first to freeze the political map of Europe and then to extend its political influence westward. *The strong Soviet interest in the Conference led the West to exploit it in three ways:*

—*to gain Soviet concessions in East-West political issues.* The successful conclusion of the Berlin agreement in 1971, the agreement between East and West Germany, and the initiation of MBFR talks all were to some degree related to the linkage established by the West between progress on these political questions and the West's gradual acceptance of a CSCE.

—*to allow governments of Western Europe, both neutrals and members of NATO, to participate in the détente process.* Western governments were thus able to respond to a strongly held public feeling that relations between East and West were changing, that the process should be encouraged and that the management of the process should not be left to the US and USSR alone.

—*to introduce into the CSCE, as a condition for its successful conclusion, the issue of human rights*—the so-called "freer movement" questions.

The United States has participated in the CSCE with restraint, wishing neither to block the efforts of its Allies nor to have the CSCE seen as a source of contention between the US and the Soviet Union. Our objectives have been to maintain Alliance cohesion; to insist that the CSCE's declarations are political, not legal; and to seek such possibilities of easing tension between East and West as might be possible.

After two years of difficult negotiation, a CSCE balance sheet shows that:

—*the Soviets have achieved a CSCE.* It will be concluded at the summit, in a historically unique event. The final declarations will give the Soviets some basis to claim that Europe's frontiers have been confirmed along their present configurations, and that the political consequences of World War II have been digested and are universally accepted.

—*the CSCE results are not wholly what the Soviets wanted.* The documents are not legally binding. The statement of principles, even if the Soviets seek to lend it the color of law, by its language falls short of supporting the Soviet objective of freezing Europe's political configuration. Peaceful change of borders is allowed; the right to self-determination is stated in sweeping terms. Our rights in Berlin have been preserved. *The Soviets did not get agreement to a post-CSCE European security arrangement designed to undermine NATO.*

—beyond that, *the philosophy which permeates most of the CSCE's declarations is that of the West's open societies.* The thrust implicit in the declarations is toward greater human rights, the freer movement of peoples and wider access to information. In response, Warsaw Pact members have tightened internal discipline.

Final judgment on the results of CSCE will depend

—*initially* on which side is able most persuasively to propagate its version of the CSCE and its version of future European security. The solemnity of the occasion will favor the Soviet Union, as will the simplicity of the Soviet message—that peace has arrived. *The West has a more complex story to tell: that CSCE achievements are modest, that the proof of the CSCE's success lies in the future, and that a strong Allied defense posture is a precondition for security and future détente.*

The Conference Documents. CSCE work has covered four major substantive areas, known as "baskets," concerning: political and military questions; economic, scientific and technological cooperation; cooperation in strengthening human contacts, the exchange of information, and cultural and educational relations; and post-conference follow-up arrangements.

Basket 1

Under the first agenda item, conference negotiators have produced a declaration of the following ten principles of interstate relations:

—Sovereign equality, respect for the rights inherent in sovereignty.

—Refraining from the threat or use of force.

—Inviolability of frontiers.

—Territorial integrity of states.

—Peaceful settlement of disputes.

—Non-intervention in internal affairs.

—Respect for human rights and fundamental freedoms, including the freedom of thought, conscience, religion or belief.

—Equal rights and self-determination of peoples.

—Cooperation among states.

—Fulfillment in good faith of international obligations.

The Soviets were especially anxious to gain Western acceptance of an unambiguous principle on inviolability of frontiers by force. Western participants made absolutely clear, however, that their agreement to this precept would in no sense constitute formal recognition of existing European frontiers or imply that present borders are immutable. The Federal Republic of Germany, with the firm support of its NATO Allies, insisted on a reference in the Declaration of Principles to the possibility of effecting border changes by peaceful means. The United States took an active role in negotiation of this key text on peaceful border changes, which is included in the principle of sovereign equality.

Also under agenda item 1, CSCE participants have negotiated limited military security measures designed to strengthen mutual trust and confidence. Specific texts were produced on two modest but significant "confidence-building measures": prior notification of military maneuvers, and exchange of observers at those maneuvers.

Basket 2

Under agenda item 2, the Geneva talks have produced a series of declarations or resolutions concerned with economic, scientific and technological, and environmental cooperation. These declarations should help broaden East-West industrial cooperation, reduce barriers to trade, increase scientific exchanges, and cooperation in the environment.

Basket 3

The third agenda item—Basket 3—deals with increased human contacts, flow of information, and cooperation in cultural and educational relations. This item was included on the CSCE agenda only as a result of energetic efforts by the United States, our Allies, and the neutral states. Here we have negotiated especially sensitive issues for both East and West, partly because they deal with "ideological coexistence," which has always been anathema to Moscow. At Geneva, agreement was reached on Basket 3 texts dealing with such issues as: family reunification, family visits, marriages between nationals of different states, the right to travel, access to printed, as well as broadcast, information, improved working conditions for journalists, and stepped-up cultural and educational cooperation.

Basket 4

Under the fourth agenda item, the conference produced a text on post-CSCE "follow-up" arrangements. The debate here turned on the degree of institutionalization and continuity to be accorded postconference activities. The final compromise text provides for unilateral, bilateral, and multilateral actions designed to carry forward the work of the conference and monitor the implementation of agreed texts. A meeting of experts will be convened in the first half of 1977 to prepare for a gathering of senior officials, later the same year, to review results of CSCE and plan for possible additional meetings in the future.

15. Cabinet Meeting, Memorandum of Conversation, August 8, 1975

Upon their return from Helsinki, Ford and then Kissinger explained the meaning of the CSCE to the cabinet. Although the Americans had not initiated the conference or played the key role in negotiations, the president and secretary of state defended the Helsinki Accords as a significant outcome of the détente process.

Source: Document 339, in *European Security*, vol. 39 of *Foreign Relations of the United States, 1969–1976*, http://history.state.gov/historicaldocuments/frus1969 -76v39/d339.

The first item is a report on CSCE and my trip in general. We stopped first in Bonn and had a good discussion with Schmidt, who is very concerned over the economic situation. I will talk in greater detail with the economic group tomorrow, because Giscard and Wilson are also concerned. From there we went to Poland where we had good talks with Gierek.

Then we went to Helsinki. There has been criticism of the meeting. But it bolstered the West and gave a greater sense of independence to the Eastern European countries. The meeting was a definite plus. The borders were settled by treaty, most of them 30 years ago. The agreement—the Final Act—specifies self-determination and peaceful change of the borders.

From there we went to Romania. That is a tough outfit, but with a fierce sense of independence. Then we stopped in Yugoslavia. I have never seen an 83-year-old sharper. We had good talks.

I met with Demirel and Karamanlis at Helsinki. The Turkish aid decision was the worst decision I have seen in my time in Congress.

I hope it will be reversed. I met with others, including Giscard and Wilson.

I had two meetings with Brezhnev. We spoke about SALT, the Middle East and other subjects. We made progress, but more flexibility is needed. That is a quick rundown. Henry–

Kissinger: CSCE was never an element of US foreign policy. We never pushed it and stayed a half step behind our allies all through the process. But we didn't want to break with our allies or confront the Soviets on it. The complaints we are seeing show the moral collapse of the academic community. They are bitching now about the borders we did nothing to change when we had a nuclear monopoly. Indeed, they beat Dulles about the head for his position. As the President said, the borders were legally established long ago. All the new things in the document are in our favor—peaceful change, human contacts, maneuver notification. At the Conference, it was the President who dominated the Conference and it was the West which was on the offensive. It was not Brezhnev who took a triumphal tour through Eastern Europe—it was the President. And even if every spectator was paid—which I don't believe—the leadership in those countries felt strongly enough about demonstrating their independence to put out so much money.

Our relations now with our allies are better than ever since the early Marshall Plan days. Our relations with the Soviets—we didn't have the impression this group was on the upswing. Anyone observing from another planet would not have thought Communism was the wave of the future.

16. Soviet Suppression of Dissidents, 1976

As a result of the Helsinki Accords, which they had signed, the Soviet authorities faced an increasingly vocal opposition on human rights issues at home. In this November 15, 1976, report to the Central Committee, the head of the KGB, Yuri Andropov, discusses the activities of the Group for the Surveillance of the Implementation of the Helsinki Accords.

Source: Original from *Rossiiskii gosudarstvennyi arkhiv noveishei istorii, Moscow (Russian State Archive for Contemporary History, RGANI)*. Published in Nicholas Wert and Gaël Moullec, eds., *Raports secrets Soviétiques: la société dans les documents confidentiels 1921–1991* (Paris: Gallimard, 1994), 513–14.

During the last years the special services and the propaganda organisations of the enemy have tried to promote the idea according to which an "internal opposition" exists within the U.S.S.R. In order to do this, they have taken all measures in order to come to the help of the instigators of anti-social manifestations and have thus objectively contributed to the reunion of various anti-social tendencies.

Thus in 1969 anti-social elements, led by Iakir and Krassin, have created "initiative groups" with the goal of tying together the groups of members of the so-called "Movement for Democracy."

In 1970, with the goal of multiplying the anti-social activities of hostile individuals, Chalidze has created a so-called "Committee of the Defence of Human Rights" which counted among his members, apart from himself, the academics Sakharov and Chafarevitch from the Academy of Sciences.

In 1973 the so-called "Russian section" of Amnesty International, directed by Tortchin and Tverdokhlebov, took on an organisational function in the regrouping of individuals sharing anti-Soviet views. The members of this organisation made contact with certain foreign anti-Soviet organisations. With the aim of discrediting the Soviet state and system they then undertook the collection and distribution of slanderous writings.

The initiatives taken by the K.G.B. have allowed for the total discrediting and the complete actual halt of the activities of the Committee of the Defence of Human Rights; the possibilities of the "Russian section" were heavily curbed.

Nevertheless the enemy who does not take note of his failures constituting an "internal opposition," continues to pursue his action in the same fashion.

On 12 March, on the initiative of Iuri Orlov, correspondent member of the Academy of Sciences of Armenia, unemployed, the anti-social elements have announced the creation of a "group for the surveillance of the implementation of the Helsinki accords."

This group reunites individuals that have already been condemned on various occasions: Ginzburg, born in 1936, Jewish, unemployed; Grigorenko, born in 1907, Ukrainian, retired; Martchenko, born in 1938, Russian, professional criminal currently serving a sentence of internal exile in the Irkoutsk region; extremist Jews: . . . Shcharansky, born in 1948, Jewish, unemployed; participants of diverse hostile actions: the wife of Sakharov—Bonner, born in 1922, Jew, retired; Landan, born in 1918, retired Jew. . . .

The above mentioned individuals have created this group for no other reason than provocation. Putting into doubt the efforts made by the U.S.S.R. to conform with the dispositions of the Final Act of the Conference for Security and Cooperation in Europe, they also try to put pressure onto the Soviet government concerning the implementation of the Helsinki accords, especially regarding questions concerning the "third pillar."

17. "To Restore America," Ronald Reagan's Campaign Address, March 31, 1976

Détente was under constant attack during the 1976 presidential campaign, and President Ford banned the public use of the word by his campaign officials. Within the Republican Party, the major critic of the policy of détente was former California governor Ronald Reagan. Although he failed to win the nomination, Reagan's message of strength echoed among those who believed that the only beneficiary of détente thus far had been the Soviet Union. Here is a sample of Reagan's 1976 "get tough" message.

Source: *Ronald Reagan's Major Speeches, 1964–89, Public Papers of President Ronald W. Reagan*, Ronald Reagan Presidential Library, http://www.reagan.utexas.edu /archives/reference/3.31.76.html.

But there is one problem which must be solved or everything else is meaningless. I am speaking of the problem of our national security. Our nation is in danger, and the danger grows greater with each passing day. Like an echo from the past, the voice of Winston Churchill's grandson was heard recently in Britain's House of Commons warning that the spread of totalitarianism threatens the world once again [and] the democracies are "wandering without aim."

"Wandering without aim" describes the United States' foreign policy. Angola is a case in point. We gave just enough support to one side to encourage it to fight and die, but too little to give them a chance of winning. And while we're disliked by the winner, distrusted by the loser, and viewed by the world as weak and unsure. If détente were the two-way street it's supposed to be, we could have told the Soviet Union to stop its trouble-making and leave Angola to the Angolans. But it didn't work out that way.

Now, we are told Washington is dropping the word "détente," but keeping the policy. But whatever it's called, the policy is what's at fault. What is our policy? Mr. Ford's new Ambassador to the United Nations attacks our longtime ally, Israel. In Asia, our new relationship with mainland China can have practical benefits for both sides. But that doesn't mean it should include yielding to demands by them, as the administration has, to reduce our military presence on Taiwan where we have a longtime friend and ally, the Republic of China.

And, it's also revealed now that we seek to establish friendly relations with Hanoi. To make it more palatable, we're told that this might help us learn the fate of the men still listed as Missing in Action. Well, there's no doubt our government has an obligation to end the agony of parents, wives and children who've lived so long with uncertainty. But, this should have been one of our first demands of Hanoi's patron saint, the Soviet Union, if détente had any meaning at all. To present it now as a reason for friendship with those who have already violated their promise to provide such information is hypocrisy.

In the last few days, Mr. Ford and Dr. Kissinger had taken us from hinting at invasion of Cuba, to laughing it off as a ridiculous idea. Except, that it was their ridiculous idea. No one else suggested it. Once again—what is their policy? During this last year, they carried on a campaign to befriend Castro. They persuaded the Organization of American States to lift its trade embargo, lifted some of the U.S. trade restrictions. They engaged in cultural exchanges. And then, on the eve of the Florida primary election, Mr. Ford went to Florida, called Castro an outlaw and said he'd never recognize him. But he hasn't asked our Latin American neighbors to reimpose a single sanction, nor has he taken any action himself. Meanwhile, Castro continues to export revolution to Puerto Rico, to Angola, and who knows where else?

Mr. Ford says détente will be replaced by "peace through strength." Well now, that slogan has a—a nice ring to it, but neither Mr. Ford nor his new Secretary of Defense will say that our strength is superior to all others. In one of the dark hours of the Great Depression, Franklin Delano Roosevelt said, "It is time to speak the truth frankly and boldly." Well, I believe former Secretary of Defense James Schlesinger was trying to speak the truth frankly and boldly to his fellow citizens. And that's why he is no longer Secretary of Defense.

The Soviet Army outnumbers ours more than two-to-one and in reserves four-to-one. They out-spend us on weapons by 50 percent. Their Navy outnumbers ours in surface ships and submarines two-to-one. We're outgunned in artillery three-to-one and their tanks outnumber ours four-to-one. Their strategic nuclear missiles are larger, more powerful and more numerous than ours. The evidence mounts that we are Number Two in a world where it's dangerous, if not fatal, to be second best. Is this why Mr. Ford refused to invite Alexander Solzhenitsyn to the White House? Or, why Mr. Ford traveled halfway 'round the world to sign the Helsinki Pact, putting our stamp of approval on Russia's enslavement of the captive nations? We gave away the freedom of millions of people—freedom that was not ours to give.

Now we must ask if someone is giving away our own freedom. Dr. Kissinger is quoted as saying that he thinks of the United States as Athens and the Soviet Union as Sparta. "The day of the U.S. is past and today is the day of the Soviet Union." And he added, " . . . My Job as Secretary of State is to negotiate the most acceptable second-best position available." Well, I believe in the peace of which Mr. Ford spoke—as much as any man. But peace does not come from weakness or from retreat. It comes from the restoration of American military superiority.

Ask the people of Latvia, Estonia, Lithuania, Czechoslovakia, Poland, Hungary—all the others: East Germany, Bulgaria, Romania—ask them what it's like to live in a world where the Soviet Union is Number One. I don't want to live in that kind of world; and I don't think you do either. Now we learn that another high official of the State Department, Helmut Sonnenfeldt, whom Dr. Kissinger refers to as his "Kissinger," has expressed the belief that, in effect, the captive nations should give up any claim of national sovereignty and simply become part of the Soviet Union. He says, "their desire to break out of the Soviet straightjacket" threatens us with World War III. In other words, slaves should accept their fate.

Well, I don't believe the people I've met in almost every State of this Union are ready to consign this, the last island of freedom, to the dust bin of history, along with the bones of dead civilizations of the past. Call it mysticism, if you will, but I believe God had a divine purpose in placing this land between the two great oceans to be found by those who had a special love of freedom and the courage to leave the countries of their birth. From our forefathers to our modern-day immigrants, we've come from every corner of the earth, from every race and every ethnic background, and we've become a new breed in the world. We're Americans and we have a rendezvous with destiny.

18. Carter-Ford Debate about Détente, October 6, 1976

Gerald Ford, the incumbent, lost the 1976 presidential election to a relatively unknown former governor of Georgia, James E. Carter. A key message of the Carter campaign had been a relentless critique of the "immorality" and secrecy of American foreign policy during the Nixon and Ford presidencies. This line of argumentation—as well as the claim that America had been weakened by détente—came across during a televised presidential debate only weeks before Election Day. Ford's defense of the Republican record was marred by his famous statement denying that Poland was a Soviet satellite.

Source: John T. Woolley and Gerhard Peters, eds., *The American Presidency Project,* http://www.presidency.ucsb.edu/ws/?pid=6414.

MR. FRANKEL. Governor, since the Democrats last ran our foreign policy, including many of the men who are advising you, the country has been relieved of the Vietnam agony and the military draft; we've started arms control negotiations with the Russians; we've opened relations with China; we've arranged the disengagement in the Middle East; we've regained influence with the Arabs without deserting Israel. Now, maybe, we've even begun a process of peaceful change in Africa.

Now, you've objected in this campaign to the style with which much of this was done, and you've mentioned some other things that you think ought to have been done. But do you really have a quarrel with this Republican record? Would you not have done any of those things?

MR. CARTER. Well, I think this Republican administration has been almost all style and spectacular and not substance. We've got a chance tonight to talk about, first of all, leadership, the character of our country, and a vision of the future. In every one of these instances, the Ford administration has failed. And I hope tonight that I and Mr. Ford will have a chance to discuss the reason for those failures.

Our country is not strong anymore; we're not respected anymore. We can only be strong overseas if we're strong at home, and when I become President, we'll not only be strong in those areas but also in defense—a defense capability second to none.

We've lost, in our foreign policy, the character of the American people. We've ignored or excluded the American people and the Congress from participation in the shaping of our foreign policy. It's been one of secrecy and exclusion.

In addition to that, we've had a chance to become now, contrary to our long-standing beliefs and principles, the arms merchant of the whole world. We've tried to buy success from our enemies, and at the same time we've excluded from the process the normal friendship of our allies.

In addition to that, we've become fearful to compete with the Soviet Union on an equal basis. We talk about detente. The Soviet Union knows what they want in detente, and they've been getting it. We have not known what we've wanted, and we've been out-traded in almost every instance.

The other point I want to make is about our defense. We've got to be a nation blessed with the defense capability that's efficient, tough, capable, well organized, narrowly focused fighting capability. The ability to fight if necessary is the best way to avoid the chance for or the requirement to fight.

And the last point I want to make is this: Mr. Ford, Mr. Kissinger have continued on with the policies and failures of Richard Nixon. Even the Republican platform has criticized the lack of leadership in Mr. Ford, and they've criticized the foreign policy of this administration. This is one instance where I agree with the Republican platform.

I might say this in closing, and that is, that as far as foreign policy goes, Mr. Kissinger has been the President of this country. Mr. Ford has shown an absence of leadership and an absence of a grasp of what this country is and what it ought to be. That's got to be changed, and that is one of the major issues in this campaign of 1976.

THE MODERATOR. President Ford, would you like to respond?

THE PRESIDENT. Governor Carter again is talking in broad generalities. Let me take just one question that he raises—the military strength and capability of the United States. Governor Carter, in November of 1975, indicated that he wanted to cut the defense budget by $15 billion. A few months later he said he wanted to cut the defense budget by $8 billion or $9 billion. And more recently he talks about cutting the defense budget by $5 billion to $7 billion. There is no way you can be strong militarily and have those kinds of reductions in our military appropriations.

Now let me just tell you a little story. About late October of 1975, I asked the then Secretary of Defense, Mr. Schlesinger, to tell me what had to be done if we were going to reduce the defense budget by $3 to $5 billion. A few days later Mr. Schlesinger came back and said if we cut the defense budget by $3 to $5 billion, we will have to cut military personnel by 250,000, civilian personnel by 100,000, jobs in America by 100,000. We would have to stretch out our aircraft procurement. We would have to reduce our naval construction program. We would have to reduce the research and development for the Army, the Navy, the Air Force, and Marines by 8 percent. We would have to close 20 military bases in the United States immediately. That's the kind of a defense program that Mr. Carter wants.

Let me tell you this straight from the shoulder: You don't negotiate with Mr. Brezhnev from weakness. And the kind of a defense program that Mr. Carter wants will mean a weaker defense and a poorer negotiating position.

MR. FRANKEL. Mr. President, I'd like to explore a little more deeply our relationship with the Russians. They used to brag, back in Khrushchev's day, that because of their greater patience and because of our greed for business deals, that they would sooner or later get the better of us. Is it possible that, despite some setbacks in the Middle East, they've proved their point? Our allies in France and Italy are now flirting with communism; we've recognized a permanent Communist regime in East Germany; we virtually signed, in Helsinki, an agreement that the Russians have dominance in Eastern Europe; we bailed out Soviet agriculture with our huge grain sales, we've given them large loans, access to our best technology, and if the Senate hadn't interfered with the Jackson Amendment, maybe you would have given them even larger loans. Is that what you call a two-way street of traffic in Europe?

THE PRESIDENT. I believe that we have negotiated with the Soviet Union since I've been President from a position of strength. And let me cite several examples.

Shortly after I became President, in December of 1974, I met with General Secretary Brezhnev in Vladivostok. And we agreed to a mutual cap on the ballistic missile launchers at a ceiling of 2,400, which means that the Soviet Union, if that becomes a permanent agreement, will have to make a reduction in their launchers that they now have or plan to have. I negotiated at Vladivostok with Mr. Brezhnev a limitation on the MIRVing of their ballistic missiles at a figure of 1,320, which is the first time that any President has achieved a cap either on launchers or on MIRV's.

It seems to me that we can go from there to the grain sales. The grain sales have been a benefit to American agriculture. We have achieved a 5 3/4-year sale of a minimum of 6 million metric tons, which means that they have already bought about 4 million metric tons this year and are bound to buy another 2 million metric tons, to take the grain and corn and wheat that the American farmers have produced in order to have full production. And these grain sales to the Soviet Union have helped us tremendously in meeting the cost of the additional oil and the oil that we have bought from overseas.

If we turn to Helsinki—I am glad you raised it, Mr. Frankel—in the case of Helsinki, 35 nations signed an agreement, including the Secretary of State for the Vatican. I can't under any circumstances believe that His Holiness the Pope would agree, by signing that agreement, that the 35 nations have turned over to the

Warsaw Pact nations the domination of Eastern Europe. It just isn't true. And if Mr. Carter alleges that His Holiness, by signing that, has done it, he is totally inaccurate.

Now, what has been accomplished by the Helsinki agreement? Number one, we have an agreement where they notify us and we notify them of any military maneuvers that are to be undertaken. They have done it in both cases where they've done so. There is no Soviet domination of Eastern Europe, and there never will be under a Ford administration.

MR. FRANKEL. I'm sorry, could I just follow—did I understand you to say, sir, that the Russians are not using Eastern Europe as their own sphere of influence and occupying most of the countries there and making sure with their troops that it's a Communist zone, whereas on our side of the line the Italians and the French are still flirting with the possibility of communism?

THE PRESIDENT. I don't believe, Mr. Frankel, that the Yugoslavians consider themselves dominated by the Soviet Union. I don't believe that the Romanians consider themselves dominated by the Soviet Union. I don't believe that the Poles consider themselves dominated by the Soviet Union. Each of those countries is independent, autonomous; it has its own territorial integrity. And the United States does not concede that those countries are under the domination of the Soviet Union. As a matter of fact, I visited Poland, Yugoslavia, and Romania, to make certain that the people of those countries understood that the President of the United States and the people of the United States are dedicated to their independence, their autonomy, and their freedom.

THE MODERATOR. Governor Carter, have you a response?

MR. CARTER. Well, in the first place, I am not criticizing His Holiness the Pope. I was talking about Mr. Ford.

The fact is that secrecy has surrounded the decisions made by the Ford administration. In the case of the Helsinki agreement, it may have been a good agreement at the beginning, but we have failed to enforce the so-called Basket 3 part, which ensures the right of people to migrate, to join their families, to be free to speak out. The Soviet Union is still jamming Radio Free Europe. Radio Free Europe is being jammed.

We've also seen a very serious problem with the so-called Sonnenfeldt document which, apparently, Mr. Ford has just endorsed, which said that there is an organic linkage between the Eastern European countries and the Soviet Union. And I would like to see Mr. Ford convince the Polish Americans and the Czech Americans and the Hungarian Americans in this county that those countries don't live under the domination and supervision of the Soviet Union behind the Iron Curtain.

We also have seen Mr. Ford exclude himself from access to the public. He hasn't had a tough, cross-examination-type press conference in over 30 days. One press conference he had without sound.

He's also shown a weakness in yielding to pressure. The Soviet Union, for instance, put pressure on Mr. Ford, and he refused to see a symbol of human freedom recognized around the world—Alexander Solzhenitsyn. . . .

19. Jimmy Carter's Letter to Leonid Brezhnev, February 15, 1977

Having narrowly defeated Gerald Ford in November 1976, Jimmy Carter set out to implement his human rights–oriented foreign policy while simultaneously building upon the nuclear arms control agreements of the past. In his first top secret exchanges of letters with Soviet general secretary Brezhnev, Carter attempted to extend the détente process, while making clear that he expected Soviet cooperation in areas such as human rights.

Source: Jussi Hanhimäki and Odd Arne Westad, eds., *The Cold War: A History in Documents and Eyewitness Accounts* (Oxford: Oxford University Press, 2003), 535–36.

Dear Mr. General Secretary,

I am very pleased to note that our first exchange of letters has brought us at once to consideration of the central questions of universal peace. Our two great countries share a special responsibility not only for doing everything possible for the lessening of tension, but also for working out a series of mutual understandings which can lead to a more reliable and less dangerous political climate in the world.

I know the history of your country and admire it. As a child I developed my literary taste reading your classics. I also know how much suffering your people endure[d] very recently, during the last war. I know about your own role in this war and about the losses suffered by each Soviet family. That is why I believe that we both are sincere in our declarations about our devotion to peace, and that gives me hope for the future.

The question is how we can turn this devotion into reality. How can we start a process which could widen our cooperation and simultaneously restrain and finally limit our rivalry. This rivalry—it is real, extremely expensive, and undeniable—can at any moment become very dangerous, which is why we must not allow it to develop without restraint. In my opinion, this demands, at least, first, work to widen where possible our coordinated efforts, especially in the area of limitation of nuclear weapons; and second, to demonstrate highly deliberate restraint towards those unstable regions of the world where direct confrontation could arise between us. . . .

I agree that in our exchanges of opinion and in the conversations which Secretary of State Vance will have in Moscow at the end of March we must concentrate mainly on the question of achieving an agreement on the second stage of strategic arms limitation, possibly including some significant reductions of the level of forces. Maybe we could bring these negotiations to a successful conclusion if we agree that this is only the first step in the process which could lead to bigger reductions in our respective nuclear arsenals. . . .

I can assure you that in the analysis of our arms control policy which I am carrying out at the present time, all applicable proposals will be considered. As I said during a conversation with your Ambassador, I hope that we can consider not only the question of possible sharp reductions of the total quantity of nuclear weapons, i.e. the question of the minimum number of missiles which would allow every country to feel secure from a first blow, but also the question of restrictions on throw weights, of the possibility of a ban on all mobile missiles, of refusal to take any long-term preparatory measures in the field of civil defense, and also of such additional confidence building measures as preliminary warning of all missile tests and achieving an agreement on the nonarming of satellites and an agreement to reject development of capability to destroy observation satellites. We also have to study practical means to satisfy our mutual desire that our agreements be observed. Such measures as on-site inspection and uninterrupted observation from space must [be] the subject of correct interpretation. These are the means, which can be used to achieve progress, and to win society's support and understanding of our efforts. . . .

We expect cooperation in the realization of further steps toward the fulfill-ment of the agreements reached in Helsinki relating to human rights. As I said to Ambassador Dobrynin, we hope that all aspects of these agreements can be real-ized. It is not our intention to interfere in the internal affairs of other countries. We do not wish to create problems with the Soviet Union, but it will be necessary for our Administration from time to time to publicly express the sincere and deep feelings which our people and I feel. Our obligation to help promote human rights will not be expressed in an extreme form or by means not proportional to achiev-ing reasonable results. We would also welcome, of course, personal, confidential exchanges of views on these delicate questions. . . .

Permit me to say a few words about our efforts to improve the situation in other areas, where there exists disagreements and potential conflicts. . . . In south-ern Africa, we believe that the Africans should solve their problems without out-side interference. It is with this goal in mind that we support a peaceful solution, which corresponds to the will of the majority, and have limited actions which could increase the potential for violence.

20. Jimmy Carter's Commencement Address
at Notre Dame University, May 22, 1977

Carter's dual policy of human rights promotion and nuclear disarmament was on pub-lic display throughout the first year of his presidency, including in this speech at Notre Dame University.

Source: John T. Woolley and Gerhard Peters, *The American Presidency Project*, http://www.presidency.ucsb.edu/ws/?pid=7552.

I have a quiet confidence in our own political system. Because we know that democracy works, we can reject the arguments of those rulers who deny human rights to their people.

We are confident that democracy's example will be compelling, and so we seek to bring that example closer to those from whom in the past few years we have been separated and who are not yet convinced about the advantages of our kind of life.

We are confident that the democratic methods are the most effective, and so we are not tempted to employ improper tactics here at home or abroad.

We are confident of our own strength, so we can seek substantial mutual reductions in the nuclear arms race.

And we are confident of the good sense of American people, and so we let them share in the process of making foreign policy decisions. We can thus speak with the voices of 215 million, and not just of an isolated handful.

Democracy's great recent successes—in India, Portugal, Spain, Greece— show that our confidence in this system is not misplaced. Being confident of our own future, we are now free of that inordinate fear of communism which once led us to embrace any dictator who joined us in that fear. I'm glad that that's being changed.

For too many years, we've been willing to adopt the flawed and erroneous principles and tactics of our adversaries, sometimes abandoning our own values for theirs. We've fought fire with fire, never thinking that fire is better quenched with water. This approach failed, with Vietnam the best example of its intellectual and moral poverty. But through failure we have now found our way back to our own principles and values, and we have regained our lost confidence.

By the measure of history, our Nation's 200 years are very brief, and our rise to world eminence is briefer still. It dates from 1945, when Europe and the old international order lay in ruins. Before then, America was largely on the periphery of world affairs. But since then, we have inescapably been at the center of world affairs.

Our policy during this period was guided by two principles: a belief that Soviet expansion was almost inevitable but that it must be contained, and the corresponding belief in the importance of an almost exclusive alliance among non-Communist nations on both sides of the Atlantic. That system could not last forever unchanged. Historical trends have weakened its foundation. The unifying threat of conflict with the Soviet Union has become less intensive, even though the competition has become more extensive.

The Vietnamese war produced a profound moral crisis, sapping worldwide faith in our own policy and our system of life, a crisis of confidence made even more grave by the covert pessimism of some of our leaders.

In less than a generation, we've seen the world change dramatically. The daily lives and aspirations of most human beings have been transformed. Colonialism is nearly gone. A new sense of national identity now exists in almost 100 new countries that have been formed in the last generation. Knowledge has become more widespread. Aspirations are higher. As more people have been freed from traditional constraints, more have been determined to achieve, for the first time in their lives, social justice.

The world is still divided by ideological disputes, dominated by regional conflicts, and threatened by danger that we will not resolve the differences of race and wealth without violence or without drawing into combat the major military powers. We can no longer separate the traditional issues of war and peace from the new global questions of justice, equity, and human rights.

It is a new world, but America should not fear it. It is a new world, and we should help to shape it. It is a new world that calls for a new American foreign policy—a policy based on constant decency in its values and on optimism in our historical vision.

We can no longer have a policy solely for the industrial nations as the foundation of global stability, but we must respond to the new reality of a politically awakening world.

We can no longer expect that the other 150 nations will follow the dictates of the powerful, but we must continue—confidently—our efforts to inspire, to persuade, and to lead.

Our policy must reflect our belief that the world can hope for more than simple survival and our belief that dignity and freedom are fundamental spiritual requirements. Our policy must shape an international system that will last longer than secret deals.

We cannot make this kind of policy by manipulation. Our policy must be open; it must be candid; it must be one of constructive global involvement, resting on five cardinal principles.

I've tried to make these premises clear to the American people since last January. Let me review what we have been doing and discuss what we intend to do.

First, we have reaffirmed America's commitment to human rights as a fundamental tenet of our foreign policy. In ancestry, religion, color, place of origin, and cultural background, we Americans are as diverse a nation as the world has ever seen. No common mystique of blood or soil unites us. What draws us together, perhaps more than anything else, is a belief in human freedom. We want the world to know that our Nation stands for more than financial prosperity.

This does not mean that we can conduct our foreign policy by rigid moral maxims. We live in a world that is imperfect and which will always be imperfect—a world that is complex and confused and which will always be complex and confused.

I understand fully the limits of moral suasion. We have no illusion that changes will come easily or soon. But I also believe that it is a mistake to undervalue the power of words and of the ideas that words embody. In our own history, that power has ranged from Thomas Paine's "Common Sense" to Martin Luther King, Jr.'s "I Have a Dream."

In the life of the human spirit, words are action, much more so than many of us may realize who live in countries where freedom of expression is taken for granted. The leaders of totalitarian nations understand this very well. The proof is that words are precisely the action for which dissidents in those countries are being persecuted.

Nonetheless, we can already see dramatic, worldwide advances in the protection of the individual from the arbitrary power of the state. For us to ignore this trend would be to lose influence and moral authority in the world. To lead it will be to regain the moral stature that we once had.

The great democracies are not free because we are strong and prosperous. I believe we are strong and influential and prosperous because we are free.

Throughout the world today, in free nations and in totalitarian countries as well, there is a preoccupation with the subject of human freedom, human rights. And I believe it is incumbent on us in this country to keep that discussion, that debate, that contention alive. No other country is as well-qualified as we to set an example. We have our own shortcomings and faults, and we should strive constantly and with courage to make sure that we are legitimately proud of what we have.

Second, we've moved deliberately to reinforce the bonds among our democracies. In our recent meetings in London, we agreed to widen our economic cooperation, to promote free trade, to strengthen the world's monetary system, to seek ways of avoiding nuclear proliferation. We prepared constructive proposals for the forthcoming meetings on North-South problems of poverty, development, and global well-being. And we agreed on joint efforts to reinforce and to modernize our common defense.

You may be interested in knowing that at this NATO meeting, for the first time in more than 25 years, all members are democracies. Even more important, all of us reaffirmed our basic optimism in the future of the democratic system. Our spirit of confidence is spreading. Together, our democracies can help to shape the wider architecture of global cooperation.

Third, we've moved to engage the Soviet Union in a joint effort to halt the strategic arms race. This race is not only dangerous, it's morally deplorable. We must put an end to it.

I know it will not be easy to reach agreements. Our goal is to be fair to both sides, to produce reciprocal stability, parity, and security. We desire a freeze on further modernization and production of weapons and a continuing, substantial reduction of strategic nuclear weapons as well. We want a comprehensive ban on all nuclear testing, a prohibition against all chemical warfare, no attack capability against space satellites, and arms limitations in the Indian Ocean.

We hope that we can take joint steps with all nations toward a final agreement eliminating nuclear weapons completely from our arsenals of death. We will persist in this effort.

Now, I believe in detente with the Soviet Union. To me it means progress toward peace. But the effects of detente should not be limited to our own two countries alone. We hope to persuade the Soviet Union that one country cannot impose its system of society upon another, either through direct military intervention or through the use of a client state's military force, as was the case with Cuban intervention in Angola.

Cooperation also implies obligation. We hope that the Soviet Union will join with us and other nations in playing a larger role in aiding the developing world, for common aid efforts will help us build a bridge of mutual confidence in one another.

21. National Security Council Meeting on the Horn of Africa, March 2, 1978

By 1978 the war between Ethiopia and Somalia caused key members of the Carter administration to worry about the breakdown of superpower détente. In March Secretary of State Cyrus Vance, Secretary of Defense Harold Brown, and National

Security Adviser Zbigniew Brzezinski held a meeting from which the excerpts below are taken.

Source: Hanhimäki and Westad, eds., *The Cold War*, 542–44.

C[yrus] V[ance]: I want you to know what I said in hearings before Congress yesterday. I was asked, "Is there linkage between what is going on in the Horn and SALT?" I replied, "There is not." I did have to recognize that what is happening could affect the political atmosphere. I made a speech for about two minutes on the importance of SALT.

Z[bigniew] B[rzezinski]: The President said in response to a question this noon that there is no linkage but Soviet actions may impose such linkage.

H[arold] B[rown] & CV: That is wrong.

CV: I think it is wrong to say that this is going to produce linkage, and it is of fundamental importance.

ZB: It is going to poison the atmosphere.

CV: We will end up losing SALT and that will be the worst thing that could happen. If we do not get a SALT treaty in the President's first four years, that will be a blemish on his record forever.

ZB: It will be a blemish on his record also if a treaty gets rejected by the Senate.

CV: Zbig, you yesterday and the President today said it may create linkage and I think it is wrong to say that.

V[ice] P[resident Walter Mondale]: How would you see that playing out, Cy?

CV: It will toughen the Russians' position. What is more, we are getting ourselves in a problem here at home. The problem is that people will say that if the Russians are good, are we going to give in to them on something in SALT?

HB: There is going to be linkage—but we should not encourage it.

ZB: What we are saying is that if there is an aggravation of tensions because of what the Soviets are doing in the Horn, there is going to be linkage. That is a statement of fact.

HB: Not all statements of fact should be made.

ZB: The Soviets should be made aware of the fact that they are poisoning the atmosphere.

HB: We should find something else to beat the Soviets with.

CV: I do not think there is much leverage anyway on this issue. . . .

ZB: Let's go to item no. 2: showing our displeasure to the Soviets. Frank Press has developed a memorandum on bilateral relationships—space, transportation and housing seem to be the areas in which we have the least interest. . . .

HB: It most favors them and these are the ones we want to find.

ZB: I am convinced about the moondoggle.

HB: I think we should consider cancelling the meeting—not just postponing it.

VP: It is all pretty puny.

ZB: None of this amounts to much by itself except to convey displeasure on the Horn.

HB: The Salyut one they will feel. . . .

HB: I have an idea re China. The Chinese are less concerned about the aggressor. Why don't we get together with the Chinese in Warsaw and issue a joint statement of concern about the Horn and append to it a statement that we will consult on other areas where we have a joint interest? That would get the Soviets' attention.

CV: That would get their attention but we are at the point where we are on the brink of ending up with a real souring of relations between ourselves and the Soviet Union and it may take a helluva long while to change and may not be changed for years and I think that is a very important step to take—we should examine it carefully before we go down that road.

HB: It is an important step—it is not like postponing or cancelling a meeting on space. I am struck by the approach the Chinese ambassador made the other day to our ambassador in the Sudan. They want to be in close touch with us.

ZB: On this business of souring relations with the Soviets, the real question is why are they being soured? Do the Soviets want to sour these relations? If they can do what they want in the Horn without getting evidence of concern from us, we are going to have major problems with them in the south. We should communicate to the Soviets that they do not have a free hand and that what they do entails risks. Otherwise, what will they think? . . .

CV: I think the key still remains SALT. If we make progress on SALT, then a lot of things will fall into place that do not fall into place otherwise.

HB: I do not think a SALT treaty would make any difference—if we had it now, they would be reacting in the same way.

ZB: They must understand that there are consequences in their behavior. If we do not react, we are destroying our own posture—regionally and internationally and we are creating the conditions for domestic reaction.

CV: This is where you and I part. The consequences of doing something like this are very dangerous.

22. Brezhnev's Speech to the Politburo on the International Situation, June 8, 1978

After his discussions with President Carter in Washington in May 1978, Foreign Minister Andrei Gromyko returned to the Soviet Union to brief the Politburo on American policy goals. Reflecting upon this report and other developments, General Secretary Brezhnev expressed serious pessimism about the prospects for détente in his speech to the Politburo in early June 1978.

Source: Document #5034F5A8-96B6-175C-9DD9D17B9F404E16, Digital Archive, Cold War International History Project, Woodrow Wilson Center, http://www.wilsoncenter.org/digital-archive.

Com. Gromyko has performed considerable and useful work during his time in America both in terms of participation in the special session of the General Assembly of the UN, as well as in the course of his negotiations with Carter and Vance, and also at the time of bilateral meetings and discussions with representatives of many countries. I think that it is fitting to approve this work and to record this in our resolution.

But it would be, probably, incorrect to limit ourselves only to this. From the report of com. Gromyko, and likewise from the extensive information which has reached us recently through various channels, it is completely apparent that we are experiencing a very complicated period in the development of international relations. A serious deterioration and exacerbation of the situation has occurred. And the primary source of this deterioration is the growing aggression of the foreign policy of the Carter government, the continually more sharply anti-Soviet character of the statements of the President himself and of his closest colleagues—in the first instance those of Brzezinski.

Judging from appearances, Carter is not simply falling under the usual influence of the most shameless anti-Soviet types and ringleaders of the military-industrial complex of the USA, but is intent upon struggling for his election to a new term as President of the USA under the banner of anti-Soviet policy and a return to the "cold war."

This line of the government of the USA is putting its stamp on the policy of the Western powers both in the NATO bloc, and in Africa, and in relation to China.

The question arises, how are we to react to all of this?

I think that passivity here is inadmissible. We must fight actively and persistently for peace and détente. We must do all that is possible in order to hinder the policy, which is fraught with the threat of a new world war. Here we need energetic steps, noticeable for the whole world.

Concretely, if we are speaking of the immediate period, it would be possible, it seems to me, to do the following.

First. We should come forward in our press (simultaneously in all of the main newspapers) with a large and serious declaration, calling it, let's say, "Concerning the policy of the Carter government." We should publish this declaration without any sort of signature—this will even attract more attention to it. In it we should say directly, that in the policy of the USA changes are taking place which are dangerous for the affairs of peace. Under the curtain of lies and slander on the USSR and other socialist countries, concrete matters are being perpetrated, directed against peace and detente. The course of negotiations with the Soviet Union on the limitations of strategic arms is intentionally being retarded. Attempts at clumsy interference in our internal affairs are being perpetrated, in fact, the ties between both countries are being curtailed. New extensive plans for the arms race are being made, and for decades in advance, at the very time when the peoples hoped for disarmament. The current creators of American policy, it seems, have already found a common language with the aggressive anti-Soviet rulers of China, who, as it is known, declare peace and detente to be a fraud, and war to be the single realistic prospect.

The government of the USA has become the inspiration for a new colonialism in Africa—the policy of armed intervention and open interference in the affairs of African governments, the merciless suppression of revolutionary liberation processes.

It is all of these current tendencies in the foreign policy of the Carter government which have lent the central color to the work of the last session of the Council of NATO in Washington. Encouraging its adherents, dragging after itself those who waver and doubt, putting pressure on the dissenting participants of this bloc, the USA is attempting once again to push it onto the road of the "cold war" and of active preparation for a hot war.

So all of these dangerous sides of the current policies of Carter should be [described], without excessive dramatization, but clearly shown in such a document. It is necessary to show both to other countries and to communities in the USA itself, just how dangerous a game Carter, Brzezinski, and their likes are starting.

We should conclude this text with a calm and clear confirmation of our course towards detente and towards the development of good, mutually beneficial relations with the United States.

Second. We should come forward with a collective declaration of governments—participants in the Warsaw Pact regarding the results of the session of the Council of NATO. This document, taking into consideration the necessity of its approval, among others by the Romanians, should be made less sharp, with emphasis on the constructive elements of our policy.

We should note with regret, that the work of the session of the Council of NATO and its resolutions do not serve detente or the consolidation of peace, but the exacerbation of the international situation and the intensification of military preparations, the arms race. Urgent calls for the increase of allotments, the agitation of the NATO representatives for neutron, chemical, bacteriological arms, the forcing through of long-term programs for the production of arms of all types—this is the real meaning of this session and of that which follows after it.

The countries of the Warsaw Pact condemn this policy and are certain that the peoples of other countries will condemn it. There is an attempt to impose on us a continually broader competition in arms. But we decisively come forward for keeping in check the arms race, for concrete agreements on these questions in all forums. The Soviet Union is doing all that is dependent on it for the successful completion of negotiations with the USA concerning SALT. The socialist countries occupy a flexible position and are developing concrete constructive initiatives at the Vienna talks. The countries of the Warsaw Pact are coming forward for the strict observance of the principles of peaceful coexistence, against interference in the internal affairs of other countries—whether in the form of armed intervention or subversive activities of another sort.

And we should conclude this document with a persistent call to return to the path of detente, to the path of mutual respect and mutually beneficial cooperation, which is clearly indicated in the document of the Helsinki Summit, in Soviet-American and other bilateral documents, and in numerous resolutions of the UN.

Third. We should come forward with a special Declaration of the Soviet government on African affairs. In this document we should categorically refute and expose the imperialist intentions with regard to the policy of the Soviet Union and other socialist countries in Africa, among them the region of the Horn of Africa, in Zaire, etc. Briefly and in calm tones we should say how it is in reality. At the same time with all sharpness we should condemn the policy of armed intervention, subversive activity and other forms of interference in African affairs by the governments of NATO headed by the USA. We should show how the contemporary colonizers, operating with the hypocritical slogan, "African solidarity," enlist accomplices for themselves in Africa from the numbers of reactionary, anti-popular regimes, for carrying out their own policy. We should express our conviction that genuine African solidarity will take hold—the single will of independent countries and the free peoples of Africa, their resoluteness to assert the independence of their countries and the freedom of their internal development.

These are the three documents, it seems to me, that it would be possible to prepare in the immediate future and come forth with them. Of course, this is not to be done in one day, but somehow intelligently distributed over time.

Simultaneously it would be possible to prepare instructions for our ambassadors in progressive and other more or less independent governments in Africa for carrying out the corresponding work with their guidance.

23. Ambassador Dobrynin on U.S.-Soviet Relations, July 11, 1978

As the longstanding Soviet ambassador to Washington, Anatoly Dobrynin often had deep insight into U.S. foreign policy making. In the summer of 1978 his pessimism about the future of détente was palpable, evidenced throughout the excerpts of this report on the state of Soviet-American relations that he sent to the Politburo in July.

Source: Document #5034F5B8-96B6-175C-9405378C6C223C5B, Digital Archive, Cold War International History Project, Woodrow Wilson Center, http://www.wilsoncenter.org/digital-archive.

Almost eighteen months ago—January 20, 1977—the new, 39th President of the United States, J. Carter, stepped across the threshold of the White House. Since that time, a definite policy has been conducted by his administration, the basic elements of which are the subject of the review in the present political letter.

As has already been noted by the Embassy, Soviet-American relations during the Carter Administration have been characterized by instability, major swings, which to a great extent are due to its calculations of the state of affairs in both its internal and external dimensions.

In the middle of April of this year, Carter, as is well known, conducted in his country residence, Camp David, a meeting of the members of his cabinet and closest advisors, at which was taken a decision to carry out a regular reevaluation of Soviet-American relations. The initiative for this affair came from Brzezinski and several Presidential advisors on domestic affairs, who convinced Carter that he would succeed in stopping the process of worsening of his position in the country if he would openly initiate a harsher course vis a vis the Soviet Union.

Africa (events on the Horn of Africa, and then in the Shaba Province of Zaire) was chosen as the pretext around which the Administration would begin earnestly to create tension in Soviet-American relations. In fact, in connection to these African events it was decided to attempt a review of the entire concept of the policy of detente, subordinating it to the needs of the Administration, not stopping even before publicly putting under threat the chances of concluding a new agreement on the limitation of offensive strategic weapons (by artificially linking it with other issues).

In the country, however, by the way pretty unexpectedly for Carter, this "harsh" course, which had been firmly and clearly rejected by the Soviet Union, caused a reaction in which was evident a clear apprehension among broad strata of the American population regarding the long-term condition and fate of Soviet-

American relations. There was expressed the depth of the American mood in support of the policy of detente, which had developed in the course of the last few years and which in the minds of the unsophisticated residents of this country is associated with a simple thesis: detente mitigates the threat of confrontation with the Soviet Union, and thus, of nuclear war with it. Characteristically, there were such apprehensions even in the Congress, the representatives of which began to demand explanations of the Administration, where anyway the matter of relations with the Soviet Union is heading and wasn't the Administration trying to bring about some sort of big changes in these relations without the consent of the Congress.

And so, Carter became convinced that detente is not a "faucet" which he can turn on and off whenever he feels so disposed. The Administration was obliged to quickly make some adjustments in its position (particularly in light of the speech of L.I. Brezhnev, and also our answer in Pravda to Carter's speech in Annapolis, which he had found to be unexpectedly firm). The President, having let Vance go out front, decided to restrain Brzezinski a bit. Vance usually stresses the positive accomplishments in Soviet-American relations without leaving out, however, the negative things which are associated with Carter himself (for example, the notorious policy of "defense of human rights" or "dissidents") . . .

Consequently, in so far as it is possible to judge on the basis of information which the Embassy has at its disposal, the Carter Administration has come to its own variety of a selective, half-hearted conception of detente (of which Brzezinski himself first accused us). Detente in its current concrete application by the White House is, as if, being partitioned. It is seen as important and necessary—in support of the national interests of the United States itself and the corresponding formation of public opinion—regarding problems associated with nuclear weapons, issues of war and peace (limitation of strategic weapons, a total ban on nuclear tests, certain other disarmament-related issues). As far as the majority of other questions is concerned, as in the past it is applied subject to the "behavior" of the Soviet Union in Africa, in the Middle East, in relation to "human rights," and so on. The reaction of the Administration to the recently-begun Shcharansky process is in this regard sufficiently instructive.

The Carter Administration variously denies that it is supporting a return to the "Cold War." It seems that it fears a decline of relations with the Soviet Union to a level when the threat of a serious, to say nothing of a military conflict with us would be interpreted by the American people, and also in other countries of the world, as something real. Carter, evidently has come to realize that this would cause deep alarm among the population of the country and would for him be a political loss, and maybe would represent a catastrophe in the 1980 presidential elections. In this regard the choice—"cooperation or confrontation"—which he tried to pose for us in his speech in Annapolis, seemed in its essence directed in the United States itself to him personally; the heartland is expecting from Carter himself an answer to that choice, and he—thanks to the adherence to principal [sic] in our position—has turned out to have not quite as free a choice as he tried to present it.

24. NATO's Double-Track Decision, December 1979

On December 12, 1979, less than two weeks before the Soviet invasion of Afghanistan commenced, NATO allies decided to introduce the new American medium-range Pershing II and cruise missiles in Western Europe. This excerpt from the meeting's official communiqué explains the decision, which was, in essence, a response to new Soviet missile deployments.

Source: Special Meeting of Foreign and Defense Ministers, NATO, http://www.nato.int/cps/en/natolive/official_texts_27040.htm?selectedLocale=en.

3. The Warsaw Pact has over the years developed a large and growing capability in nuclear systems that directly threaten Western Europe and have a strategic significance for the Alliance in Europe. This situation has been especially aggravated over the last few years by Soviet decisions to implement programmes modernising and expanding their long-range nuclear capability substantially. In particular, they have deployed the SS-20 missile, which offers significant improvements over previous systems in providing greater accuracy, more mobility, and greater range, as well as having multiple warheads, and the Backfire bomber, which has a much better performance than other Soviet aircraft deployed hitherto in a theatre role. During this period, while the Soviet Union has been reinforcing its superiority in Long-Range Theatre Nuclear Forces (LRTNF) both quantitatively and qualitatively, Western LRTNF capabilities have remained static. Indeed these forces are

increasing in age and vulnerability and do not include land-based, long-range theatre nuclear missile systems.

4. At the same time, the Soviets have also undertaken a modernisation and expansion of their shorter-range TNF and greatly improved the overall quality of their conventional forces. These developments took place against the background of increasing Soviet inter-continental capabilities and achievement of parity in inter-continental capability with the United States.

5. These trends have prompted serious concern within the Alliance, because, if they were to continue, Soviet superiority in theatre nuclear systems could undermine the stability achieved in inter-continental systems and cast doubt on the credibility of the Alliance's deterrent strategy by highlighting the gap in the spectrum of NATO's available nuclear response to aggression.

6. Ministers noted that these recent developments require concrete actions on the part of the Alliance if NATO's strategy of flexible response is to remain credible. After intensive consideration, including the merits of alternative approaches, and after taking note of the positions of certain members, Ministers concluded that the overall interest of the Alliance would best be served by pursuing two parallel and complementary approaches of TNF modernisation and arms control.

7. Accordingly Ministers have decided to modernise NATO's LRTNF by the deployment in Europe of US ground-launched systems comprising 108 Pershing II launchers, which would replace existing US Pershing I-A, and 464 Ground-Launched Cruise Missiles (GLCM), all with single warheads. All the nations currently participating in the integrated defence structure will participate in the programme: the missiles will be stationed in selected countries and certain support costs will be met through NATO's existing common funding arrangements. . . .

9. . . . . Ministers fully support the decision taken by the United States following consultations within the Alliance to negotiate arms limitations on LRTNF and to propose to the USSR to begin negotiations as soon as possible along the following lines which have been elaborated in intensive consultations within the Alliance:

a. Any future limitations on US systems principally designed for theatre missions should be accompanied by appropriate limitations on Soviet theatre systems.

b. Limitations on US and Soviet long-range theatre nuclear systems should be negotiated bilaterally in the SALT III framework in a step-by-step approach.

c. The immediate objective of these negotiations should be the establishment of agreed limitations on US and Soviet land-based long-range theatre nuclear missile systems.

d. Any agreed limitations on these systems must be consistent with the principle of equality between the sides. Therefore, the limitations should take the form of de jure equality both in ceilings and in rights.

e. Any agreed limitations must be adequately verifiable. . . .

11. The Ministers have decided to pursue these two parallel and complementary approaches in order to avert an arms race in Europe caused by the Soviet TNF build-up, yet preserve the viability of NATO's strategy of deterrence and defence and thus maintain the security of its member States.

a. A modernisation decision, including a commitment to deployments, is necessary to meet NATO's deterrence and defence needs, to provide a credible response to unilateral Soviet TNF deployments, and to provide the foundation for the pursuit of serious negotiations on TNF.

b. Success of arms control in constraining the Soviet buildup can enhance Alliance security, modify the scale of NATO's TNF requirements, and promote stability and détente in Europe in consonance with NATO's basic policy of deterrence, defence and détente as enunciated in the Harmel Report. NATO's TNF requirements will be examined in the light of concrete results reached through negotiations.

25. Reasons to Invade Afghanistan, December 27, 1979

By late 1979, with détente in rapid decline on other issues, the Soviet leadership reversed its earlier decision not to intervene directly in Afghanistan. In this personal

memorandum to Soviet leader Brezhnev from early December 1979, the head of the
KGB, Yuri Andropov, set out the key arguments for an invasion.

Source: Document #B66BA25A-FF9E-199E-171756AA7EDBA860, Digital
Archive, Cold War International History Project, Woodrow Wilson Center,
http://www.wilsoncenter.org/digital-archive.

After the coup and the murder of Taraki in September of this year, the situation
in Afghanistan began to undertake an undesirable turn for us. The situation in the
party, the army and the government apparatus has become more acute, as they
were essentially destroyed as a result of the mass repressions carried out by Amin.

At the same time, alarming information started to arrive about Amin's secret
activities, forewarning of a possible political shift to the West. [These included:]
Contacts with an American agent about issues which are kept secret from us.
Promises to tribal leaders to shift away from USSR and to adopt a "policy of neu-
trality." Closed meetings in which attacks were made against Soviet policy and
the activities of our specialists. The practical removal of our headquarters in Kabul,
etc. The diplomatic circles in Kabul are widely talking of Amin's differences with
Moscow and his possible anti-Soviet steps.

All this has created, on the one hand, the danger of losing the gains made
by the April [1978] revolution (the scale of insurgent attacks will increase by
spring) within the country, while on the other hand—the threat to our positions
in Afghanistan (right now there is no guarantee that Amin, in order to protect his
personal power, will not shift to the West). [There has been] a growth of anti-
Soviet sentiments within the population.

2. Recently we were contacted by [a] group of Afghan communists abroad. In the
course of our contact with Babrak [Karmal] and [Asadullah] Sarwari, it became
clear (and they informed us of this) that they have worked out a plan for opposing Amin and creating new party and state organs. But Amin, as a preventive
measure, has begun mass arrests of "suspect persons" (300 people have been shot).

In these conditions, Babrak and Sarwari, without changing their plans of opposition, have raised the question of possible assistance, in case of need, including military.

We have two battalions stationed in Kabul and there is the capability of rendering such assistance. It appears that this is entirely sufficient for a successful

operation. But, as a precautionary measure in the event of unforeseen complications, it would be wise to have a military group close to the border. In case of the deployment of military forces we could at the same time decide various questions pertaining to the liquidation of gangs.

The implementation of the given operation would allow us to decide the question of defending the gains of the April revolution, establishing Leninist principals in the party and state leadership of Afghanistan, and securing our positions in this country.

26. Jimmy Carter, Address to the Nation on the Soviet Invasion of Afghanistan, January 4, 1980

The December 1979 Soviet invasion of Afghanistan was a surprise to the Carter administration. Its reaction was swift and understandably negative. In early January 1980 the president delivered a nationally televised address in which he relayed a series of punitive actions against the USSR.

Source: John T. Woolley and Gerhard Peters, eds., *The American Presidency Project*, http://www.presidency.ucsb.edu/ws/?pid=32911.

I come to you this evening to discuss the extremely important and rapidly changing circumstances in Southwest Asia.

I continue to share with all of you the sense of outrage and impatience because of the kidnapping of innocent American hostages and the holding of them by militant terrorists with the support and the approval of Iranian officials. Our purposes continue to be the protection of the long-range interests of our Nation and the safety of the American hostages.

We are attempting to secure the release of the Americans through the International Court of Justice, through the United Nations, and through public and private diplomatic efforts. We are determined to achieve this goal. We hope to do so without bloodshed and without any further danger to the lives of our 50 fellow Americans. In these efforts, we continue to have the strong support of the world community. The unity and the common sense of the American people under such trying circumstances are essential to the success of our efforts.

Recently, there has been another very serious development which threatens the maintenance of the peace in Southwest Asia. Massive Soviet military forces have invaded the small, nonaligned, sovereign nation of Afghanistan, which had hitherto not been an occupied satellite of the Soviet Union.

Fifty thousand heavily armed Soviet troops have crossed the border and are now dispersed throughout Afghanistan, attempting to conquer the fiercely independent Muslim people of that country.

The Soviets claim, falsely, that they were invited into Afghanistan to help protect that country from some unnamed outside threat. But the President, who had been the leader of Afghanistan before the Soviet invasion, was assassinated— along with several members of his family—after the Soviets gained control of the capital city of Kabul. Only several days later was the new puppet leader even brought into Afghanistan by the Soviets.

This invasion is an extremely serious threat to peace because of the threat of further Soviet expansion into neighboring countries in Southwest Asia and also because such an aggressive military policy is unsettling to other peoples throughout the world.

This is a callous violation of international law and the United Nations Charter. It is a deliberate effort of a powerful atheistic government to subjugate an independent Islamic people.

We must recognize the strategic importance of Afghanistan to stability and peace. A Soviet-occupied Afghanistan threatens both Iran and Pakistan and is a steppingstone to possible control over much of the world's oil supplies.

The United States wants all nations in the region to be free and to be independent. If the Soviets are encouraged in this invasion by eventual success, and if they maintain their dominance over Afghanistan and then extend their control to adjacent countries, the stable, strategic, and peaceful balance of the entire world will be changed. This would threaten the security of all nations including, of course, the United States, our allies, and our friends.

Therefore, the world simply cannot stand by and permit the Soviet Union to commit this act with impunity. Fifty nations have petitioned the United Nations Security Council to condemn the Soviet Union and to demand the immediate withdrawal of all Soviet troops from Afghanistan. We realize that under the United Nations Charter the Soviet Union and other permanent members may veto action of the Security Council. If the will of the Security Council should be thwarted in this manner, then immediate action would be appropriate in the General Assembly of the United Nations, where no Soviet veto exists.

In the meantime, neither the United States nor any other nation which is committed to world peace and stability can continue to do business as usual with the Soviet Union.

I have already recalled the United States Ambassador from Moscow back to Washington. He's working with me and with my other senior advisers in an immediate and comprehensive evaluation of the whole range of our relations with the Soviet Union.

The successful negotiation of the SALT II treaty has been a major goal and a major achievement of this administration, and we Americans, the people of the Soviet Union, and indeed the entire world will benefit from the successful control of strategic nuclear weapons through the implementation of this carefully negotiated treaty.

However, because of the Soviet aggression, I have asked the United States Senate to defer further consideration of the SALT II treaty so that the Congress and I can assess Soviet actions and intentions and devote our primary attention to the legislative and other measures required to respond to this crisis. As circumstances change in the future, we will, of course, keep the ratification of SALT II under active review in consultation with the leaders of the Senate.

The Soviets must understand our deep concern. We will delay opening of any new American or Soviet consular facilities, and most of the cultural and economic exchanges currently under consideration will be deferred. Trade with the Soviet Union will be severely restricted.

I have decided to halt or to reduce exports to the Soviet Union in three areas that are particularly important to them. These new policies are being and will be coordinated with those of our allies.

I've directed that no high technology or other strategic items will be licensed for sale to the Soviet Union until further notice, while we revise our licensing policy.

Fishing privileges for the Soviet Union in United States waters will be severely curtailed.

The 17 million tons of grain ordered by the Soviet Union in excess of that amount which we are committed to sell will not be delivered. This grain was not intended for human consumption but was to be used for building up Soviet livestock herds.

I am determined to minimize any adverse impact on the American farmer from this action. The undelivered grain will be removed from the market through storage and price support programs and through purchases at market prices. We will also increase amounts of grain devoted to the alleviation of hunger in poor countries, and we'll have a massive increase of the use of grain for gasohol production here at home.

After consultation with other principal grain-exporting nations, I am confident that they will not replace these quantities of grain by additional shipments on their part to the Soviet Union.

These actions will require some sacrifice on the part of all Americans, but there is absolutely no doubt that these actions are in the interest of world peace and in the interest of the security of our own Nation, and they are also compatible with actions being taken by our own major trading partners and others who share our deep concern about this new Soviet threat to world stability.

Although the United States would prefer not to withdraw from the Olympic games scheduled in Moscow this summer, the Soviet Union must realize that its continued aggressive actions will endanger both the participation of athletes and the travel to Moscow by spectators who would normally wish to attend the Olympic games.

Along with other countries, we will provide military equipment, food, and other assistance to help Pakistan defend its independence and its national security against the seriously increased threat it now faces from the north. The United States also stands ready to help other nations in the region in similar ways.

Neither our allies nor our potential adversaries should have the slightest doubt about our willingness, our determination, and our capacity to take the measures I have outlined tonight. I have consulted with leaders of the Congress, and I am confident they will support legislation that may be required to carry out these measures.

History teaches, perhaps, very few clear lessons. But surely one such lesson learned by the world at great cost is that aggression, unopposed, becomes a contagious disease.

The response of the international community to the Soviet attempt to crush Afghanistan must match the gravity of the Soviet action.

With the support of the American people and working with other nations, we will deter aggression, we will protect our Nation's security, and we will preserve the peace.

The United States will meet its responsibilities.

Thank you very much.

27. Soviet Analysis of the Impact of the Soviet Intervention in Afghanistan, January 20, 1980

In this excerpt Academician O. Bogomolov of the Institute of the Economy of the World Socialist System gives a rather pessimistic analysis of the broad impact that the introduction of Soviet troops into Afghanistan is likely to have on the USSR's international position. The analysis was sent to the Central Committee of the CPSU and the KGB in January 1980.

Source: Document #5034E08A-96B6-175C-942922BAB585B8C7, Digital Archive, Cold War International History Project, Woodrow Wilson Center, http://www.wilsoncenter.org/digital-archive. Translated for CWIHP by Gary Goldberg from A. A. Lyakhovskiy's "Plamya Afgana" ("Flame of the Afghanistan veteran"), Iskon, Moscow, 1999.

The introduction of Soviet troops did not lead to the abatement of armed struggle by the opposition against the government. The Islamic fundamentalists have sharply stepped up their propaganda activity among the population using a new slogan: fight against foreign troops. Attempts have been stepped up at joining all Islamic groups into a single anti-government and anti-Soviet front.

After the introduction of the Soviet troops the United States, their allies, some Arab and Muslim countries, and also China announced their support and aid to the opposition. This aid had been given earlier, but now it has grown considerably. Afghanistan ended up isolated at the international level and relies only on the socialist camp, mainly the Soviet Union.

With the introduction of troops into Afghanistan our policy . . . crossed the permissible bounds of confrontation in the "Third World." The advantages of this action turned out to be insignificant compared to the damage which was inflicted on our interests:

1. In addition to the confrontations on two fronts—in Europe against NATO and in East Asia against China—a third dangerous hotbed of military and political tension on the USSR's southern flank has arisen for us in unfavorable geographic and sociopolitical conditions. . . .

2. A considerable expansion and consolidation of the anti-Soviet front of countries surrounding the USSR from west to east has taken place.

3. The influence of the USSR on the Non-Aligned Movement, has suffered considerably, especially in the Muslim world.

4. Détente has been blocked and the political prerequisites to limit the arms race have been destroyed.

5. Economic and technological pressure on the Soviet Union have risen sharply.

6. Western and Chinese propaganda have received strong trump cards to expand a campaign against the Soviet Union in order to undermine its prestige in Western public opinion, developing countries, and also the socialist countries.

7. The Afghan events have eliminated the preconditions for a possible normalization of Soviet-Chinese relations for a long time.

8. These events have served as a catalyst to overcome the crisis relations and for a reconciliation between the Iran and the US.

9. Mistrust toward Soviet policy has been intensified and Yugoslavia, Romania, and North Korea have distanced themselves from it. Even in the Hungarian and Polish press signs have been observed of a restraint in connection with Soviet actions in Afghanistan. Evidently they reflect the sentiments of the public and the fears of the leaders of these countries of being drawn into the global actions of the Soviet Union, for which our partners do not have sufficient resources to participate.

10. The nuanced policy of the Western powers has been intensified and it has switched to a new tactic of active intrusion into the sphere of relations between the Soviet Union and other socialist countries, openly playing on the contradictions and incompatibility of interests between them.

11. The burden of economic aid to Afghanistan has rested on the Soviet Union. . . .

28. Reagan's Televised Address, "A Strategy for Peace in the '80s," October 19, 1980

In the last weeks of the 1980 presidential campaign, polls showed that the sizable lead the Republican challenger had enjoyed over the summer was diminishing. As part of his successful effort to stop Carter's last-minute momentum, Ronald Reagan spoke on national television, criticizing the Carter administration's approach to foreign and security policy.

Source: *Ronald Reagan's Major Speeches, 1964–89, Public Papers of President Ronald W. Reagan,* Ronald Reagan Presidential Library, http://www.reagan.utexas.edu /archives/Reference/10.19.80.html.

Let us base our decisions about peace and security on the facts, on what we need to know and not on what we are told we must fear.

There can be no doubt about what is the major issue in this campaign concerning the question of peace.

It is whether you believe Mr. Carter's words and deeds have brought the United States closer to or further away from the goal of peace based on confidence in the strength of our nation.

As a presidential candidate four years ago, he said: " . . . it is imperative that the world know that we will meet obligations and commitments to our allies and that we will keep our nation strong."

Did he keep his promise? That's the real peace issue in 1980. And that's an issue for you to decide. Has he kept our nation strong? Are you willing to risk four more years of what we have now? Has the registration and the possible draft of your sons and daughters contributed to your peace of mind? Is the world safer for you and your family?

Whatever else history may say about my candidacy. I hope it will be recorded that I appealed to our best hopes, not our worst fears, to our confidence rather than our doubts, to the facts, and not to fantasies.

And these three—hope, confidence, and facts—are at the heart of my vision of peace.

We have heard the phrase "peace through strength" so often, its meaning has become blurred through overuse.

The time has come for America to recall once more the basic truths behind the familiar words.

Peace is *made* by the fact of strength—economic, military, and strategic.

Peace is *lost* when such strength disappears or—just as bad—is seen by an adversary as disappearing.

We must build peace upon strength. There is no other way. And the cold, hard fact of the matter is that our economic, military, and strategic strength under President Carter is eroding.

Only if *we* are strong will peace be strong.

Throughout Scripture, we see reference to peace-makers—those who through their actions—not just their words—take the material of this imperfect world and, with hard work and God's help, fashion from that material peace for the world.

In recent weeks you've been hearing from a lot of other people as to what they say I believe about peace. Well, tonight let me tell you what I believe.

Understanding of how peace is obtained—through competence and hard work, confidence, and patience—must guide and inspire this nation in the years ahead.

And at the center of such peace-making is the need to restore our historic American tradition of bipartisanship.

The cause of peace knows no party. The cause of peace transcends personal ambition. The cause of peace demands appeals for unity, not appeals to divisiveness.

These are truisms—which Mr. Carter has forgotten—or chosen to ignore.

Senator Ted Kennedy said earlier this year, in reference to him, that "no president should be reelected because he happened to be standing there when his foreign policy collapsed around him."

I cannot believe this administration's defense policies reflect the thinking of millions of rank-and-file Democrat party members. The Carter administration, dominated as it is by the McGovernite wing of the party, has broken sharply with the views and policies of Harry Truman, John Kennedy, and many contemporary Democratic leaders.

A great American tradition of bipartisanship—where domestic political differences end at the water's edge—has been lost at a time when we are faced with growing instability and crisis abroad. I believe the bipartisan tradition is too deep and sound to be destroyed by one man in the space of four years, but still, damage has been done and it will take a determined effort to repair it.

I pledge, if elected President, to take every step necessary to restore the bipartisan tradition in American national security and foreign policy; to work with congressional leaders of both parties to design and conduct a truly bipartisan tradition in American national security and foreign policy. And, I intend to have this bipartisan spirit reflected during my presidency in key foreign and defense policy appointive positions. As in the past, our domestic differences will end at the water's edge.

29. Ayatollah Khomeini's Message, 1980

The establishment of the Islamic Republic of Iran was a major setback to American foreign policy. Yet, in 1979–1980 the left wing and the Communists lost the struggle for power in Iran. Instead, groups that promoted a political version of Islam—often referred to as Islamism—took over the government. They were led by the eighty-year-old Ayatollah Ruhollah Khomeini, who issued the following challenge to both the United States and the Soviet Union in his message to pilgrims in September 1980.

Source: Ruhollah Khomeini, *Islam and Revolution: Writings and Declarations*, trans. by Hamid Algar (London: KPI, 1981), 300–306.

Now it is necessary for me to bring certain matters to our attention, free Muslims who have gathered at the site of revelation in order to fulfill a duty that relates both to worship and politics, so that you may be made aware of what is happening in the Muslim countries; what plans are underway to subjugate, exploit, and dominate the Muslims; and what impure hands are engaged in kindling the fires of division.

At a time when all the Muslims in the world are about to join together and achieve mutual understanding between the different schools of thought of Islam, in order to deliver their nations from the foul grasp of the superpowers; at a time when the arms of the Eastern and Western oppressors are about to be foreshortened in Iran, by means of unity and purpose and reliance on God Almighty—precisely at this time, the Great Satan has summoned its agents and instructed them to show dissention among the Muslims by every imaginable means, giving rise to hostility and dispute among brothers in faith who share the belief in *tauhid*, so that nothing will stand in the way of complete domination and plunder. Fearing the Islamic Revolution of Iran will spread to other countries, Muslim and non-Muslim alike, and thus compel it to remove its foul hands from the lands it dominates, the Great Satan is resorting to another stratagem now, after the failure of both the economic boycott and the military attack. It is attempting to distort the nature of our Islamic Revolution in the eyes of Muslims throughout the world in order to set the Muslims at each others' throats while it continues its exploitation and oppression of the Muslim countries. Thus it is that precisely at the time Iran is waging a determined struggle to ensure the unity of all Muslims in the world on the basis of *tauhid* and true Islam, the Great Satan gives its orders to one of the pawns in the region, one of the dead Shah's friends, to obtain decrees from Sunni *fuqaha* and *muftis* to the effect that the Iranians are unbelievers. These pawns of America say that the Islam of Iran is different from the Islam of those who support the pawns of America, like Sadat and Begin, who extend the hand of friendship to the enemies of Islam and flaunt the commands of God Almighty, and who leave no lie and calumny unuttered in their efforts to create disunity among the Muslims. The Muslims of the world must be aware of these people who are attempting to spread dissension, and must frustrate their foul conspiracy.

At a time when the superpowers are attacking Muslim countries like Afghanistan, inflicting pitiless and savage massacres on the Afghan Muslims who wish the destiny of their country to be free from foreign interference, at a time when America has a hand in every form of corruption; at a time when criminal Israel in unleashing a comprehensive onslaught against the Muslims in its beloved Lebanon and Palestine, and is preparing to transfer its capital to Jerusalem and intensify and extend its crimes against the Muslims it has driven from their homelands; in short, at a time when the Muslims stand in greater need than ever of unity, Sadat, the traitor and servant of America, the friend and brother of Begin and the dead, deposed Shah, and Saddam, another humble servant of America, are trying to sow dissension among the Muslims and will not hesitate to commit any crime their masters enjoin upon them in order to achieve their goal. America is engaged in continuous attacks on Iran, sending spies in the hope of defeating our Islamic Revolution and conspiring with Sadat to diffuse (by way of Iraq) lies and false propaganda concerning the leaders of the Islamic government. The Muslims must beware of the treason to Islam and the Muslims that these agents of America engage in. . . .

Muslims the world over who believe in the truth of Islam, arise and gather beneath the banner of *tauhid* and the teachings of Islam. Repel the treacherous superpowers from your countries and your abundant resources. Restore the glory of Islam, and abandon your selfish disputes and differences, for you possess everything! Rely on the culture of Islam, resist Western imitation, and stand on your own feet. Attack those intellectuals who are infatuated with the West and the East, and recover your true identity. Realize that intellectuals in the pay of foreigners have inflicted disaster upon their people and countries. As long as you remain disunited and fail to place your reliance in true Islam, you will continue to suffer what you have suffered already. We are now in an age when the masses act as the guides to the intellectuals and are rescuing them from abasement and humiliation by the East and the West. For today is the day that the masses of the people are on the move; they are the guides to those who previously sought to be the guides themselves. . . .

Neutral countries, I call upon you to witness that America plans to destroy us, all of us. Come to your senses and help us achieve our common goal. We have turned our backs on the East and the West, on the Soviet Union and America, in order to run our country ourselves. Do we therefore deserve to be attacked by the East and the West? The position we have attained is an historical exception, given the present conditions in the world, but our goal will certainly not be lost if *we* are to die, martyred and defeated.

NOTES

Introduction

1. Richard Nixon, "Oath of Office and Second Inaugural Address," January 20, 1973, in *The American Presidency Project*, ed. John T. Woolley and Gerhard Peters, http://www.presidency.ucsb.edu/ws/?pid=4141.
2. X, "The Sources of Soviet Conduct," *Foreign Affairs* 25, no. 4 (1947): 566–82.
3. Richard Nixon, "Address to the Bohemian Club," July 29, 1967, in *Foundations of Foreign Policy*, vol. 1 of *Foreign Relations of the United States, 1969–76* (hereafter cited as *FRUS* followed by the title years), http://history.state.gov /historicaldocuments/frus1969-76v01/d2.

1. Roots of Détente: Crises, Challenges, and the Quest for Stability

1. Robert Lochner, interview for CNN's Cold War series, http://www.cnn.com/SPECIALS/cold.war/episodes/09/reflections/ (accessed October 5, 2010, site discontinued).
2. The best overviews of the German question and the Cold War are Marc Trachtenberg, *A Constructed Peace* (Princeton, NJ: Princeton University Press, 1999); and William Glenn Grey, *Germany's Cold War: The Global Campaign to Isolate East Germany, 1949–1969* (Chapel Hill: University of North Carolina Press, 2007).
3. Hope Harrison, *Driving the Soviets Up the Wall: Soviet-East German Relations, 1953–1961* (Princeton, NJ: Princeton University Press, 2003; Alexander Furusenko and Timothy Naftali, *Khrushchev's Cold War: The Inside Story of an American Adversary* (New York: Norton, 2007), 367–408.
4. Dwight Eisenhower, cited in William Taubman, *Khrushchev: The Man and His Era* (New York: Norton, 2003), 464.
5. A vivid description of these events can be found in Frederick Taylor, *The Berlin Wall: A World Divided* (New York: Harper, 2008).
6. See ibid., 355–428. See also John P. S. Gearson and Kori Schake, eds., *The Berlin Wall Crisis: Perspectives on Cold War Alliances* (Basingstoke: Palgrave, 2002).

7. On the United States and the Cuban revolution, see Thomas G. Paterson, *Contesting Castro: The United States and the Triumph of the Cuban Revolution* (New York: Oxford University Press, 1995). The most recent detailed account of the failed overthrow of the Castro regime is Howard Jones, *The Bay of Pigs* (New York: Oxford University Press, 2008).

8. It would be fruitless to start listing all the books about the Cuban missile crisis. This account benefited greatly from Anatoly Furusenko and Timothy Naftali, *"One Hell of a Gamble": Khrushchev, Castro and Kennedy, 1958–1964* (New York: Norton, 1998); and Michael Dobbs, *One Minute to Midnight: Kennedy, Khrushchev, and Castro on the Brink of Nuclear War* (New York: Knopf, 2008).

9. William Burr and David Alan Rosenberg, "Nuclear Competition in an Era of Stalemate, 1963–1975," in *Crises and Détente*, vol. 2 of *The Cambridge History of the Cold War*, ed. Melvyn P. Leffler and Odd Arne Westad (Cambridge: Cambridge University Press, 2010), 96–98.

10. Anatoly Dobrynin, *In Confidence: Moscow's Ambassador to Six Cold War Presidents (1962–1986)* (New York: Random House, 1995), 91.

11. John F. Kennedy, "Commencement Address at American University in Washington," June 10, 1963, in *American Presidency Project*, http://www.presidency.ucsb.edu /ws/index.php?pid=9266&st=&st1= (accessed November 5, 2010).

12. For a series of essays on de Gaulle's role in France, see Hugh Gough and John Horne, eds., *De Gaulle and Twentieth Century France* (London: Edward Arnold, 1994); and Frédéric Bozo, *Two Strategies for Europe: De Gaulle, the United States and the Atlantic Alliance* (New York: Rowman and Littlefield, 2000).

13. Thomas Schwartz, *In the Shadow of Vietnam: Lyndon Johnson and Europe* (Cambridge, MA: Harvard University Press, 2003).

14. Particularly significant for this discussion were the essays in Andreas Wenger, Christian Nünlist, and Anna Locher, eds., *Transforming NATO in the Cold War: Challenges beyond Deterrence in the 1960s* (London: Routledge, 2007).

15. The Harmel Report was the result of a study group, set up in December 1966, on the future role of NATO after the French withdrawal. It was named after Belgian foreign minister Pierre Harmel, the chairman of the study group. See Frédéric Bozo, "Détente versus Alliance: France, the United States and the Politics of the Harmel Report," *Contemporary European History* 7, no. 3 (1998): 343–60; and Andreas Wenger, "Crisis and Opportunity: NATO and the Multilateralization of Détente, 1966–68," *Journal of Cold War Studies* 6, no. 1 (Winter 2004): 22–74. For alliance politics in general see Vojtech Mastny, "The New History of Cold War Alliances," *Journal of Cold War Studies* 4, no. 2 (Spring 2002): 55–84.

16. The "empire by invitation" thesis is usually associated with Geir Lundestad, but it has many adherents. Lundestad, "'Empire' by Invitation? United States and Western Europe, 1945–1952," *Journal of Peace Research* 23, no. 3 (1986): 263–77. On the Warsaw Pact see Vojtech Mastny and Malcolm Byrne, eds., *A Cardboard Castle? An Inside History of the Warsaw Pact, 1955–1991* (Budapest: Central European University Press, 2005).

17. Very little has been written about Albania during the Cold War. For a general account see, for example, R. J. Crampton, *The Balkans, Since the Second World War* (London: Longman, 2002).

18. On Romania, see Stephen Fischer-Galati, *20th Century Rumania* (New York: Columbia University Press, 1991), 159–82; and Katherine Verdery, *National Ideology under Socialism: Identity and Cultural Politics in Ceausescu's Romania* (Los Angeles: University of California Press, 1995).

19. Kennedy, "Commencement Address"; Zbigniew Brzezinski and William E. Griffith, "Peaceful Engagement in Eastern Europe," *Foreign Affairs* 39 (July 1961): 642-65. See also Jussi M. Hanhimäki, "The First Line of Defense or a Springboard for Disintegration: European Neutrals in American Foreign and Security Policy, 1945–1961," *Diplomacy and Statecraft* 7, no. 2 (July 1996): 378–403.

20. Bennett Kovrig, *Of Walls and Bridges: The United States and Eastern Europe* (New York: New York University Press, 1991), esp. 247–49.

21. Quoted in Joseph F. Harrington, "Romanian-American Relations during the Kennedy Administration," *East European Quarterly* 18, no. 2 (June 1984): 225. See also Kovrig, *Of Walls and Bridges*, 247–48.

22. Joseph Harrington and Bruce Courtney, "Romanian-American Relations during the Johnson Administration," *East European Quarterly* 22, no. 2 (June 1988): 225. In his memoir, Lyndon Johnson wrote, poignantly, "The East-West trade bill became a victim of the war in Vietnam," while Dean Rusk called it a "casualty of Viet Nam." Lyndon B. Johnson, *The Vantage Point: Perspectives of the Presidency, 1963–1969* (New York: Holt, Rinehart and Winston, 1971), 473. Rusk in Frank Costigliola, "Lyndon B. Johnson, Germany, and the 'End of the Cold War,'" in Warren I. Cohen and Nancy Bernkopf Tucker, eds., *Lyndon Johnson Confronts the World: American Foreign Policy, 1963–1969* (New York: Cambridge University Press, 1994), 207 fn.132.

23. U.S. exports to Eastern Europe (excluding the USSR and Yugoslavia) grew from about $87.5 million in 1961 to $135 million in 1967. Kovrig, *Of Walls and Bridges*, 251. For a fuller analysis of East-West trade politics in this period see Michael Mastanduno, *Economic Containment: CoCom and the Politics of East-West Trade* (Ithaca, NY: Cornell University Press, 1992), 107–42.

24. "National Security Action Memorandum (NSAM) 352: Bridge Building," July 8, 1966, in *Eastern Europe Region*, vol. 17 of *FRUS, 1964–68*, 54–55, http://history.state.gov/historicaldocuments/frus1964-68v17/d15 (accessed July 29, 2012).

25. There is no more exhaustively studied issue in post-1945 U.S. foreign policy than the Vietnam War. Some of the more recent works that were useful for writing this account include Seth Jacobs, *Cold War Mandarin: Ngo Dinh Diem and the Origins of America's War in Vietnam, 1950–1963* (Lanham, MD: Rowman and Littlefield, 2006); Frederick Logevall, *Choosing War: The Lost Chance for Peace and the Escalation of War in Vietnam* (Berkeley: University of California Press, 1999); and Andrew Preston, *War Council: McGeorge Bundy, the NSC, and Vietnam* (Cambridge: Harvard University Press, 2010).

26. For Vietnam and domestic politics, see Melvin Small, *At the Water's Edge: American Politics and the Vietnam War* (Chicago: Ivan R. Dee, 2005).

27. Thomas Borstelman, *The Cold War and the Color Line: American Race Relations in the Global Arena* (Cambridge, MA: Harvard University Press, 2001); idem, *Apartheid's Reluctant Uncle: The United States and Southern Africa in the Early Cold War* (New York: Oxford University Press, 1993); Mary Dudziak, *Cold War Civil Rights: Race and the Image of American Democracy* (Princeton, NJ: Princeton University Press, 2000); Penny M. Von Eschen, *Race Against Empire: Black Americans and Anticolonialism, 1937–1957* (Ithaca, NY: Cornell University Press, 1997); Gerald L. Horne, *From the Barrel of a Gun: The U.S. and the War against Zimbabwe, 1965–1980* (Chapel Hill: University of North Carolina Press, 2001); Michael L. Krenn, *Black Diplomacy: African-Americans and the State Department, 1945–1969* (Armonk, NY: M. E. Sharpe, 1999); Brenda Gayle Plummer, *Rising Wind: African-Americans and U.S. Foreign Affairs, 1935–1960* (Chapel Hill: University of North Carolina Press, 1996). See also "Symposium: African-Americans and U.S. Foreign Relations," *Diplomatic History* 20 (Fall 1996): 531–650, with contributions from Carol Anderson, Helen Laville, Scott Lucas, Michael L. Krenn, Gerald Horne, Penny M. Von Eschen, and Brenda Gayle Plummer; and Cary Fraser, "Crossing the Color Line in Little Rock: The Eisenhower Administration and the Dilemma of Race for U.S. Foreign Policy," *Diplomatic History* 24 (Spring 2000): 233–64.

28. Dudziak, *Cold War Civil Rights*, 3–5.

29. Borstelman, *Cold War and the Color Line*; Dudziak, *Cold War Civil Rights*; Krenn, *Black Diplomacy*; Plummer, *Rising Wind*; and Fraser, "Crossing the Color Line."

30. Martin Luther King, "Beyond Vietnam," cited in Mary Robbins, ed., *Against the Vietnam War: Writings by Activists* (New York: Rowman and Littlefield, 2007), 109.

31. See Borstelman, *Cold War and the Color Line*; and Dudziak, *Cold War Civil Rights*.

32. For further discussion on the Port Huron Statement, see Tom Hayden, *The Port Huron Statement: The Vision Call of the 1960s Revolution* (New York: Public Affairs, 2005).

2. 1968: Revolution, War, and the Birth of Détente

1. *New York Times* article, cited in Mark Kurlansky, *1968: The Year That Rocked the World* (New York: Random House, 2005), 3.

2. The most comprehensive account is David F. Schmitz, *The Tet Offensive: Politics, War, and Public Opinion* (Lanham, MD: Rowman and Littlefield, 2005). For a brief accounting, see James H. Willbanks, *The Tet Offensive: A Concise History* (New York: Columbia University Press, 2007).

3. For the military aspects of the Tet offensive, see James Arnold, *Tet Offensive 1968: Turning Point in Vietnam* (Oxford: Osprey Publishing, 1990).

4. Willbanks, *Tet Offensive*, 66–78.

5. Lyndon Johnson, "President Lyndon B. Johnson's Address to the Nation Announcing Steps to Limit the War in Vietnam and Reporting His Decision Not to Seek Reelection," March 31, 1968, Selected Speeches and Messages of Lyndon Baines Johnson, Lyndon Baines Johnson Library and Museum,

http://www.lbjlib.utexas.edu/johnson/archives.hom/speeches.hom/680331.asp (accessed July 29, 2012).

6. On the background of the Prague Spring, see Vladimir Kusin, *The Intellectual Origins of the Prague Spring: The Development of Reformist Ideas in Czechoslovakia, 1956–1967* (Cambridge: Cambridge University Press, 2002).

7. Kieran Willliams, *The Prague Spring and Its Aftermath: Czechoslovak Politics, 1968–1970* (Cambridge: Cambridge University Press, 1997), 63–111; Jiri Valenta, *Soviet Intervention in Czechoslovakia, 1968: Anatomy of a Decision* (Baltimore: Johns Hopkins University Press, 1991), 123–53. See also the documentation in Jaromir Navratil, ed., *The Prague Spring 1968: A National Security Archive Documentary Reader* (Budapest: Central European University Press, 2006); and Mastny and Byrne, eds., *Cardboard Castle.*

8. On the aftermath, see Williams, *Prague Spring,* 112–225.

9. Although Brezhnev gave his speech in November, the arguments that would be referred to as the Brezhnev Doctrine had already been published in the Soviet daily, *Pravda,* in September. "Unofficial Enunciation of the 'Brezhnev Doctrine,' September 26, 1968 (Excerpts)," Document 128, in Navratil, ed., *Prague Spring 1968,* 502–3.

10. Matthew J. Ouimet, *The Rise and Fall of the Brezhnev Doctrine in Soviet Foreign Policy* (Chapel Hill: University of North Carolina Press, 2003), esp. pp. 9–64.

11. On the Johnson administration's response to the Warsaw Pact intervention, see Mitch Lerner, "'Trying to Find the Guy Who Invited Them': Lyndon Johnson, Bridge Building, and the End of the Prague Spring," *Diplomatic History* 32, no. 1 (January 2008): 77–103.

12. "Notes of Cabinet Meeting, August 22, 1968," Document 84, in *Eastern Europe,* vol. 12 of *FRUS, 1964–68,* http://www.state.gov/www/about_state/history/vol _xvii/j.html (accessed November 3, 2010).

13. On Robert Kennedy's campaign, see Thurston Clarke, *The Last Campaign: 82 Days That Inspired America* (Chicago: Henry Holt, 2008).

14. David Culbert, "Television's Impact on Decision-Making in the USA, 1968: The Tet Offensive and Chicago's Democratic National Convention," *Journal of Contemporary History* 33, no. 3 (1998): 419–44. Ribicoff is cited on p. 428.

15. Nixon's success and strategy is discussed in Robert Mason, *Richard Nixon and the Quest for a New Majority* (Chapel Hill: University of North Carolina Press, 2004), 5–36.

16. Nixon's early career is detailed in Rick Perlstein, *Nixonland: The Rise of a President and the Fracturing of America* (New York: Scribner, 2008).

17. Jussi Hanhimäki, *The Flawed Architect: Henry Kissinger and American Foreign Policy* (New York: Oxford University Press, 2004), 15.

18. These well-known episodes can be found in all Nixon biographies; in addition to sources already cited, see, for example, Melvin Small, *The Presidency of Richard Nixon* (Lawrence: University Press of Kansas, 1999).

19. Jeremi Suri, *Henry Kissinger and the American Century* (Cambridge, MA: Harvard University Press, 2007). Suri's is the only work that truly explores the impact that being Jewish had on Kissinger's career.

20. Hanhimäki, *Flawed Architect*, 23–24; Robert Dallek, *Nixon and Kissinger: Partners in Power* (New York: HarperCollins, 2007), 89–103.

21. Richard Nixon, "Campaign Speech in Omaha, Nebraska," May 6, 1968, in *Foundations of Foreign Policy*, vol. 1 of *FRUS, 1969–76*, http://history.state.gov/historicaldocuments/frus1969-76v01/d5 (accessed July 29, 2012).

22. Richard Nixon, "Asia after Vietnam," *Foreign Affairs*, October 1967, http://www.foreignaffairs.org/19671001faessay46107/richard-m-nixon/asia-after-viet-nam.html (accessed November 1, 2010).

23. Nixon, "Address to the Bohemian Club."

24. Henry Kissinger, *American Foreign Policy: Three Essays* (New York: W. W. Norton, 1969), 15.

25. "Presidential Adviser Kissinger: New Approaches to Friend and Foe," *Time*, February 14, 1969.

26. John L. Gaddis, *Strategies of Containment: A Critical Appraisal of Postwar American National Security Policy during the Cold War* (New York: Oxford University Press, 2005), 305–6.

3. "Three for Three": Triangulation

1. Wilson was but one of Nixon's heroes; the other former president that he admired most was, ironically, Wilson's great adversary, Theodore Roosevelt.

2. Richard Nixon, "Inaugural Address," January 20, 1969, in *American Presidency Project*, http://www.presidency.ucsb.edu/ws/index.php?pid=1941 (accessed September 12, 2010).

3. Ibid.

4. Henry Kissinger, *White House Years* (Boston: Little, Brown, 1979), 57, 64. Hereafter cited as *WHY*.

5. *Haldeman Diaries*, 47, 48, 51 (March 9, 10, and 17, 1969). For an extensive discussion of Operation Menu, see Jeffrey Kimball, *Nixon's Vietnam War* (Lawrence: University Press of Kansas, 1998), 124–45.

6. See William Bundy, *A Tangled Web: The Making of Foreign Policy in the Nixon Presidency* (New York: Hill and Wang, 1998), 155; Kimball, *Nixon's Vietnam War*, 131–35; Hanhimäki, *Flawed Architect*, 42–46.

7. *WHY*, 980–81; Nelson D. Lankford, *The Last American Aristocrat: The Biography of David K. E. Bruce, 1898–1977* (Boston: Little, Brown, 1996), 360–61.

8. See Bundy, *Tangled Web*, 64–65.

9. Ibid., 65; Kimball, *Nixon's Vietnam War*, 137–39.

10. Richard Nixon, "Informal Remarks in Guam with Newsmen," July 25, 1969, in *American Presidency Project*, http://www.presidency.ucsb.edu/ws/index.php?pid=2140&st=&st1= (accessed September 15, 2010).

11.   In fact, the last combat troops left Vietnam in August 1972.

12.   *WHY*, 265.

13.   Cited in Hanhimäki, *Flawed Architect*, 39.

14.   Ole R. Holsti, *Public Opinion and American Foreign Policy* (Ann Arbor: University of Michigan Press, 1997), 68.

15.   Memorandum of conversation (Memcon): Nixon, Kissinger, Toon, Dobrynin, February 17, 1969, Box 340: USSR Memcons Dobrynin/President, NSC Subject Files, Nixon Presidential Materials Project (NPMP), National Archives (NA), College Park, MD.

16.   Odd Arne Westad, "Introduction," in Westad, ed., *Brothers in Arms: The Rise and Fall of the Sino-Soviet Alliance, 1945–1963* (Stanford, CA: Stanford University Press, 1998), 29.

17.   Ibid.

18.   Hanhimäki, *Flawed Architect*, 42.

19.   Ibid., 147.

20.   John Ashbrook, cited in Seymour Hersh, *The Price of Power: Kissinger in the Nixon White House* (New York: Summit Books, 1983), 550.

21.   On the agreements and criticism, see Bundy, *Tangled Web*, 323–27, 345–47; and Raymond Garthoff, *Détente and Confrontation: American Soviet Relations from Nixon to Reagan*, 2nd ed. (Washington, DC: Brookings Institution, 1994), 188–98, 298–301. Hyland is cited in Walter Isaacson, *Kissinger* (New York: Simon & Schuster, 1992), 436.

22.   Garthoff, *Détente and Confrontation*, 290.

23.   Henry Kissinger, cited in ibid., 292.

24.   Memcon: Kissinger, Gromyko et.al., May 28, 1972, and Memcon: Nixon, Brezhnev, Kissinger and Aleksandrov-Agentov, May 29, 1972, both in Box 73: Mr. Kissinger's Conversations in Moscow May 1972, Henry A. Kissinger (HAK) Office Files, NSC, NPMP, NA.

25.   Henry Kissinger, cited in Hanhimäki, *Flawed Architect*, 225. Italics added.

26.   Richard Nixon, "Address to a Joint Session of the Congress on Return from Austria, the Soviet Union, Iran, and Poland," June 1, 1972, in *American Presidency Project*, http://www.presidency.ucsb.edu/ws/index.php?pid=3450&st=&st1= (accessed November 1, 2010).

27.   This episode is described in detail in Hanhimäki, *Flawed Architect*, 228–29.

28.   McGovern carried only Massachusetts and the District of Columbia and lost the electoral college vote by 520 to 17.

29.   Nixon, "Oath of Office and Second Inaugural Address."

4. Nixon, Kissinger, and Détente in Europe

1.   Memcon: Kissinger, Mao and Zhou, February 18, 1973, in *Kissinger Transcripts: The Top Secret Talks with Moscow and Beijing*, ed. William Burr (New York: New Press, 1999), 86–101.

2.   Kissinger, *American Foreign Policy*, 78.

3. Memcon: Nixon-Wilson, February 24, 1969, "President Nixon's Trip to Europe 2/23/69-3/2/69, Vol. I of VIII," Box 489: Executive Secretariat Conference Files, 1966–1972, Record Group (RG) 59, Department of State Records (DSR), NA.

4. Further on this, see chapter 4 in Jussi M. Hanhimäki, Benedikt Schoenborn, and Barbara Zanchetta, *Transatlantic Relations since 1945: An Introduction* (London: Routledge, 2012).

5. See Frédéric Bozo, "France, 'Gaullism,' and the Cold War," in *Cambridge History of the Cold War*, 2:158–78.

6. Benedikt Schoenborn, "NATO Forever? Willy Brandt's heretical thoughts on an Alternative Future," in *Routledge Handbook of Transatlantic Security*, ed. Basil Germond, Jussi Hanhimäki, and Georges-Henri Soutou (London: Routledge: 2010), 79–81.

7. For an outline of Ostpolitik, see Michael J. Sodaro, *Moscow, Germany, and the West from Khrushchev to Gorbachev* (Ithaca, NY: Cornell University Press, 1990).

8. Gerry A. Andrianopoulos, *Kissinger and Brzezinski: The NSC and the Struggle for Control of US National Security Policy* (London: Macmillan, 1991), 232.

9. Kissinger to Nixon, February 16, 1970, Box 683: Germany Vol. IV, NSC Country Files, NPMP, NA.

10. *WHY*, 410.

11. Memcons: Nixon, Rogers, Kissinger, Brandt, Kiesinger, February 26, 1969, Box 484, Conference Files, 1966–72, CF 340-CF342, RG 59, DSR, NA.

12. Kissinger to Nixon (drafted by Sonnenfeldt), October 14, 1969, VIP Visits, Box 917, NSC, NPMP, NA; and Kissinger to Nixon, October 20, 1969, Box 682: Germany Vol. III, NSC Country Files, NPMP, NA. Bahr's memcon in *Akten zur Auswartigen Politik der Bundesrepublik Deutschland 1969* (Munich: Oldenbourg, 2000), Band II, 1114–18 . Kissinger and Bahr's versions are also in their memoirs: *WHY*, 410–12; and Egon Bahr, *Zu Meiner Zeit* (Munich: Karl Blessing Verlag, 1996), 271–73.

13. Willy Brandt, *Erinnerungen* (Frankfurt: Propyläen Verlag, 1989), 176; *WHY*, 416; Rush to Rogers, April 2, 1970; Kissinger to Nixon (drafted by Sonnenfeldt), April 3, 1970, VIP Visits, Box 917, NSC, NPMP, NA.

14. *WHY*, 424; Memcon: Brandt, Schmidt, Nixon, Rogers, Laird, Kissinger, VIP Visits, Box 917, NSC, NPMP, NA.

15. Sodaro, *Moscow, Germany, and the West*, 174–79, 183–85; Bundy, *Tangled Web*, 173–79; Hanhimäki, *Flawed Architect*, 85–90.

16. Memcon: Dobrynin and Kissinger, April 26, 1971, "Dobrynin/Kissinger 1971, Vol. 5 part 1," Box 490, NSC, NPMP, NA; *WHY*, 823–33; Bahr, *Zu Meiner Zeit*, 358–71; Garthoff, *Détente and Confrontation*, 136–39; Hanhimäki, *Flawed Architect*, 171–92.

17. Davignon Report, cited in Trevor Salmon and William Nicoll, eds., *Building the European Union: A Documentary History and Analysis* (Manchester: Manchester University Press, 1997), 107–10.

18. "The USSR and the Changing Scene in Europe," NIE 12–72, NIEs, 1951–83, Box 5, CIA, RG 263, NA.

19. Kissinger to Nixon, January 31, 1973, VIP Visits, Box 492, NSC, NPMP, NA.

20. The speech can be found in James Mayall and Cornelia Navari, *The End of the Post-War Era* (Cambridge, UK: Cambridge University Press, 1980), 360–67. Much of this part is based on Hanhimäki, *Flawed Architect*, 275–77.

21. James Reston, "A Plea for Partnership," *New York Times*, April 24, 1973.

22. Frank Costigliola, *France and the United States: The Cold Alliance since World War II* (New York: Twayne, 1992), 174.

23. Brandt, *Erinnerungen*, 175.

24. Edward Heath, *Course of My Life* (London: Pimlico, 1998), 493.

25. Memcon: Kissinger and Jobert, May 22, 1973, "French Memcons Jan–May 1973," Box 56, HAK Office Files, NPMP, NA.

26. "Kissinger to Nixon: 'We Helped' Coup Forces in Chile," September 16, 1973, in *The Kissinger Telcons: The Kissinger Telcons on Chile*, National Security Archive Electronic Briefing Book No. 123, ed. Peter Kornbluh (Washington, DC: National Security Archive, 2004), www.gwu.edu/~nsarchiv/NSAEBB/NSAEBB123 /chile.htm (accessed November 3, 2010).

27. For useful overviews of these developments, see James E. Goodby, *Europe Undivided: The New Logic of Peace in U.S.-Russian Relations* (Washington, DC: U.S. Institute of Peace Press, 1998), 47–49.

28. More detailed overviews in John J. Maresca, *To Helsinki: The Conference on Security and Cooperation in Europe, 1973–1975* (Durham, NC: Duke University Press, 1985); Goodby, *Europe Undivided*; and John van Oudenaren, *Détente in Europe: The Soviet Union and the West since 1953* (Durham, NC: Duke University Press, 1991).

29. Jussi M. Hanhimäki, "'They Can Write It in Swahili': Kissinger, the Soviets, and the Helsinki Accords, 1973–1975," *Journal of Transatlantic Studies* 1, no. 1 (Spring 2003): 37–58.

30. For a thorough analysis, see Daniel C. Thomas, *The Helsinki Effect: International Norms, Human Rights, and the Demise of Communism* (Princeton, NJ: Princeton University Press, 2001).

31. This is evident in both the documentation now available as well as the memoirs of most participants. For a good treatment, see also sources cited in the previous notes and, in particular, Thomas, *Helsinki Effect*. On the Davignon Report and European foreign policy cooperation, see Michael E. Smith, *Europe's Foreign and Security Policy: The Institutionalization of Cooperation* (New York: Cambridge University Press, 2004).

32. Elliott to Callaghan, July 29, 1974, in *Documents on British Policy Overseas*, Series 3, Vol. 2, *The Conference on Security and Cooperation in Europe, 1972–1975*, ed. G. Bennett and K. A. Hamilton (London: TSO, 1997), 317–26.

33. For a detailed account of these issues, see Hanhimäki, "'They Can Write It in Swahili.'"

34. Lundestad, *United States and Western Europe since 1945*, 190–93.

35. American troop levels in Europe actually increased in the early 1970s: from about 246,000 to 264,000 between 1970 and 1973. On Pompidou, see George-Henri Soutou, "Le President Pompidou et les relations entre les Etats-Unis et l'Europe," *Journal of European Integration History* 6, no. 2 (2000): 111–46.

5. Détente Halted: Domestic Critics and Regional Crises

1. Henry Kissinger, "Anatomy of Crisis," *Newsweek*, August 11, 2003.

2. On Watergate, see Keith W. Olson, *Watergate: The Presidential Scandal That Shook America* (Lawrence: University Press of Kansas, 2003).

3. The "McGovernite Congress" appears repeatedly in Henry Kissinger, *Years of Renewal* (New York: Simon & Schuster, 1999). Citation in Kissinger's foreword to Richard Helms, *A Look over My Shoulder: A Life in the Central Intelligence Agency*, with William Hood (New York: Random House, 2003), xi.

4. Memcon: Ford, Kissinger, and Scowcroft, January 4, 1975, Box 8, NSC Memoranda of Conversations, 1973–77, Gerald Ford Library (GFL), Ann Arbor, Michigan.

5. Dobrynin, *In Confidence*, 329.

6. Henry Jackson, cited in Hanhimäki, *Flawed Architect*, 221.

7. Based on Isaacson, *Kissinger*, 611–21; Robert G. Kaufman, *Henry M. Jackson: A Life in Politics* (Seattle: University of Washington Press, 2000), 266–68; Bundy, *Tangled Web*, 348–50.

8. See Garthoff, *Détente and Confrontation*, 367–69; Dobrynin, *In Confidence*, 266–70; Richard Nixon, *RN: The Memoirs of Richard Nixon* (New York: Grosset & Dunlap, 1978), 830–52; Stanley I. Kutler, *The Wars of Watergate: The Last Crisis of Richard Nixon* (New York: Norton, 1992), 309–20.

9. Memcon: Nixon, Brezhnev et al., June 18 and 19, 1973, Box 75: "Brezhnev Visit, June 18–25, 1973, Memcons," NSC Country Files, NPMP, NA.

10. Memcon: Kissinger, Sonnenfeldt, Hartman, etc., March 18, 1974, in *Kissinger Transcripts*, 222–28. On March 6 and 15 Kissinger met with Jackson, but the senator persisted in his demand for an explicit Soviet guarantee of 100,000 annual exit visas. This, in part, explains Kissinger's anger at the March 18 meeting. Kissinger, *Years of Upheaval* (Boston: Little, Brown, 1982), 991–94; Kaufman, *Henry M. Jackson*, 268–78.

11. NSC Meeting, December 2, 1974, Box 1, NSC Meeting Minutes, GFL.

12. For the principals' accounts of the Vladivostok discussions, see Kissinger, *Years of Renewal*, 291–96; Gerald Ford, *A Time to Heal: The Autobiography of Gerald R. Ford* (New York: Harper and Row, 1979), 213–19; and Dobrynin, *In Confidence*, 327–32. A good overview can be found in Garthoff, *Détente and Confrontation*, 494–500.

13. Henry Jackson, cited in Kaufman, *Henry M. Jackson*, 288.

14. Garthoff, *Détente and Confrontation*, 512. For a general overview of the Trade Act debacle, see ibid., 505–16; Paula Stern, *Water's Edge: Domestic Politics and the*

Making of American Foreign Policy (Westport, CT: Greenwood Press, 1979), 173–90; and Kissinger's perspective in *Years of Renewal*, 302–9.

15. Garthoff, *Détente and Confrontation*, 508, 510–12; Dobrynin, *In Confidence*, 336–37; Kissinger, *Years of Renewal*, 304–9. Paul Miltich to Ford, "National Security: Salt Treaties," December 12, 1974, Box 32, Presidential Handwriting File, GFL.

16. Kissinger, *Years of Upheaval*; Kissinger, *Crisis*, 421.

17. Kissinger to Nixon (via Scowcroft), December 19 and 21, 1973, Box 43, Trip Files, HAK Office Files, NSC, NPMP, NA.

18. Memcon: Nixon, Kissinger, Gromyko, Dobrynin, Sonnenfeldt, Stoessel, February 4, 1974, Box 72: "US/USSR Presidential Exchanges," HAK Office Files, NSC, NPMP, NA.

19. Kissinger to Nixon, March 29, 1974, Box 48, Trip Files, HAK Office Files, NSC, NPMP, NA; Memcon: Kissinger, Brezhnev et al., March 27, 1974, in *Kissinger Transcripts*, 259; comment to Callaghan in ibid., 260.

20. Meetings of the Cabinet, April 16, 1975, Box 4, James E. Connor Files, GFL.

21. John Robert Greene, *Presidency of Gerald Ford* (Lawrence: University Press of Kansas, 1995), 139–40; Bundy, *Tangled Web*, 495–97.

22. Robert Tucker, "Vietnam: The Final Reckoning," *Commentary* 59, no. 5 (May 1975), cited in Jonathan Haslam, *No Virtue Like Necessity: Realist Thought in International Relations since Machiavelli* (New Haven: Yale University Press, 2002), 98. *Time* article cited in Isaacson, *Kissinger*, 642.

23. Hanhimäki, *Flawed Architect*, 422–23.

24. Odd Arne Westad, *The Global Cold War: Third World Interventions and the Making of Our Times* (Cambridge: Cambridge University Press, 2005), 241.

25. Ibid.

26. Henry Kissinger, "The Moral Foundations of Foreign Policy" (address made on July 15, 1975), *Department of State Bulletin*, August 4, 1975, 166–67.

27. Henry Kissinger, "Building an Enduring Foreign Policy" (address made on November 24, 1975), *Department of State Bulletin*, December 15, 1975, 848–49.

28. *The Gallup Poll, 1972–1975* (Wilmington, DE: Scholarly Resources, 1978), 595.

29. Ibid., 601, 606–7. Henry Jackson's campaign was faltering, while Jimmy Carter hardly registered in late 1975 (52 percent of those interviewed said they "knew too little about him to judge"). Ibid., 598.

30. Greene, *Presidency of Gerald Ford*, 162–64; Isaacson, *Kissinger*, 693–94.

31. Memcon: Ford, Kissinger, Rumsfeld, Scowcroft, March 29, 1976, Box 18, Memoranda of Conversations, 1973–77, NSC, GFL; Isaacson, *Kissinger*, 695–97; Kissinger, *Years of Renewal*, 862–66; Robert D. Schulzinger, *Henry Kissinger: Doctor of Diplomacy* (New York: Columbia University Press, 1989), 228–29.

32. Greene, *Presidency of Gerald Ford*, 166–68.

33. Memcon: Ford, Kissinger, Scowcroft, August 30, 1976, Box 20, Memoranda of Conversations, 1973–77, NSC, GFL.

34. On Carter and his quest for the presidency, see Burton I. Kaufman, *The Presidency of James Earl Carter* (Lawrence: University Press of Kansas, 1993); Kenneth E. Morris, *Jimmy Carter, American Moralist* (Athens: University of Georgia Press, 1996); Jules Witcover, *Marathon: The Pursuit of the Presidency, 1972–1976* (New York: Viking Press, 1977), 229–58. See also essays in Gary M. Fink and Hugh Davis Graham, eds., *The Carter Presidency: Policy Choices in the Post–New Deal Era* (Lawrence: University Press of Kansas, 2001).

35. Greene, *Presidency of Gerald Ford*, 175–76.

36. Ibid.; Isaacson, *Kissinger*, 699–701; Schulzinger, *Henry Kissinger*, 230–32.

6. Reason or Morality: Carter, Human Rights, and Nuclear Peace

1. Garthoff, *Détente and Confrontation*, 629.

2. Jimmy Carter, "Inaugural Address of President Jimmy Carter," January 20, 1977, Selected Speeches of Jimmy Carter, Jimmy Carter Library and Museum, http://www.jimmycarterlibrary.gov/documents/speeches/inaugadd.phtml (accessed November 23, 2010).

3. Olav Njolstad, "The Collapse of Superpower Détente, 1975–1980," in *Endings*, vol. 3 of *The Cambridge History of the Cold War*, ed. Melvin P. Leffler and Odd Arne Westad (Cambridge: Cambridge University Press, 2010), 142–43. See also Zbigniew Brzezinski, *Power and Principle: Memoirs of the National Security Adviser, 1977–1981* (New York: Farrar, Straus, Giroux, 1983), 150.

4. Citations in John Dumbrell, *American Foreign Policy: Carter to Clinton* (London: Macmillan, 1997), 12, 13.

5. Ibid., 15; Brzezinski, *Power and Principle*, 126.

6. Hamilton Jordan, *Crisis* (New York: G. P. Putnam's Sons, 1982), 47.

7. Westad, *Global Cold War*, 248; and Njolstad, "Keys of Keys? SALT II and the Breakdown of Détente," in Odd Arne Westad, ed., *The Fall of Détente: Soviet-American Relations during the Carter Years* (Oslo: Scandinavian University Press, 1997), 17.

8. For the Brezhnev-Carter correspondence in 1977, see Westad, *Fall of Détente*, 171–86.

9. Dobrynin, *In Confidence*, 392; Garthoff, *Détente and Confrontation*, 887–89.

10. Record of Conversation between Dobrynin and Vance, February 26, 1977, in *Fall of Détente*, 186.

11. Garthoff, *Détente and Confrontation*, 906. For the negotiations, see idem, 894–906.

12. Carter, "Address Delivered before a Joint Session of Congress on the Vienna Summit Meeting," June 18, 1979, in *American Presidency Project*, http://www.presidency.ucsb.edu/ws/index.php?pid=32498&st=&st1= (accessed July 2, 2010). For the full text of the treaty, see "Treaty between the United States of American and the Union of Soviet Socialist Republics on the Limitation of Strategic Offensive Arms, Together with Agreed Statements and Common

Understandings Regarding the Treaty," June 18, 1979, http://www.fas.org/nuke/control/salt2/text/salt2-2.htm (accessed July 2, 2010).

13. Njolstad, "Keys of Keys," 57–62.

14. Garthoff, *Détente and Confrontation*, 535–37, 844–45.

15. Nancy Mitchell, "The Cold War and Jimmy Carter," in *Cambridge History of the Cold War*, 3:72–73.

16. Jimmy Carter, "The President's News Conference," February 8, 1977, in *American Presidency Project*, http://www.presidency.ucsb.edu/ws/index.php?pid =7666&st=&st1= (accessed June 29, 2010). "The Dissidents Challenge Moscow," *Time*, February 21, 1977.

17. Garthoff, *Détente and Confrontation*, 632–33.

18. On Charter 77, see John Keane, ed., *The Power of the Powerless: Citizens against the State in Central-Eastern Europe* (London: Hutchinson, 1985).

19. On the influence of John Paul II, see Owen Chadwick, *The Church in the Cold War* (London: Penguin, 1993). For an account that gives much credit to the pope's role in bringing about an end to the Cold War, see John L. Gaddis, *Cold War: A New History* (New York: Penguin, 2005). For a controversial account detailing the pope's relationship with the CIA, see Carl Bernstein and Marco Politi, *His Holiness: John Paul and the History of Our Time* (New York: Penguin, 1997). On Solidarity, see Timothy Garton Ash, *The Polish Revolution: Solidarity* (New Haven: Yale University Press, 2002).

20. Ronald Reagan, "America's Purpose in the World" (speech, 5th Annual APAC Conference, March 17, 1978), Reagan 2020, http://reagan2020 .us/speeches/Americas_World_Purpose.asp (accessed September 27, 2010).

21. Jimmy Carter, cited in Richard R. Fagen, "The Carter Administration and Latin America: Business as Usual?," *Foreign Affairs* 57, no. 3 (1978): 652–69.

22. See Kathryn Sikkink, *Mixed Signals: US Human Rights Policy and Latin America* (Ithaca, NY: Cornell University Press, 2004), ch. 6.

23. Chris Saunders and Sue Onslow, "The Cold War and Southern Africa, 1976– 1990," *Cambridge History of the Cold War*, 3:222–43. See also the essays in Sue Onslow, ed., *Cold War in Southern Africa: White Power, Black Liberation* (London: Routledge, 2009).

24. Nancy Mitchell, "Tropes of the Cold War: Jimmy Carter and Rhodesia," *Cold War History* 7, no. 2 (May 2007): 263–83. Citation in Saunders and Onslow, "Cold War and Southern Africa," 234.

25. Reagan, "America's Purpose."

26. Rosemary Foot, "The Cold War and Human Rights," in *Cambridge History of the Cold War*, 3:461.

27. "Presidential Campaign Debate," October 6, 1976, in *American Presidency Project*, http://www.presidency.ucsb.edu/ws/index.php?pid=6414&st=&st1= (accessed September 28, 1976); Jimmy Carter, speech at Notre Dame, May 1977, in *Détente and Confrontation*, 761; Carter cited in ibid., 763.

28. Roderick MacFarquhar and Michael Schoenhals, *Mao's Last Revolution* (Cambridge, MA: Harvard University Press, 2006), 262

29. James Mann, *About Face: A History of America's Curious Relationship with China, from Nixon to Clinton* (New York: Vintage, 1998), 83–84.

30. Ibid., 86–89. For Brzezinski's recollection of his visit, see Brzezinski, *Power and Principle*, 209–19.

31. Mann, *About Face*, 95–98.

32. Patrick Tyler, *A Great Wall: Six Presidents and China: An Investigative History* (New York: Century Foundation, 1999), 273–74.

33. Mann, *About Face*, 101–2.

34. "Teng's Great Leap Outward," *Time*, February 5, 1979.

35. Brezhnev's conversation with Erich Honecker, July 27, 1979, in *Fall of Détente*, 234.

36. "Signed and Sealed . . . " *Time*, July 2, 1979, http://www.time.com/time/magazine/article/0,9171,916822,00.html#ixzz0sJqTksUv (accessed July 5, 2010).

37. Brezhnev's conversation with Erich Honecker, July 27, 1979, in *Fall of Détente*, 234.

7. Crisis and Collapse: Iran, Afghanistan, and the Carter Doctrine

1. Jimmy Carter's Address to the Joint Session of Congress, September 18, 1978, in *American Presidency Project*, http://www.presidency.ucsb.edu /ws/?pid=29799 (accessed August 1, 2012).

2. Patrick Tyler, *A World of Trouble: The White House and the Middle East—from the Cold War to the War on Terror* (New York: Farrar, Straus, Giroux, 2009), 209.

3. Dobrynin, *In Confidence*, 399.

4. Zbigniew Brzezinski, cited in "Iran: The Crescent of Crisis," *Time*, January 15, 1979.

5. George Lenczowski, "The Arc of Crisis: Its Central Sector," *Foreign Affairs* 57, no. 4 (Spring 1979): 796–820.

6. For an account of the Ogaden War that uses Ethiopian sources, see Gebru Tareke, "The Ethiopia-Somalia War of 1977 Revisited," *International Journal of African Historical Studies* 33, no. 3 (2000): 635–67.

7. Westad, *Global Cold War*, 271–72.

8. Brzezinski, *Power and Principle*, 178.

9. See Barbara Zanchetta, "Human Rights versus the Cold War: The Horn of Africa, Southwest Asia and the Emergence of the Carter Doctrine," in *The Globalization of the Cold War: Diplomacy and Local Confrontation, 1975–1985*, ed. Max Guderzo and Bruna Bagato (London: Routledge, 2010), 73–91.

10. Mitchell, "Cold War and Jimmy Carter," 80.

11. Jimmy Carter, "Tehran, Iran Toasts of the President and the Shah at a State Dinner," December 31, 1977, in *American Presidency Project*, http://www.presidency.ucsb.edu/ws/?pid=7080 (accessed August 1, 2012).

12.   Peter L. Hahn, *Crisis and Crossfire: The United States and the Middle East since 1945* (Washington, DC: Potomac Books, 2005), 69–72; Tyler, *World of Trouble*, 223.

13.   Hahn, *Crisis and Crossfire*, 72–73.

14.   Amin Saikal, "Islamism, the Iranian Revolution, and the Soviet Invasion of Afghanistan," in *Cambridge History of the Cold War*, 3:119–21.

15.   Barbara Zanchetta, "The Loss of Iran," in *Routledge Handbook*, ed. Germond et al., 143–44, citation on p. 144. See also Jeffrey A. Lefebvre, *Arms for the Horn: US Security Policy in Ethiopia and Somalia, 1953–1991* (Pittsburgh, PA: University of Pittsburgh Press, 1991), 202–7.

16.   Zanchetta, "Loss of Iran," 145.

17.   For background on Afghanistan see Westad, *Global Cold War*, 299–301; Saikal, "Islamism, the Iranian Revolution, and the Soviet Invasion of Afghanistan," 121–24.

18.   Saikal, "Islamism, the Iranian Revolution, and the Soviet Invasion of Afghanistan," 124–27; Westad, *Global Cold War*, 302–5.

19.   Vladislav Zubok, *The Failed Empire: The Soviet Union in the Cold War from Stalin to Gorbachev* (Chapel Hill: University of North Carolina Press, 2007), 261–64; Westad, *Global Cold War*, 317–26, Brezhnev cited on p. 325.

20.   Jimmy Carter, "Soviet Invasion of Afghanistan: Address to the Nation," January 4, 1980, in *American Presidency Project*, http://www.presidency.ucsb.edu/ws/?pid=32911 (accessed August 1, 2012).

21.   Mitchell, "Cold War and Jimmy Carter," 85.

22.   Jimmy Carter, "The State of the Union Address," January 23, 1980, in *American Presidency Project*, http://www.presidency.ucsb.edu/ws/?pid =33079 (accessed November 1, 2010).

23.   Saikal, "Islamism, the Iranian Revolution and the Soviet Invasion of Afghanistan," 129–34.

24.   Ronald Reagan, "Ronald Reagan's Announcement for Presidential Candidacy," November 13, 1979, Ronald Reagan's Major Speeches, 1964–89, Public Papers of President Ronald W. Reagan, Ronald Reagan Presidential Library, http://www.reagan.utexas.edu/archives/reference /11.13.79.html (accessed November 2, 2010).

25.   Ronald Reagan, "Republican National Convention Acceptance Speech," July 17, 1980, *Ronald Reagan's Major Speeches, 1964–89, Public Papers of President Ronald W. Reagan*, Ronald Reagan Presidential Library, http://www.reagan.utexas.edu/archives/reference/7.17.80.html (accessed November 2, 2010).

26.   Ronald Reagan, "Televised Address by Governor Ronald Reagan 'A Strategy for Peace in the '80s,'" October 19, 1980, Ronald Reagan's Major Speeches, 1964–89, Public Papers of President Ronald W. Reagan, Ronald Reagan Presidential Library, http://www.reagan.utexas.edu/archives/Reference/10.19.80.html (accessed November 2, 2010).

27. On the election, see Kaufman, *Presidency of James Earl Carter*, 197–206.

28. Ronald Reagan, "Inaugural Address," January 20, 1981, *Ronald Reagan's Major Speeches, 1964–89, Public Papers of President Ronald W. Reagan*, Ronald Reagan Presidential Library, http://www.reagan.utexas.edu /archives/speeches/1981/12081a.htm (accessed November 2, 2010).

29. Yuri Andropov, cited in Zubok, *Failed Empire*, 271.

8. Cold War Transformed: The Paradox of Détente

1. Ronald Reagan, "The President's News Conference," January 29, 1981, in *American Presidency Project*, http://www.presidency.ucsb.edu/ws/index .php?pid=44101&st=Soviet+Union&st1= (accessed November 5, 1981).

2. Ronald Reagan, "Excerpts from an Interview with Walter Cronkite of CBS News," March 3, 1981, in *American Presidency Project*, http://www.presidency.ucsb.edu/ws/index.php?pid=43497&st=Soviet+Union&st 1= (accessed November 5, 2010).

3. Charles Krauthammer, "The Reagan Doctrine," *Time*, April 1, 1985, http://www.time.com/time/magazine/article/0,9171,964873,00.html#ixzz17Viff 4Q5 (accessed August 1, 2012).

4. A good place to start exploring this debate is the chapters by Archie Brown, Beth A. Fischer, Alex Pravda, and Adam Roberts in *Cambridge History of the Cold War*, vol. 3.

5. Henry Kissinger, *Diplomacy* (New York: Simon & Schuster, 1994), 713.

6. Gaddis, *Strategies of Containment*, 274.

7. Nixon, "Address to the Bohemian Club."

8. "Presidential Adviser Kissinger."

9. Richard Nixon, cited in Hanhimäki, *Flawed Architect*, 197.

10. Henry Kissinger, cited in ibid., 11

11. Kissinger, *Years of Renewal*, 635.

12. Andrei Gromyko, cited in Dobrynin, *In Confidence*, 346.

13. Thomas, *Helsinki Effect*.

14. Westad, *Global Cold War*, 4.

15. Ibid. See also Christopher Andrew, *The World Was Going Our Way: The KGB and the Battle for the Third World* (New York: Basic Books, 2005).

SELECTED BIBLIOGRAPHY

Andrew, Christopher. *The World Was Going Our Way: The KGB and the Battle for the Third World*. New York: Basic Books, 2005.

Andrianopoulos, Gerry A. *Kissinger and Brzezinski: The NSC and the Struggle for Control of US National Security Policy*. London: Macmillan, 1991.

Asselin, Pierre. *A Bitter Peace: Washington, Hanoi, and the Making of the Paris Agreement*. Chapel Hill: University of North Carolina Press, 2002.

Bahr, Egon. *Zu Meiner Zeit*. Munich: Karl Blessing Verlag, 1996.

Bernstein, Carl, and Marco Politi, *His Holiness: John Paul and the History of Our Time*. New York: Penguin, 1997.

Bozo, Frédéric. "Détente versus Alliance: France, the United States and the Politics of the Harmel Report." *Contemporary European History* 7, no. 3 (1998): 343–60.

———. *Two Strategies for Europe: De Gaulle, the United States and the Atlantic Alliance*. New York: Rowman and Littlefield, 2000.

Brandt, Willy. *Erinnerungen*. Frankfurt: Propyläen Verlag, 1989.

Brzezinski, Zbigniew. *Power and Principle: Memoirs of the National Security Adviser, 1977–1981*. New York: Farrar, Straus, Giroux, 1983.

Bundy, William. *A Tangled Web: The Making of Foreign Policy in the Nixon Presidency*. New York: Hill and Wang, 1998.

Burr, William, ed. *The Kissinger Transcripts: The Top Secret Talks with Beijing and Moscow*. New York: New Press, 1999.

Cahn, Anne Hessing. *Killing Détente: The Right Attacks the CIA*. University Park: Pennsylvania State University Press, 1998.

Chadwick, Owen. *The Church in the Cold War*. London: Penguin, 1993.

Cohen, Warren I., and Nancy Bernkopf Tucker, eds. *Lyndon Johnson Confronts the World: American Foreign Policy, 1963-1969*. New York: Cambridge University Press, 1994.

Costigliola, Frank. *France and the United States: The Cold Alliance since World War II*. New York: Twayne, 1992.

Dallek, Robert. *Nixon and Kissinger: Partners in Power*. New York: HarperCollins, 2007.

Dobbs, Michael. *One Minute to Midnight: Kennedy, Khrushchev, and Castro on the Brink of Nuclear War*. New York: Knopf, 2008.

Dobrynin, Anatoly. *In Confidence: Moscow's Ambassador to Six Cold War Presidents (1962–1986)*. New York: Random House, 1995.

Dumbrell, John. *American Foreign Policy: Carter to Clinton*. London: Macmillan, 1997.

———, and Axel Schäfer, eds. *America's "Special Relationships."* London: Routledge, 2009.

Fink, Gary M., and Hugh Davis Graham, eds. *The Carter Presidency: Policy Choices in the Post-New Deal Era*. Lawrence: University Press of Kansas, 2001.

Foot, Rosemary. *The Practice of Power: U.S. Relations with China since 1949*. Oxford: Oxford University Press, 1995.

Ford, Gerald R. *A Time to Heal: The Autobiography of Gerald R. Ford*. New York: Harper and Row, 1979.

Fosdick, Dorothy, ed. *Staying the Course: Henry M. Jackson and National Security*. Seattle: University of Washington Press, 1987.

Furusenko, Alexander, and Timothy Naftali. *Khrushchev's Cold War: The Inside Story of an American Adversary*. New York: Norton, 2007.

———. *"One Hell of a Gamble": Khrushchev, Castro and Kennedy, 1958–1964*. New York: Norton, 1998.

Gaddis, John L. *Strategies of Containment: A Critical Appraisal of Postwar American National Security Policy*. New York: Oxford University Press, 1982. Revised and updated, 2005.

Garthoff, Raymond. *Détente and Confrontation: American Soviet Relations from Nixon to Reagan*. 2nd ed. Washington, DC: Brookings Institution, 1994.

Gearson, John P. S., and Kori Schake, eds. *The Berlin Wall Crisis: Perspectives on Cold War Alliances*. Basingstoke: Palgrave, 2002.

Germond, Basil, Jussi Hanhimäki, and Georges-Henri Soutou, eds. *Routledge Handbook of Transatlantic Security*. London: Routledge, 2010.

Gleijeses, Piero. *Conflicting Missions: Havana, Washington, and Africa, 1959–1976*. Chapel Hill: University of North Carolina Press, 2002.

Goodby, James E. *Europe Undivided: The New Logic of Peace in U.S.-Russian Relations*. Washington, DC: U.S. Institute of Peace Press, 1998.

Gough, Hugh, and John Horne, eds. *De Gaulle and Twentieth Century France*. London: Edward Arnold, 1994.

Greene, John Robert. *The Limits of Power: The Nixon and Ford Administrations*. Bloomington: Indiana University Press, 1992.

———. *The Presidency of Gerald R. Ford*. Lawrence: University Press of Kansas, 1995.

Grey, William Glenn. *Germany's Cold War: The Global Campaign to Isolate East Germany, 1949–1969*. Chapel Hill: University of North Carolina Press, 2007.

Guderzo, Max, and Bruna Bagato, eds. *The Globalization of the Cold War: Diplomacy and Local Confrontation, 1975–1985*. London: Routledge, 2010.

Hahn, Peter L. *Crisis and Crossfire: The United States and the Middle East since 1945*. Washington, DC: Potomac Books, 2005.

Hanhimäki, Jussi M. "The First Line of Defense or a Springboard for Disintegration: European Neutrals in American Foreign and Security Policy, 1945–1961." *Diplomacy and Statecraft* 7, no. 2 (July 1996): 378–403.

———. *The Flawed Architect: Henry Kissinger and American Foreign Policy*. New York: Oxford University Press, 2004.

———. "'They Can Write It in Swahili': Kissinger, the Soviets, and the Helsinki Accords, 1973–1975." *Journal of Transatlantic Studies* 1, no. 1 (Spring 2003): 37–58.

———, Benedikt Schoenborn, and Barbara Zanchetta. *Transatlantic Relations since 1945: An Introduction*. London: Routledge, 2012.

Hanhimäki, Jussi M., and Odd Arne Westad, eds. *The Cold War: A History in Documents and Eyewitness Accounts*. Oxford: Oxford University Press, 2003.

Harrison, Hope. *Driving the Soviets Up the Wall: Soviet-East German Relations, 1953-1961*. Princeton, NJ: Princeton University Press, 2003.

Hayden, Tom. *The Port Huron Statement: The Vision Call of the 1960s Revolution*. New York: Public Affairs, 2005.

Hersh, Seymour. *The Price of Power: Kissinger in the Nixon White House*. New York: Summit Books, 1983.

Hoff, Joan. *Nixon Reconsidered*. New York: Basic Books, 1994.

Holsti, Ole R. *Public Opinion and American Foreign Policy*. Ann Arbor: University of Michigan Press, 1997.

Hyland, William G. *Mortal Rivals: Superpower Relations from Nixon to Reagan*. New York: Random House, 1987.

Isaacson, Walter. *Kissinger*. New York: Simon & Schuster, 1992.

Jacobs, Seth. *Cold War Mandarin: Ngo Dinh Diem and the Origins of America's War in Vietnam, 1950–1963*. Lanham, MD: Rowman and Littlefield, 2006.

Johnson, Lyndon B. *The Vantage Point: Perspectives of the Presidency, 1963–1969*. New York: Holt, Rinehart and Winston, 1971.

Kaufman, Burton I. *The Presidency of James Earl Carter*. Lawrence: University Press of Kansas, 1993.

Kaufman, Robert G. *Henry M. Jackson: A Life in Politics*. Seattle: University of Washington Press, 2000.

Kissinger, Henry A. *American Foreign Policy: Three Essays*. New York: W. W. Norton, 1969.

———. *Diplomacy*. New York: Simon & Schuster, 1994.

———. *White House Years*. Boston: Little, Brown, 1979

———. *Years of Renewal*. New York: Simon & Schuster, 1999.

———. *Years of Upheaval*. Boston: Little, Brown, 1982.

Kimball, Jeffrey. *Nixon's Vietnam War*. Lawrence: University Press of Kansas, 1998.

Kovrig, Bennett. *Of Walls and Bridges: The United States and Eastern Europe*. New York: New York University Press, 1991.

Kurlansky, Mark. *1968: The Year That Rocked the World*. New York: Random House, 2005.

Kutler, Stanley I. *The Wars of Watergate: The Last Crisis of Richard Nixon*. New York: Norton, 1992.

Lefebvre, Jeffrey A. *Arms for the Horn: US Security Policy in Ethiopia and Somalia 1953–1991*. Pittsburgh, PA: University of Pittsburgh Press, 1991.

Leffler, Melvyn P., and Odd Arne Westad, eds. *Crises and Détente*. Vol. 2 of *The Cambridge History of the Cold War*. Cambridge: Cambridge University Press, 2010.

———. *Endings*. Vol. 3 of *The Cambridge History of the Cold War*. Cambridge: Cambridge University Press, 2010.

Lenczowski, George. "The Arc of Crisis: Its Central Sector," *Foreign Affairs* 57, no. 4 (Spring 1979): 796–820.

Lerner, Mitch. "'Trying to Find the Guy Who Invited Them': Lyndon Johnson, Bridge Building, and the End of the Prague Spring." *Diplomatic History* 32, no. 1 (January 2008): 77–103.

Litwak, Robert S. *Détente and the Nixon Doctrine: Foreign Policy and the Pursuit of Stability*. Cambridge, UK: Cambridge University Press, 1984.

Logevall, Frederick. *Choosing War: The Lost Chance for Peace and the Escalation of War in Vietnam*. Berkeley: University of California Press, 1999.

———, and Andrew Preston, eds. *Nixon in the World: American Foreign Relations, 1969–1977*. New York: Oxford University Press, 2008.

Loth, Wilfried, and Soutou, Georges-Henri, eds. *The Making of Détente: Eastern and Western Europe in the Cold War, 1965–1975*. London: Routledge, 2008.

Lundestad, Geir. *The United States and Western Europe since 1945*. Oxford: Oxford University Press, 2003.

MacFarquhar, Roderick, and Michael Schoenhals. *Mao's Last Revolution*. Cambridge, MA: Harvard University Press, 2006.

Mann, James. *About Face: A History of America's Curious Relationship with China, from Nixon to Clinton*. New York: Vintage, 1998.

Maresca, John. *To Helsinki: The Conference on Security and Cooperation in Europe, 1973–1975*. Durham, NC: Duke University Press, 1985.

Mason, Robert. *Richard Nixon and the Quest for a New Majority*. Chapel Hill: University of North Carolina Press, 2004.

Mastanduno, Michael. *Economic Containment: CoCom and the Politics of East-West Trade*. Ithaca, NY: Cornell University Press, 1992.

Mastny, Vojtech. "The New History of Cold War Alliances." *Journal of Cold War Studies* 4, no. 2 (Spring 2002): 55–84.

————, and Malcolm Byrne, eds. *A Cardboard Castle? An Inside History of the Warsaw Pact, 1955–1991*. Budapest: Central European University Press, 2005.

Mitchell, Nancy. "Tropes of the Cold War: Jimmy Carter and Rhodesia." *Cold War History* 7, no. 2 (May 2007): 263–83.

Morris, Kenneth E. *Jimmy Carter, American Moralist*. Athens: University of Georgia Press, 1996.

Nelson, Keith L. *The Making of Détente: Soviet-American Relations in the Shadow of Vietnam*. Baltimore: Johns Hopkins University Press, 1995.

Nixon, Richard. *RN: The Memoirs of Richard Nixon*. New York: Grosset & Dunlap, 1978.

Olson, Keith W. *Watergate: The Presidential Scandal That Shook America*. Lawrence: University Press of Kansas, 2003.

Onslow, Sue, ed. *Cold War in Southern Africa: White Power, Black Liberation*. London: Routledge, 2009.

Ouimet, Matthew J. *The Rise and Fall of the Brezhnev Doctrine in Soviet Foreign Policy*. Chapel Hill: University of North Carolina Press, 2003.

Perlstein, Rick. *Nixonland: The Rise of a President and the Fracturing of America*. New York: Scribner, 2008.

Preston, Andrew. *War Council: McGeorge Bundy, the NSC, and Vietnam*. Cambridge: Harvard University Press, 2010.

Quandt, William B. *Peace Process: American Policy toward the Arab-Israeli Conflict*. Berkeley: University of California Press, 1984.

Schulz, Mathias, and Schwartz, Thomas, eds. *Strained Alliance: US-European Relations from Nixon to Carter*. Cambridge: Cambridge University Press, 2010.

Schulzinger, Robert D. *Henry Kissinger: Doctor of Diplomacy*. New York: Columbia University Press, 1989.

Schwartz, Thomas. *In the Shadow of Vietnam: Lyndon Johnson and Europe*. Cambridge, MA: Harvard University Press, 2003.

Sikkink, Kathryn. *Mixed Signals: US Human Rights Policy and Latin America*. Ithaca, NY: Cornell University Press, 2004.

Small, Melvin. *At the Water's Edge: American Politics and the Vietnam War*. Chicago: Ivan R. Dee, 2005.

————. *The Presidency of Richard Nixon*. Lawrence: University Press of Kansas, 1999.

Smith, Gerard C. *Doubletalk: The Story of the First Strategic Arms Limitation Talks*. Garden City, NY: Doubleday, 1980.

Sodaro, Michael J. *Moscow, Germany, and the West from Khrushchev to Gorbachev*. Ithaca, NY: Cornell University Press, 1990.

Soutou, Georges-Henri. "Le President Pompidou et les relations entre les Etats-Unis et l'Europe." *Journal of European Integration History*, 6, no. 2 (2000): 111–46.

Stern, Paula. *Water's Edge: Domestic Politics and the Making of American Foreign Policy*. Westport, CT: Greenwood Press, 1979.

Suri, Jeremi. *Henry Kissinger and the American Century*. Cambridge, MA: Harvard University Press, 2007.

————. *Power and Protest: Global Revolution and the Origins of Détente*. Cambridge, MA: Harvard University Press, 2003.

Tareke, Gebru. "The Ethiopia-Somalia War of 1977 Revisited," *International Journal of African Historical Studies* 33, no. 3 (2000): 635–67.

Taubman, William. *Khrushchev: The Man and His Era*. New York: Norton, 2003.

Taylor, Frederick. *The Berlin Wall: A World Divided*. New York: Harper, 2008.

Thomas, Daniel C. *The Helsinki Effect: International Norms, Human Rights, and the Demise of Communism*. Princeton, NJ: Princeton University Press, 2001.

Thornton, Richard C. *The Carter Years: Toward a New Global Order*. New York: Paragon Press, 1992.

————. *The Nixon-Kissinger Years: Reshaping America's Foreign Policy*. New York: Paragon House, 1989.

Trachtenberg, Marc. *A Constructed Peace*. Princeton, NJ: Princeton University Press, 1999.

Tucker, Nancy Bernkopf. *China Confidential: American Diplomats and Sino-American Relations, 1945–1996*. New York: Columbia University Press, 2001.

Tyler, Patrick. *A Great Wall: Six Presidents and China: An Investigative History*. New York: Century Foundation, 1999.

————. *A World of Trouble: The White House and the Middle East—from the Cold War to the War on Terror*. New York: Farrar, Straus, Giroux, 2009.

Vaïsse, Maurice. *L'Europe et la crise de Cuba*. Paris: Armand Colin, 1993.

Valenta, Jiri. *Soviet Intervention in Czechoslovakia, 1968: Anatomy of a Decision*. Baltimore: Johns Hopkins University Press, 1991.

van Oudenaren, John. *Détente in Europe: The Soviet Union and the West since 1953*. Durham, NC: Duke University Press, 1991.

Wenger, Andreas. "Crisis and Opportunity: NATO and the Multilateralization of Détente, 1966–68." *Journal of Cold War Studies* 6, no. 1 (Winter 2004): 22–74.

Wenger, Andreas, Christian Nünlist, and Anna Locher, eds. *Transforming NATO in the Cold War: Challenges beyond Deterrence in the 1960s*. London: Routledge, 2007.

Westad, Odd Arne, ed. *Brothers in Arms: The Rise and Fall of the Sino-Soviet Alliance, 1945-1963*. Stanford, CA: Stanford University Press, 1998.

———, ed. *The Fall of Détente: Soviet-American Relations during the Carter Years*. Oslo: Scandinavian University Press, 1997.

———. *The Global Cold War: Third World Interventions and the Making of Our Times*. Cambridge: Cambridge University Press, 2005.

Williams, Kieran. *The Prague Spring and Its Aftermath: Czechoslovak Politics, 1968–1970*. Cambridge: Cambridge University Press, 1997.

Winand, Pascaline. *Eisenhower, Kennedy, and the United States of Europe*. Basingstoke: Macmillan, 1993.

Witcover, Jules. *Marathon: The Pursuit of the Presidency, 1972–1976*. New York: Viking Press, 1977.

Zubok, Vladislav. *The Failed Empire: The Soviet Union in the Cold War from Stalin to Gorbachev*. Chapel Hill: University of North Carolina Press, 2007.

INDEX

ABM (anti-Ballistic Missile) Treaty, 53–54, 55, 80
Acheson, Dean, 146
address to nation on Soviet invasion of Afghanistan, Carter's, 225–29
address to nation on strategy for peace, Reagan's, 231–33
Adenauer, Konrad, 11, 168
Afghan Communist Party, 134
Afghanistan
 Soviet invasion, 126, 127, 133, 134–38, 144, 223–30, 234
 US, 133, 144, 153, 154
African decolonization, 22, 91–92
Agnew, Spiro T., 34, 80
Agreement on the Prevention of Nuclear War (PNW), 69, 148
Albania, 13, 74
Allende, Salvador, 113
Alvor Accord, 92
Amalrik, Andrei, 101
American University commencement address, Kennedy's, 8, 14, 157–60
American-Isreal Political Action Committee (AIPAC), 82
Amin, Hafizullah, 135, 224
Amnesty International, 197
analysis of impact of Afghanistan invasion, Soviet, 229–30
Anderson, John, 140
Andropov, Yuri

Afghanistan, 135, 224–25
 dissidents, 110, 116–17, 197–98
 Reagan administration, 141–42
Angola, 78, 92–94, 129, 144, 151, 199
anti-Ballistic Missile (ABM) Treaty, 53–54, 55, 80
anticommunism, xvii, 14, 36, 144
antiwar movement, 18–19, 22, 27, 34, 46
Aqaba, Gulf of, 166, 167
Arab League, 125
Arab nationalism, 127
arc of crisis, 126–27, 129, 132, 133, 134, 138
Argentina, 113
Army of the Republic of Vietnam (ARVN), 17, 27, 45, 46
Ashbrook, John M., 54
Atlanticism, 62, 67–71, 75–76
autonomy, European, 62, 68–69, 205

back channel negotiations, Kissinger's, 37, 49, 56, 66, 67, 147, 148
Backfire bombers, 108, 221
Bahr, Egon, 63–64, 66, 67
Bakhtiar, Shapour, 132
Barre, Mohammad Siad, 128
"Basic Principles of Soviet-American Relations," 55–56, 187–88
Basic Treaty between East and West Germany, 64
Batista, Fulgencio, 5

Bay of Pigs invasion, 6
Bazargan, Mehdi, 132
Begin, Menachem, 86, 125, 234
Beijing trips, Kissinger and Nixon, 39, 52–53, 67
Berlin, xiv, 1, 2–5, 50, 53, 64, 67, 180, 193
Berlin Wall, 1, 4–5, 23
"Beyond Vietnam" (King), 21
bin Laden, Osama, 138
bipartisanship, 232–33
Bogomolov, O., 229–30
Bohemian Club speech of Nixon, 38, 168–73
borders
    CSCE, 73, 193, 194, 196
    Eastern European, 111–12
    Sino-Soviet, 39, 51, 72
Brandt, Willy, 50
    détente, xix
    German unification, 11, 63–64
    Kennedy, 1
    Ostpolitik, 41, 63–67, 76, 178–81
    transatlantic relations, 70, 71
Bratislava Declaration, 29
Brazil, 113
Brezhnev, Leonid
    Angola, 93
    Brezhnev Doctrine, 30, 51, 241n9
    Carter administration, 106–8, 121, 206–8, 215–18
    détente, 41
    dissidents, 110–11
    Ford administration, 81, 84, 196, 204
    Middle East, 56, 86–87, 135
    Nixon, xiv, 56, 86
    nuclear arms control, 44, 81, 103, 106–7, 121–23
    speech to Politburo on international situation, 215–18
    trade with US, 82, 84
Brezhnev Doctrine, 30, 51, 241n9
Britain. See Great Britain
Brown, Harold, 212–15
Brown, Pat, 35
Brown v. Board of Education, 21
Brzezinski, Zbigniew

Africa, 103, 115, 129, 213–15
China, 117, 119–20, 148
European détente, 13–14
Kissinger, 98, 104
Middle East, 126, 127, 132–33, 136
USSR, 216, 219, 220
Vance rivalry, 103, 104–5
Bucharest Declaration, 15
budget, US military, 21, 88, 101–2, 131, 203
Bundy, McGeorge, 1
Burr, William, 6
Bush, George H.W., 118–19, 139
Bush War, Rhodesian, 114–15

Cambodia, 16, 18, 45–46, 52, 88, 89–90
Camp David Accords, 86, 125–26
Canada, 11, 15, 20, 71, 72, 191
Cape Verde, 92
Carnation Revolution, 92
Carter, Jimmy and administration
    Afghanistan, 135–36, 137–38, 226–29
    Africa, 127, 128–30, 208, 216–17, 219
    Brezhnev, 206–8, 215–18
    China, 117, 118–21
    détente, 77, 116, 149
    Dobrynin on, 219–21
    economy, 101–2
    foreign policy overview, 98–99, 101–2, 103–4, 146, 208–12
    human rights, 110, 112–14, 115–17, 121, 148
    Middle East, 86, 125–27, 130–34, 225
        (See also Afghanistan)
    Notre Dame University commencement address, 208–12
    nuclear arms control, 101–3, 106–9, 121–22
    presidential bid, 94, 97, 201–6
    presidential reelection bid, 138–41, 231–32
    on Vance and Brzezinski, 105
Carter Doctrine, 132, 134, 137–38, 141
Castro, Fidel, 5–7, 169, 172, 200
Catholic Church, 112
Ceaușescu, Nicolae, 13, 15

Central Intelligence Agency (CIA), 79–80, 92, 137–38
Central Office for South Vietnam (COSVN), 45
CFE Treaty, 109
Chai Zemin, 119
Charter 77, 111
charter for détente, 55–56, 187–88
Checkers speech of Nixon, 36
Chicago Seven, 34
Chile, 80, 98, 113
China. See People's Republic of China
Chinese Communist Party's Central Committee, 118
Church, Frank, 80
Church Committee, 79–80
CIA (Central Intelligence Agency), 79–80, 92, 137–38
civil rights, 20–22, 23, 33
Civil Rights Acts of 1964 and 1965, 21
Cold War. See also specific aspects of
détente's impact, xv, xvii, 62, 74–75, 145, 149–53
end of, 61, 74–75, 144–45, 150
globalization of, 123, 129–30
Kennedy and Johnson era, 1–2, 5, 9, 19–20, 22, 23
Nixon era, 183–84
overview, xiv, xv–xix
Reagan era, 144–45
Cold War Civil Rights (Dudziak), 20
Colombia, 114
Commentary, 91
Committee of the Defence of Human Rights, 197–98
communications link between US and USSR, 9, 161–64
communism, Nixon on, xvii, 169, 170–71
communism in Southeast Asia, 89–90
Conference on Security and Cooperation in Europe (CSCE). See CSCE
Congress on Racial Equality (CORE), 20
containment policy
antiwar movement, 32
Carter administration, 136
Kennan, xvi, 40, 146
Nixon administration, 39, 40, 146–47

Reagan administration, 141
Southeast Asia, xvii, 16
conventional forces in Europe (CFE), 109
Costa Rica, 114
COSVN (Central Office for South Vietnam), 45
covert actions of US, 92, 98–99, 131, 147
credibility, American, 27, 44, 90–91, 93, 120, 130
Crisis (Kissinger), 85
Cronkite, Walter, 143
CSCE (Conference on Security and Cooperation in Europe)
about, xiv, 50, 71–76
cabinet meeting on, 195–97
criticism, 96, 148–49, 150
human rights provisions, 116–17, 145, 151, 192, 193, 195
Kissinger preparation memo to Ford, 191–95
Cuba
Africa, 92, 93–94, 103, 115, 127–30
background, 5, 170
Cuban missile crisis, 5–10, 23, 155–57
Ford administration, 199–200
Latin America, 114
Nixon, 169, 170, 172
Soviet submarine base, 5, 50
Cuban missile crisis, 5–10, 23, 155–57
Cultural Revolution of China, 50–51, 117–18
Czechoslovakia, xvii, 13, 26, 28–32, 101, 111
Czechoslovakian Communist Party (KS), 28

Dalai Lama, 119
Daoud, Mohammed, 134
Davignon, Étienne, 68
Davignon Report, 68, 74
Davis, John W., 104
de Gaulle, Charles, 2, 4, 10–12, 63
debates, presidential
1968, 35
1976, 98–99, 106, 117, 201–6
1980, 140
decolonization, 22, 91–92, 174, 210

Democracy Wall movement, 121
Democratic Congressional Campaign
    Committee, 97
Democratic Convention of 1968, 33–34
Democratic Republic of Vietnam (DRV).
    See North Vietnam
Democratic Republic of Yemen (DRY),
    129, 133
Deng Xiaoping, 118, 119–21
Denmark, 62, 68
détente
    American foreign policy overview,
        145–47
    Brezhnev, 215–18
    Carter administration, 102, 116–17,
        202, 212, 219–21
    Carter-Ford debate, 201–6
    competing while negotiating for, 149
    criticism, 77–78, 81
    current similarities and lessons for future,
        153–54
    European, 11–12, 15, 63–67, 71–76,
        111, 169, 173–76, 192
    Ford administration, 82–84
    Horn of Africa conflict's impact on, 127
    human rights impact on, 116–17
    Johnson administration, 30–32
    Middle East's impact on, 126–27, 130,
        134, 136, 138, 141
    morality of, 77, 79, 94–95, 99, 149
    Nixon administration, 40, 48–49, 61–62
    paradox and impact of, 149–53
    prolonged Cold War question, 145
    public opinion, 219–20
    Reagan, 96, 143–44, 198–200
    "rules" of, 55–56, 187–88
    term of, xviii–xix
Diem, Ngo Dinh, 16–17
diplomacy
    Carter, 118–19, 121
    Nixon and Kissinger, 38–39, 47–48,
        50–53, 85–86, 126, 146–47, 149,
        184–87
Diplomacy (Kissinger), 146
direct communications link between US
    and USSR, 9, 161–64

disengagement accords, Middle East, 85,
    87, 202
dissidents, Soviet, 110–11, 117, 151,
    197–98, 211
Dobrynin, Anatoly
    Carter administration, 107–8, 110–11,
        126, 218–21
    Cuba, 8
    Johnson administration, 30–31
    Kissinger back channel negotiations, 49,
        51, 53, 56, 66, 67, 148
    SALT II, 81
    triangular diplomacy, 184–87
Donaldson, Sam, 143
double-track decision, 123, 143–44,
    221–23
DRV (Democratic Republic of Vietnam).
    See North Vietnam
Dubček, Alexander, 26, 28–29
DuBois, W.E.B., 20
Dudziak, Mary, 20
Dulles, John Foster, 20, 196

East Germany. *See* German Democratic
    Republic
East-West trade bill, 14–15, 239n22
economy, US, 102, 127, 140
education tax, Soviet, 82
Egypt, 84–86, 125–26, 128
Eisenhower, Dwight and administration,
    3–4, 16–17, 35, 146
El Salvador, 113–14
elections
    1974 congressional, 79, 80
    1968 presidential, 32–35
    1976 presidential, 94, 95–99, 117,
        198–200, 201–6
    1980 presidential, 138–41
Elliott, T. A. K., 74
emigration from USSR, 82–84, 95,
    188–90, 246n10
Erhardt, Ludwig, 11
Eritrea, 127
Ethiopia, 103, 126, 127–30, 133, 169
European Common Foreign and Security
    Policy, 74

European Economic Community (EEC), 62, 68–69, 70, 71
Evans, Rowland, 96
Executive Committee of the National Security Council (ExCom), 7
exit tax, Soviet, 82

Federal Bureau of Investigation (FBI), 80
Federal Republic of Germany (FRG)
  Berlin crisis, 2–4
  CSCE, 194
  German unification, 11, 63–64, 67, 73, 175, 178–81
  NATO, 71
  Ostpolitik, 63–67, 178–81
  relations with Soviet bloc, xiv, 1
  Romania, 13
Fidelistas, 5–6
FNLA (National Front for the Liberation of Angola), 92–93
Folsom, James E., 20
Ford, Gerald and administration, 139
  Africa, 92–94, 115
  Church Committee, 80
  CSCE and Helsinki Accords, 74–75, 191–96
  Kissinger, 79
  Latin America, 113
  presidential election bid, xix, 77, 95–97, 98–99, 117, 201–6
  SALT II, 81
  Solzhenitsyn, 110
  trade with USSR, 84
  transatlantic unity, 71
  Vietnam, 88, 90–91
  Watergate scandal, 80
Foreign Affairs, xvi, 38
Foreign Policy Association, 98
forward base systems, 55, 107
Four Power Agreement on Berlin, xiv, 53, 64, 67
Four Power Paris summit, 3–4
Framework for Peace in the Middle East, 125
Framework for the Conclusion of a Peace Treaty between Egypt and Israel, 125
France

Africa, 92, 128
Berlin, 2
European East-West détente, 10–12, 63, 70, 75
  NATO, 10–11, 71, 173
  nuclear arms, 10, 107
  SEATO, 16
  Vietnam, 11
Franco-German friendship treaty of 1963, 11
freedom of expression, 74, 110–11, 211
Frei, Eduardo, 113
FRG (Federal Republic of Germany). See Federal Republic of Germany
Fulbright, William J., 16, 82

Gaddis, John, 40, 146
Gallup polls, 95
Garthoff, Raymond, 55, 108
GDR (German Democratic Republic). See German Democratic Republic
Geneva Conference of 1954, 16
Geneva Peace Conference on the Middle East, 85–86
genocide in Cambodia, 89–90
German Democratic Republic (GDR)
  Berlin, 2–4, 50
  European East-West détente, 11–12, 178–81
  German unification, 11, 63–64, 67, 73, 175, 178–81
  US, 65
Gheorghieu-Dej, Gheorghe, 13, 196
Gierek, Eduard, 57
Global War on Terror (GWT), 154
Goldwater, Barry, 35, 120
Gorbachev, Mikhail, 29, 144–45
grain sales, 204, 227–28
Great Britain
  Africa, 92, 114, 115, 116, 128
  EEC, 62, 68
  Middle East, 131
  SEATO, 16
  Test Ban Treaty, 164–65
Great Leap Forward, 50, 118
Great Leap Outward, 120
Great Society, 2

Greene, Robert, 98
Griffith, William, 14
Gromyko, Andrei, 56, 67, 86, 93, 151, 215
Ground-Launched Cruise Missiles (GLCM), 222
Group of 77, 101
Guam Doctrine, 38, 46–47
Guatemala, 5, 113–14
Guinea-Bissau, 92
Gulf of Tonkin Resolution, 17–18, 167

Haig, Alexander, 77
Haldeman, Bob, 45
Halliday, Fred, 144
Halloween massacre, 79
Hallstein Doctrine, 11
Haq, Zia ul-, 137
Harmel Report, 12, 15, 63, 64, 65, 71–72, 173–76, 238n15
Harris poll, 48
Havel, Václav, 101, 111, 112
Hayden, Tom, 23
Heath, Edward, 70, 71
Helms, Jesse, 115, 116
Helsinki Accords, xiv, 72–76, 111, 191–95, 197–98, 204–5
Ho Chi Minh, 89
Ho Chi Minh Trail, 45
Honduras, 113, 114
Honecker, Erich, 121–22, 128
Horn of Africa conflict, 103, 126–30, 136, 212–15
hostage crisis, Iranian, 103, 133, 136, 140, 225
hot link between US and USSR, 9, 161–64
Hoxha, Enver, 13
Huberman, Benjamin, 119
human rights
    Africa, 114–16
    Carter, 102, 116, 206, 208, 210–11
    China, 117–18, 120–21
    CSCE, 73, 74, 145, 192–94
    Eastern Europe, 101, 111–12
    Kissinger on, 95
    Latin America, 112–14
    Middle East, 137

USSR, 76, 110–11, 116–17, 188–90, 197–98, 208, 220
Humphrey, Hubert, 26, 28, 33–35, 98, 104
Hungary, 12–13, 28, 29, 32, 109, 230
Husak, Gustav, 29
Hyland, William, 55

IAFEATURE, 92
ICBMs (intercontinental ballistic missiles), 6–7, 9, 53–54, 81, 107, 108, 166, 167
image of America, 19, 20, 21, 22, 91
inaugural addresses
    Kennedy, 15
    Nixon, xiii, 43–44, 176–78
Indochina. See Vietnam War; specific countries
inflation, 102, 140
integration, Western European, xvi, 61–62, 68–69, 75–76, 180
Intermediate-Range Nuclear Forces Treaty (INF), 144
Internal Revenue Service (IRS), 80
international system
    détente's impact, 149–50, 152, 153–54
    stability importance, 2
    US and USSR roles in, xv–xvi
International War Crimes Tribunal, 18
Inter-Services Intelligence (ISI), 137–38
Iran
    American hostages, 103, 133, 136, 140, 225
    Iranian Revolution, 127, 130–34, 233–35
    Nixon administration, 57
    Soviet invasion of Afghanistan, 153, 225, 226, 230
Iraq, 132, 154, 234
Ireland, 62, 68
Islamic fundamentalism, 127, 130, 135, 138, 229, 234–35
Islamic Government (Khomeini), 131–32
Islamic Republic, 130
Islamic Republic of Iran, establishment of, 130–34, 233–35
Israel
    Angola, 92
    Camp David Accords, 125–26

Johnson administration, 167
Khomeini, 234
Nixon administration, 37, 50, 56, 85–87
October War, 84–86
Six-Day War, 10
Soviet Jews, 82
Italy, 11

Jackson, Henry, 54, 81–83, 95, 98, 122,
    149, 246n10
Jackson Amendment, 54
Jackson-Vanik Amendment, 82–83,
    188–90, 246n10
Japan, xv, xvi, 170
Jewish emigration from USSR, 82–84,
    188–90
Jobert, François, 70–71
John Birch Society, 14
John Paul II, Pope, 111–12, 204–5
Johnson, Lyndon and administration
    civil rights, 21–22
    Eastern Europe, 14–15, 26, 31–32,
        239n22
    Kosygin talks, 165–68
    NATO, 12
    nuclear arms, 10, 30
    overview, xvii, 2
    resignation, 25, 28, 33
    USSR, 40
    Vietnam War, 16, 17–19, 26–28
Jordan, Hamilton, 105

Karmal, Babrak, 135, 224
Kekkonen, Urho, 72
Kennan, George F., xvi, 40, 146
Kennedy, Edward, 122, 140, 232
Kennedy, John F. and administration
    American University commencement
        address, 8, 14, 157–60
    Bay of Pigs, 6
    Berlin, 1, 4
    civil rights, 22–23
    Cuban missile crisis, 7–8, 155–57
    Vietnam, 15, 17
    yearn for détente, xvii, 9
Kennedy, Robert F., 7–8, 25, 27, 33
Kerry, John F., 19

KGB (Komitet Gosudarstevennoy
    Bezopasnosti), 110, 198
Khalq, the, 134–35
Khmer Rouge, 45, 89–90
Khomeini, Ayatollah Ruhollah, 131–32,
    133, 233–35
Khrushchev, Nikita
    Berlin crisis, 2–4
    Cuban missile crisis, 6, 7–8, 9
    letter to Kennedy, 155–57
Kiesinger, Kurt, 11, 64
King, Martin Luther, Jr., 21, 25, 27, 33
Kissinger, Henry
    about, 35–37, 79, 104
    Africa, 93, 115
    Carter, 98, 203
    China, 38–39, 51–53, 147
    Church Committee, 80
    CSCE and Helsinki Accords, 73, 74–75,
        191–95, 196–97
    détente, 94–96, 97, 152
    foreign policy overview, 39–41, 95–96,
        145, 146–47
    FRG, 64–67, 178–79, 180–81
    Middle East, 85–87, 131
    Nixon bond, 37–38
    press briefing on foreign policy, 181–84
    public opinion, 149
    Reagan, 199, 200–201
    SALT II, 81
    TRA, 82–83, 246n10
    USSR, xvii, 48–50, 148
    Vietnam War, xiv, 37–38, 44–47, 57–58,
        87–88, 90, 91
    Watergate scandal, 77
    Western Europe, 61–63, 68–71
Korean War, xvi–xvii
Kosygin, Alexei, 10, 51, 165–68, 172
Krauthammer, Charles, 144

Laos, 16, 18, 89, 90
Latin America, human rights in, 112–14
Le Duc Tho, 45, 57, 88
Lebanon, 234
Lenczowski, George, 126–27
Letelier, Orlando, 113

Liberation Front of Mozambique (FRELIMO), 115
Libya, 133
Linebacker I, 56, 58
Linebacker II, 57
linkage of Soviet issues, 48–50, 56, 102, 116, 213, 219
long-range strategic bombers, 6–7, 55, 81
Long-Range Theatre Nuclear Forces (LRTNF), 221–23
Luce, Henry, xvi
Lundestad, Geir, 75

MacFarquhar, Roderick, 118
Macmillan, Harold, 169
MAD (mutually assured destruction), 10, 108–9, 122–23
Man of the Year, *Time's*, 91, 119
Mao Tse-tung, 41, 50–51, 118, 185
March on Washington, 21
Marshall, George C., 70
Marshall Plan, xvi, 70
MBFR (mutually balanced forced reductions), 50, 109, 192
McCarthy, Eugene, 27, 33
McCarthyism, xvii
McGovern, George, 33–34, 58, 98, 243n28
McNamara, Robert, 27, 104, 167
memorandum from Kissinger to Ford on CSCE, 191–95
memorandum of understanding between US and USSR on communications link, 161–64
Mengistu Haile Mariam, 128
MFN status, 77, 82, 83, 188
Middle East. *See also specific countries*
  Carter administration, 85, 125–27, 130–34, 225
  Johnson administration, 166–67
  Nixon administration, 49, 50, 56, 58, 85, 86–87, 131, 171
  October War and outcome, 71, 84–86
  peace process, 78, 85, 125–26
  Six-Day War, 10, 84
migration
  Czech, 29

East German, 3, 4
Jews from USSR, 82–84, 188–90
military spending, US, 21, 88, 101–2, 131, 203
Miller, J. Irwin, 14
Miller Committee, 14
MIRVs (multiple independently targetable reentry vehicles), 54–55, 81, 106, 108, 109, 204
Molotov, Vyacheslav, 71
Mondale, Walter, 113, 115, 213
Monroe Doctrine, 30
Moose, Richard, 116
morality
  Carter, 98, 101
  détente, 77, 79, 94–95, 99, 149
Mosaddeq, Mohammad, 131
Moscow Protocols, 29
Moscow summit of 1972, xiv, 55–56, 187
most favored nation (MFN) status, 77, 82, 83, 188
Movement for Democracy, 197
Mozambique, 92, 115
MPLA (Popular Movement for the Liberation of Angola), 92–94, 129
"Mr. X" (Kennan), xvi
Mugabe, Robert, 115, 116
multiple independently targetable reentry vehicles (MIRVs), 54–55, 81, 106, 108, 109, 204
Muskie, Edmund, 98
mutually assured destruction (MAD), 10, 108–9, 122–23
mutually balanced forced reductions (MBFR), 50, 109, 192

National Association for the Advancement of Colored People (NAACP), 20
National Front for the Liberation of Angola (FNLA), 92–93
National Liberation Front (NLF), 16–18, 25, 26–27, 88
National Security Action Memorandum 352, 15
National Security Agency (NSA), 80
National Security Council, 7, 35–36, 37, 79, 212–15

National Union for the Total
Independence of Angola (UNITA),
92–93, 144
NATO
about, xv, xvi, 212
Berlin crisis, 3
Brezhnev on, 217–18
China, 119
CSCE, 71, 75, 191, 193, 194
Czechoslovakia, 32
FRG, 64–66, 180
Harmel Report, 12, 15, 63, 64, 65,
71–72, 173–76, 238n15
Iran, 132
MBFR, 109
Nixon and Humphrey views of, 26, 62,
168–69
nuclear arms, 7, 122–23, 143–44,
221–23
Western Europe position, 10–12, 63–66,
71, 169, 180
Neto, Agostinho, 93
New York Times, 25, 70, 96
Nicaragua, 113, 114, 144
Nixon, Richard M. and administration.
See also Kissinger, Henry
about, 35–37, 242n1
Africa, 169
Bohemian Club speech, 38, 168–73
China, 147–48, 185–87
communism, xvii, 169, 170–71
détente, 150, 152
foreign policy overview, xviii, 39–41, 43,
58–59, 79, 145–47, 181–84
FRG, 64–67, 180–81
inaugural addresses, xiii, 43–44, 176–78
Kissinger bond, 37–38
Latin America, 113
Middle East, 58, 85, 86–87, 131
presidential election, 28, 34–35
presidential re-election, 58, 185, 243n28
Romania, 13
Sino-Soviet relations, 38–39, 51–53
USSR, 48–50, 53–57, 82, 148
Vietnam War, 26, 37–38, 44–48, 57–58,
88, 91, 185

Watergate scandal and resignation, 77,
78–79, 80, 85
West Europe, 61–63, 68–71, 76, 169
Nixon Doctrine, 38, 46–47
Nixon-Brezhnev summits of 1972, xiv,
55–56, 187
Njolstad, Olav, 102, 108
Nkomo, Joshua, 115
Nobel Peace Prize, 21, 36, 64, 87–88, 110,
125
Non-Aggression Pact, FRG and USSR, 64,
67
Non-Proliferation Treaty (NPT), 31, 167
normalization with China, 51–53, 77,
108, 117–21, 147–48
North Korea, xvi–xvii, 92, 230
North Vietnam, 16–18, 49–50, 58, 78,
88, 89. *See also* Vietnam War
North Yemen, 133
Norway, 68
Notre Dame University commencement
address of Carter, 208–12
Novak, Robert, 96
nuclear arms control, 9–10
Carter administration, 101–3, 106–9,
121–23, 209, 212, 217–18
Kennedy administration, 9, 155–57,
158–60
NATO, 221–23
Nixon administration, 40, 43–44, 49–
50, 53–55, 80–81, 148
Reagan administration, 143–44
nuclear arms race. *See also* nuclear arms
control
Carter administration, 106, 109, 212,
216, 217
Kennedy administration, 8–10, 160
Nixon administration, 44, 53, 55
public opinion and American psyche,
xvii, 123
stockpile amounts, 6–7, 9t, 55
Nuclear Weapons and Foreign Policy
(Kissinger), 35

October War, 71, 84–86, 126
Oder-Neisse line, 64, 180
Ogaden Desert, 103, 127, 128

oil embargos, 71, 84–85, 87
oil prices, 127
Olympics, Moscow, 136, 228
Operation Danube, 29
Operation Eagle Claw, 133
Operation Menu, 45
Operation Zulu, 93
Organization of Intelligence and National
    Security (SAVAK), 131
Organization of the Petroleum Exporting
    Countries (OPEC), 71
Ostpolitik, 11, 41, 63–67, 76, 178–81

Pahlavi, Shah Mohammed Reza, 130–32,
    133, 168
Pakistan
    Afghanistan, 134, 135, 136, 137–38,
        226, 228
    SEATO, 16
    Sino-American relations, 51–52
    US embassy attack, 133
Palach, Jan, 30
Palestine, 86, 125–26, 234
pan-European security conference. *See*
    CSCE
paradox of détente, 150–53
Parcham, the, 134–35
Paris Peace Accords on Vietnam, 50,
    57–58, 78, 88, 147, 149
Pathet Lao, 89
Patocka, Jan, 111
Patriotic Front, Zimbabwean, 115, 116
peace
    Kennedy on, 157–60
    Nixon on, xiii, 43, 44, 146, 172–73,
        177–78
    Reagan on, 139–40, 141, 231–32
People's Democratic Party of Afghanistan
    (PDPA), 134
People's Democratic Republic of
    Afghanistan (PDRA), 135
People's Democratic Republic of Yemen
    (PDRY), 129, 133
People's Republic of China (PRC), xvi, xix
    Africa, 128
    Albania, 13

Carter administration, 102–3, 117–21,
    214
détente impact, 152
France, 11, 63
Nixon and Humphrey views of, 26, 170
Nixon and Kissinger, 38–41, 44, 77,
    147–48, 172
Reagan, 199
SEATO, 16
Sino-American relations, 51–53, 77,
    108, 117–21, 147–48
Sino-Soviet relations, 50–51, 53, 118,
    184–87, 229–30
Vietnam, 89–90, 120
People's Republic of Kampuchea, 90
perestroika, 117
Pershing missiles, 221, 222
Pinochet, Augusto, 113
PNW (Agreement on the Prevention of
    Nuclear War), 69, 148
Pol Pot, 89–90
Poland, xiv, 29, 64, 66, 111–12, 180
Polish United Workers' Party, 30
polls
    opinion on USSR, 48
    presidential election, 95–96, 97–98, 140,
        231, 247n29
Pompidou, Georges, 63, 70, 71, 75
Popular Movement for the Liberation of
    Angola (MPLA), 92–94, 129
Port Huron Statement, 22–23
Portugal, 92
Portuguese Guinea, 92
poverty, 2, 19, 21–22
power, US, xv–xvi
Powers, Frances Gary, 3–4
Prague Spring, 25–26, 28–32, 51, 72
press briefing on foreign policy, Kissinger's,
    181–84
Prevention of Nuclear War (PNW)
    Agreement, 69, 148
protests
    antiwar, 18–19, 34
    civil rights, 20–21
Puzanov, Aleksandr, 134

Quang-Duc, Thich, 17

race riots, 33
racial discrimination, 19–22
Radio Free Europe, 205–6
Rathaus Schöneberg, 1
Reagan, Ronald and administration
  Afghanistan, 138
  China, 120
  détente, 77, 149
  foreign policy, xiv
  human rights, 112–13, 114, 116
  presidential bids, 34, 96–97, 127,
    138–41, 198–200, 231–33
  Soviet relations, 138–39, 141–42,
    143–44, 146
Reagan Doctrine, 144
Reagan Revolution, 140–41
religious freedom, 111–12
Republic of Vietnam (RVN). *See* South
  Vietnam
Reston, James, 70
Rhodesia, 114–15, 116
Ribicoff, Abraham, 34
Robeson, Paul, 20
Rockefeller, Nelson, 34, 35, 38
Rogers, William P., 37, 66, 103, 104
Romania
  Angola, 92
  China, 51, 52
  Soviet independence, 13, 29, 72, 96,
    196, 205, 230
Romanian Communist Party Congress, 51
Roosevelt, Franklin D., 200
Rosenberg, David, 6
rules of détente, 55–56, 187–88
Rumsfeld, Donald, 97
Rush, Kenneth, 67
Rusk, Dean, 14, 30–32, 167, 239n22
Russell, Bertrand, 18

Sadat, Anwar, 85, 86, 125–26, 234
Saigon collapse, 88–89, 90, 91
Sakharov, Andrei, 110, 197, 198
SALT I Agreement
  about, xiii–xiv, 53, 80, 108, 109, 148, 153
  criticism and concerns, 54–55, 69, 81
  negotiations and signing, 44, 49
SALT II Agreement
  about, 148
  Carter administration, 103, 106–9,
    121–23, 129–30, 136, 207, 213–15,
    227
  Ford administration, 81, 83, 93, 192,
    196
  Reagan on, 141
Sampson, Edith, 20
Sandinistas, 144
Scheel, Walter, 67
Schlesinger, James, 200, 203
Schoenhals, Michael, 118
scientific socialism, 128, 133
Scowcroft, Brent, 80, 97
SEATO, xv–xvi, 16
Selassie, Haile, 128
Senate Foreign Relations Committee, 82,
  105
Senate Select Committee to Study
  Governmental Operations with Respect
  to Intelligence Activities, 79–80 .
Shanghai communiqué, 52, 147–48
Sihanouk, Norodom, 45
Sino-American relations, 51–53, 77, 108,
  117–21, 147–48
Sino-Soviet relations, 50–51, 53, 118,
  184–87, 229–30
Six-Day War, 10, 84
SLBMs (submarine-launched ballistic
  missiles), 53–54, 81, 108
Smith, Ian, 115–16
Social Democratic Party (SDP), FRG's, 63
Solidarity movement, Polish, 112
Solzhenitsyn, Alexander, 96, 110, 200, 206
Somalia, 103, 126, 127, 128–30, 133
Somoza, Anastasio, 114
Sonnenfeldt, Helmur, 96, 201, 205–6
Sonnenfeldt Doctrine, 96–97
South Africa, 92–93, 115
South Vietnam, 15–18, 21, 26–27, 57, 58,
  77, 88, 90. *See also* Vietnam War
Soviet Union. *See* USSR
Soviet-American summit of 1961, 4
Soviet-American summit of 1972, 53–57
Soviet-American trade agreement of 1972,
  84

Special Committee on US Trade Relations with Eastern Europe and the Soviet Union, 14
Sputnik, 6
SS-20 missiles, 122, 221
Stalin, Joseph, 50
State Department, US
  China, 118, 120, 121
  civil rights, 20
  East-West trade, 14
  human rights, 101, 121
  Kissinger, 67
  Vance-Brzezinski conflict, 104, 105
State of the Union Address of Carter, 137
stockpiles of nuclear weapons, 6–7, 9t, 55
Strategic Arms Limitation Talks Agreements. See SALT I; SALT II
"Strategy for Peace in the '80's, A" speech (Reagan), 139–40, 231–33
Students for Democratic Society (SDS), 22–23
submarine base in Cuba, 50
submarine-launched ballistic missiles (SLBMs), 53–54, 81, 108
Sulzberger, C.L., 96
summitry, Soviet-American, xiii–xiv, 148–49, 150. See also specific summits
superiority, military and nuclear, 6–7, 32, 54–55, 170, 172–73, 221–22
Suri, Jeremi, 36
Syria, 84–86, 87

Tabeev, Fikrat, 135
Taiwan
  China, 52, 77, 85, 117, 118–20, 147–48, 199
  economy, 170
Taiwan Relations Act, 120
Taraki, Noor Mohammad, 135
telegram from Dobrynin to Soviet Foreign Ministry, 184–87
telephone link between US and USSR, 9, 161–64
televised address of Reagan, 139–40, 231–33
Test Ban Treaty of 1963, 9, 164–65
Tet offensive, 25, 26–27

Thatcher, Margaret, 116
Theatre Nuclear Forces (TNF) modernization, 222–23
Thieu, Nguyen Van, 46, 88, 89
Tibet, 119
Time
  American credibility, 91
  arc of crisis, 126
  China, 118–19, 121
  EEC, 68
  Kissinger, 39, 91
  Soviet dissidents, 110
  US foreign policy, 147
"To Restore America" (Reagan), 198–200
Toon, Malcolm, 49
trade, US and USSR
  Carter administration, 136, 227–28
  Johnson administration, 14–15, 239n22–23
  Nixon administration, 82–84, 173, 188–90
Trade Law of 1974, 82–83, 188–90, 239n22
Trade Reform Act (TRA), 82–84
Trades Unions Congress of Ghana, 20
transatlantic relationship and unity, 62, 67–71, 75–76
transnationalism, 151
Treaty of Friendship and Cooperation, USSR and Somalia, 128
triangular diplomacy
  Carter, 118–19, 121
  Nixon and Kissinger, 39, 47–48, 50–53, 184–87
troop levels, US
  Vietnam, 18, 27, 47, 242n11
  Western Europe, 32, 109, 246n35
Truman, Harry, 146, 232
Truman Doctrine, 146
Tucker, Robert, 91
Tulane University convocation address of Ford, 91
Turkey, 7–8, 196
Tyler, Patrick, 126

U-2 spy flights, 3, 7
Ulbricht, Walter, xix, 66

underground nuclear testing, 156, 165
unemployment, 102, 140
unification of Germany, 11, 63–64, 67, 73, 175, 178–81
unilaterlism, 56, 78, 86–87, 93–94, 126, 149, 188
UNITA (National Union for the Total Independence of Angola), 92–93, 144
United Nations (UN)
    Africa, 114, 115, 169
    Cuban missile crisis, 7
    Czechoslovakia, 31–32, 111
    Middle East, 84
    NATO, 176
    Soviet invasion of Afghanistan, 226–27
unity
    Soviet bloc, 12–14
    Western, 12, 32, 62, 66–71, 75–76, 174
urban violence, 33
US Helsinki Watch Committee, 117
USSR
    Afghanistan, 126, 127, 133, 134–38, 144, 223–30, 234
    Africa, 92–94, 103, 115, 127–30, 213–15, 216–18
    Carter, 212, 219–21
    China, 38–40, 44, 50–51, 53, 118–19, 121, 184–87, 229–30
    collapse of, 144–45
    communications link with US, 9, 161–64
    dissidents, 110–11, 117, 151, 197–98, 211
    emigration, 82–84, 95, 188–90, 246n10
    FRG, xiv
    human rights, 76, 110–11, 116–17, 188–90, 197–98, 208, 220
    impact of détente, 151–53
    Middle East, 84–85, 86–87, 126–27, 131, 132–33 (See also Afghanistan)
    Nixon and administration, xvii, 48–50, 53–57, 82, 148, 171–73
    nuclear arms control, 122–23, 222–23 (See also nuclear arms control)
    Reagan, 138–39, 141–42, 143–44
    role in international system, xvi
    trade with US (See trade, US and USSR)

triangular relationship with US and China, 47–48, 184–87
Vietnam, 78, 89
Ustinov, Dmitri, 135

Vance, Cyrus
    about, 103–5
    Africa, 115, 129–30, 212–15
    China, 117, 118, 120
    human rights, 101
    Middle East, 132, 133
    SALT II, 106–8
    USSR, 220
Vanik, Charles, 82
Venezuela, 114
Vienna talks, 121–22
Vietnam. See also North Vietnam; South Vietnam; Vietnam War
    unification and post unification, 89–91
Vietnam Veterans Against the War, 19
Vietnam War, xvii, 23, 32
    Ford administration, 88–91
    Johnson administration, 11, 17–19, 25–28, 37, 167
    Kennedy administration, 15–17
    Nixon administration, 37–38, 40, 44–48, 49, 52, 56–58, 87–88
    Vance on, 105
Vietnamization, 38, 46–47
Vladivostok agreement, 81, 83, 106, 108, 148, 204
Voting Rights Act, 21

Wałesa, Lech, 112
Wallace, George, 35, 98
War Powers Act, 88
Warsaw Five invasion of Czechoslovakia, 29–32
Warsaw Pact. See also specific countries
    Albania, 13
    Bucharest Declaration, 15
    Czechoslovakia, 13, 26, 29–32
    FRG, 63–64
    NATO, 12, 15, 63, 71–72, 75, 109, 123, 173–76
    nuclear arms control, 123, 217–18, 221
Washington Post, 96

Watergate scandal, xviii, 36, 58, 77,
78–79, 80, 85
Wei Jingsheng, 121
Wenger, Andreas, 12
West German-Polish Treaty, 64
West Germany. *See* Federal Republic of
Germany
Westad, Odd Arne, 51, 94, 151
Westmoreland, William, 27
White, Walter, 20
White House background press briefing by
Kissinger, 181–84
White Revolution, 131
Wilson, Harold, 11, 62, 191, 196
Wilson, Jimmy, 20
Wilson, Woodrow, 43
Woodcock, Leonard, 119

Xuan Thuy, 45

Year of Europe, 68–71, 76
Year Zero, 89
Yemen, 129, 133
Young, Andrew, 115
Yugoslavia, 31, 196, 205, 230

Zaire, 92–93, 218, 219
Zambia, 115
Zhou, En-lai, 51, 52, 53
Zimbabwe, 114–15
Zimbabwe African National Union
(ZANU), 114–15
Zimbabwe African People's Union
(ZAPU), 115
Zionism, 127

ABOUT THE AUTHOR

Jussi M. Hanhimäki is a professor of international history at the Graduate Institute of International and Development Studies in Geneva, Switzerland. His most recent publications include *Transatlantic Relations since 1945: An Introduction* (2012, with Benedikt Schoenborn and Barbara Zanchetta); *The United Nations: A Very Short Introduction* (2008); *The Flawed Architect: Henry Kissinger and American Foreign Policy* (2004); and *The Cold War: A History in Documents and Eyewitness Accounts* (2003, with Odd Arne Westad). He is one of the founding editors of the journal *Cold War History* and a member of the editorial boards of *Relations internationales*, *Refugee Survey Quarterly*, and *Ulkopolitiikka*. In 2006 he was named Finland Distinguished Professor by the Academy of Finland.